THE
CHOCOLATE
CONSCIENCE

THE CHOCOLATE CONSCIENCE

Gillian Wagner

CHATTO & WINDUS

LONDON

Published in 1987 by
Chatto & Windus Ltd
30 Bedford Square
London WC1B 3RP

British Library Cataloguing in Publication Data
Wagner, Gillian
The chocolate conscience.
1. Confectionery – Great Britain – History
– 19th century
I. Title
338.4′7664153′0941   HD9999.C73G7

ISBN 0-7011-2475-X

Designed by Behram Kapadia

Photoset in Linotron Goudy Old Style by
Rowland Phototypesetting Ltd
Bury St Edmunds, Suffolk
Printed in Great Britain by
Redwood Burn Ltd
Trowbridge, Wiltshire

Contents

List of Illustrations

Acknowledgements for the illustrations are made with thanks to the following:
Rowntree Mackintosh Ltd, plates 2, 6, 7, 12, 13, 14, 17, 20, 22, 24, 27, 30, 31,
32, 33, 34, 35, 38; Cadbury Schweppes PLC, 1, 9, 25, 26; *The Cadbury family*,
John Crosfield, 3, 4, 5, 8, 10, 11, 15, 16, 18, 19, 21, 23, 28, 29; The Guildhall
Library, London, 37, The British Library Newspaper Library, Colindale, 36.

Acknowledgements

I would like to thank Cadbury Schweppes and Rowntree Mackintosh for their courtesy and help. I am particularly grateful to Sir Adrian Cadbury for his generosity in lending me books and papers and to Basil Murray, sometime archivist at Cadbury Schweppes, for bringing much new material to my notice. I thank the chairman of Rowntree Mackintosh for allowing me to make use of archive material and my special thanks go to the librarian, Colin Murray, and his assistant, Bill Bushell, for their unfailing courtesy and kindness, and their patience in dealing with my many queries. I am also indebted to Dr David Jeremy, editor of the *Dictionary of Business Biography*, for his help; to Francis Goodall, who generously shared with me the fruits of his research; and to Sarah Silcox. My requests for information were invariably answered by the many Cadbury and Rowntree trusts. I thank Robin Guthrie, director of the Joseph Memorial Trust, Steven Burkeman, director of the Joseph Rowntree Memorial Trust and Lord Chitnis of the Joseph Rowntree Social Services Trust for both talking about the work of the trust and making information available. My thanks go also to Anthony Wilson, secretary to several of the Cadbury family trusts, and to Mrs Sylvia Gale, secretary to the William Cadbury Trust. I am greatly indebted to Lewis Waddilove, who not only showed me round New Earswick but spent time talking to me about the work of the trusts.

I would particularly like to thank Lord Seebohm, one of the first to whom I spoke about the project and who gave me much helpful advice; the late William Kenrick who drove me round Bournville; Jose Harris, who kindly read the text, as did Betty Askwith and Lucy Wagner; and John Crosfield, who allowed me to see his book on the Cadbury family before it was published. For many unforeseen reasons this book took much longer to complete than expected, so the number of people who helped me at different times is very great and I thank them all. The staff at the British Library, Colindale, the London Library, Birmingham University Library, the library at the Society of Friends and the Aldeburgh branch of the Suffolk County Library have all made my task easier and I am grateful to them. Thanks of a different order go to my husband, for without his steady support this book would never have been finished, and to my publishers for their patience.

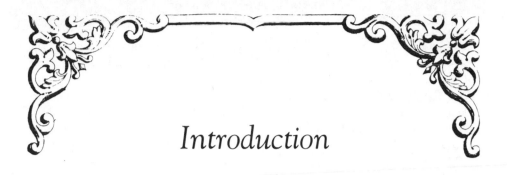

Introduction

The Chocolate Conscience does not purport to be an exhaustive account of either the Frys, Cadburys or Rowntrees, but aims rather to look at some of the moral dilemmas that those families had to face while coming to terms with the power which their recently acquired wealth brought them. Joseph Storrs Fry II, George Cadbury and Joseph Rowntree had much in common, all three being cocoa and chocolate manufacturers at a time when demand for their products was increasing so fast that their business doubled and quadrupled in size during their lifetimes. All three came from families that had long been members of the Society of Friends, and were themselves active Quakers. The Frys were already well established as chocolate and cocoa manufacturers when the Cadburys and Rowntrees entered the business. From modest beginnings the Cadbury and Rowntree business empires grew, overtaking and eventually engulfing that of J. S. Fry & Sons. All three businesses owed their astonishing success in the nineteenth and twentieth centuries to the upsurge in popular taste for products made from the previously underrated cocoa bean. I have long been fascinated by the link between the modest little bean and the great fortunes which were made as a consequence of its exploitation, not least because of the uses to which those fortunes were put.

Victorian Quakerism sanctioned and encouraged the pursuit of wealth. Nevertheless there seems to be an inherent contradiction between the simple life, which was an intrinsic part of the ethos of the Society of Friends, and the acquisition of great personal wealth. It is a contradiction that Quakers today, perhaps, also feel. In an attempt to define the kind of people who are now Quakers, George Goyman in a recent handbook called 'Introducing Quakers' wrote, 'Generally Quakers are thought to be "good", so good in fact that they are quite impossible to live with. Many people persist in thinking of Quakers as wealthy philanthropists: others associate them with reforming movements but regretfully imagine that they became extinct with the death of Elizabeth Fry.' Elizabeth Fry's name is remembered for her reforming zeal, but by no means could she be said to have been a wealthy philanthropist. Indeed, her husband ran into business difficulties and was declared bankrupt at one time, creating yet another paradox. For although Victorian Quakers encouraged the pursuit of wealth, the corollary to this was that failure in business

— 3 —

was punished, and had not Elizabeth's rich relatives, the Gurneys, come to the rescue, the couple would have been compelled to give up membership of the Society of Friends. So if people do think of Quakers as wealthy philanthropists, it is more than likely that they are remembering some of the successful nineteenth-century Quaker businessmen who became known for their philanthropic activities; and the names of George Cadbury and Joseph Rowntree must be among those pre-eminent in this field.

The fact that successful businesses are, in general, no longer owned or run by Quakers poses a quite different question. But among the many complex reasons for this, one trend was noted as early as 1832 by Henry Ashworth, the wealthy cotton manufacturer, who warned his brother-in-law 'that with very few exceptions the third generation of the rich leave our Society'.

Precluded by their religious affiliation from going to university, and by their beliefs from joining the army or navy, or taking part in politics, with all frivolous social intercourse frowned upon and any untoward interest in the arts discouraged, it is little wonder that so many Quakers turned to business to find fulfilment and satisfaction. The nineteenth century was a time of great opportunity with a rapidly growing domestic market in Britain. With only occasional bad periods, the general employment position improved between 1850 and 1910 and money wages almost doubled during that time. Cheap imports of such commodities as sugar, cocoa and fats, mass production and multiple retailing all help to explain why food prices from 1874 began to fall and the consumption of tea, sugar, chocolate and cocoa doubled.

The Quakers' circle of religious and kinship relationships was another factor that contributed to their success. Certainly by training and inheritance Quaker businessmen were well placed to take advantage of the opportunities that lay before them. George Cadbury attributed his success in business to iron parsimony in the early years and hard work, qualities which were very much part of the Protestant work ethic. But energy, imagination, ambition, a willingness to take risks and an element of ruthlessness, all qualities which have little to do with religion, were also needed, as well as favourable economic and social conditions.

Great wealth creates its own problems and for members of the Society of Friends the spending of that wealth might seem to pose even more problems. While Joseph Storrs Fry followed the conventional path of giving to a multitude of organisations and good causes, both George Cadbury and Joseph Rowntree gave much thought to how they could best use the power that their wealth had brought them. Both men believed that money should be spent during their own lifetimes, but Joseph Rowntree, having become wealthy only late in life, made special provision, through interlinked trusts, to enable the support he had given to special causes to be carried on for a limited period after his death by his sons and nephews.

Andrew Carnegie, a contemporary from Scotland who had made far more money in America from steel than any of the chocolate manufacturers, never forgot that his father, a handloom weaver, had been thrown out of work as a result of the mechanisation of the industry and forced to emigrate. Needing to justify his wealth, with no deep religious beliefs to guide him, he sought to hammer out a philosophy that would satisfy his own radicalism, and under the title of 'Gospel of Wealth' tried to create a framework for what he called his principles of 'scientific phil-anthropy'. Like Cadbury and Rowntree he rejected inheritance in favour of the distribution of wealth in the lifetime of the owner for the public benefit. But he went further than them and believed an ideal state was possible when the surplus wealth of the few

will become, in the best sense, the property of the many because administered for the common good and this wealth passing through the hands of the few can be a much more potent force for the elevation of our race than if distributed in small sums to the people themselves . . . The man of wealth thus becomes the mere trustee and agent for his poorer brethren, bringing to their service his superior wisdom, experience and ability to administer, doing for them better than they would or could do for themselves.

Carnegie's thesis was soon refuted, but it is interesting nonetheless as an attempt to justify great wealth. Neither George Cadbury nor Joseph Rowntree saw any need to be defensive about their personal fortunes, but they both saw the spending of their wealth as a great responsibility. Joseph Rowntree believed that money well spent could change the face of the nation, and George Cadbury spent largely to promote causes that he believed to be for the public good. It has to be said that in spite of their good intentions, neither Carnegie nor Cadbury succeeded in divesting himself of all his great wealth, and both died millionaires. Joseph Rowntree left a more modest inheritance.

When it became financially practicable, both Cadbury and Rowntree built modern factories outside the towns in which they lived, thus giving their labour forces greatly improved conditions of work. The management of large units of industrial employment was a relatively new art and the way in which social relationships in industry developed depended to a large extent on the industrialists themselves. They had to solve problems of discipline and regularity of work at a time when there was little or no public welfare provision or public pressure to ameliorate the social problems that industrialisation brought with it. It is in that context that the new model factory built at Bournville by the Cadbury brothers should be judged.

Built in the country outside Birmingham, the workshops were well lit and ventilated and plenty of space for recreation was provided. Both George Cadbury and Joseph Rowntree admitted that it was to their advantage to have a happy and contented work force and that their businesses were more successful as a result. At a time when the state played little part in either encouraging industrial progress or helping its social casualties, their actions might be construed as being merely enlightened self-interest, but there is no doubt that a genuine concern for the wellbeing of their workers formed part of their business philosophy. In George Cadbury's case, however, there was something in the public parade of virtue, in the way the business continuously advertised the fact that they were model employers while at the same time promoting their products, that irked some. When the opportunity presented itself, their opponents did not hesitate to use the Cadburys' self-proclaimed virtues as employers as an excuse to mount an attack on them over the question of slave labour in the cocoa-producing islands of São Tomé and Principe.

It was in the realm of public affairs that both men encountered most criticism; they took their stand on high moral ground, thus leaving themselves open to attack. When they stepped outside the restricted world of business onto the public stage by trying to influence national policy through their ownership of newspapers, their actions were seen as being controversial. They were at their most vulnerable when through their newspapers they attempted to influence public opinion to their way of thinking. The public distrusted too much moralising and when the two cocoa manufacturers failed to ban racing news in two of their newspapers after denouncing the evils of gambling, this latent hostility was given voice.

Besides their businesses and their newspaper proprietorships, George Cadbury and Joseph Rowntree left enduring monuments in the shape of the model villages, Bournville and New Earswick. Both villages were built as a contribution to the solution of the problem of providing working-class housing at reasonable rents at a time when the state played no part in the provision of housing. Trusts were set up to administer the villages. Many of George Cadbury's children and nephews created a large number of further trusts to give support to causes in which they believed, and the tradition has continued to the third generation. Joseph Rowntree set up two more trusts to promote social research, in which he and his sons were interested. The trusts have continued and multiplied in a way that would have surprised their founder. Yet, in spite of so many benefactions and so much public virtue, there is something in the Quaker character that gives rise to a certain amount of cynicism, as unkindly expressed by an unknown author:

> Take a dozen Quakers, be sure they're sweet and pink
> Add one discussion programme to make the people think
> . . . Garnish with compassion – just a touch will do
> Serve with deep humility your philanthropic stew.

Unfair probably, uncharitable certainly, but representing a feeling that behind so much unrelieved goodness there must also be a certain amount of humbug; that the dividing line between self-interest and the public interest has been somewhat blurred; that in any case the Quaker notion of what is in the public interest discounts too many aspects of life, for example the important role played by the creative arts, which to many people is of vital importance. These are in the main unformulated opinions, prejudices maybe. By highlighting some of the very positive contributions as well as some of the more controversial happenings in which the chocolate manufacturers and their successors have been involved, I hope to have made a small contribution to answering the unasked question that lies behind the title – what was the chocolate conscience?

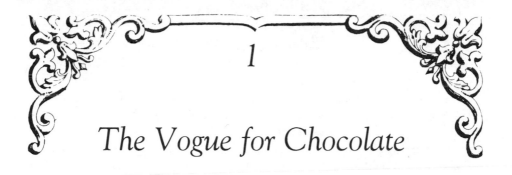

1

The Vogue for Chocolate

Chocolate, one of the cheapest luxuries in the world, is now enjoyed by hundreds of millions of people. Considering the many centuries that the cacao bean has been known to man, it has taken a long time for chocolate and cocoa to become popular and to become established as a household food. Long before any foreigner set foot in America, the peoples of the central and southern regions knew and enjoyed the fruit of the cacao tree, drinking a beverage made from its seeds mixed with spices. The Europeans discovered the cacao bean in the sixteenth century, but were, perhaps not surprisingly, slow to understand its latent delights. The process of turning the slimy white cacao seeds inside the pods into cocoa and chocolate as it is known today involves many delicate and complex operations. During the seventeenth and eighteenth centuries chocolate, then only served in the form of a drink, remained the exclusive preserve of the rich and fashionable.

Industrial developments in the nineteenth century so revolutionised the manufacture of cocoa and chocolate that imports to Europe and North America increased dramatically, prices dropped, consumption became more widespread and a new industry was born. In Britain, in 1825, the consumption of raw cocoa totalled only 143 tons. A century later, the figure had gone up to 56,000 tons. From being a luxury only for the wealthy, this richly nutritious food had become so cheap that a destitute child seeking a night's shelter in one of the refuges in the East End of London was given, as a matter of routine, a mug of cocoa and a slice of bread.

The people of the Amazon, Orinoco and Mexico had known, long before Christopher Columbus (1451–1506) discovered America, how to make use of the strange green pods which hang in an unlikely way direct from the trunk of their trees, as though artificially attached. The cacao tree is small, standing only 20 feet high. It needs a rich alluvial soil with abundant moisture and good drainage, it is sensitive to drought and wind and will only grow in tropical regions above 250 feet. The pods, which hang on a short thick stalk, contain about thirty to forty gleaming white seeds or beans covered in a mucilaginous pulp. They contain protein, fat, carbohydrate, calcium, phosphorus, iron, sodium, potassium, vitamin A, thiamine, riboflavin, starch, theobromine and caffeine. Linnaeus, the great Swedish botanist

(1707–78), in 1735 christened the tree *Theobroma cacao*, which translated means 'food of the Gods'. Few would disagree with Linnaeus's graceful compliment.

Cacao beans were among the specimen plants and fruits that Columbus brought back with him for his patron, Ferdinand of Spain, on his return from his epic journey of discovery in 1492. He was the first European to see the beans used, but their value went unrecognised and they were thrown away as useless.

When Hernán Cortés (1485–1547), the Spanish soldier who conquered Mexico, landed in that country in 1519 he saw the bean widely grown and used, for chocolate or *xocolatl* as it was called, was the national drink of the Aztecs. When Cortés was received by their emperor, Montezuma (1466–1520), a sovereign whose riches were immense and whose power was absolute, he would certainly have been offered chocolate to drink. William Prescott (1796–1859), the American historian, recorded in his *History of the Conquest of Mexico* that the emperor took

> no other beverage than chocolatl, a potation of chocolate flavoured with vanilla and other spices, and so prepared as to be reduced to a froth the consistency of honey, which gradually dissolved in the mouth and was taken cold. This beverage was served in golden goblets with spoons of the same metal or tortoiseshell finely wrought. The emperor was exceedingly fond of it, to judge by the quantity – no less than fifty jars or pitchers being prepared for his own daily consumption; two thousand more were allowed for that of his household.

The Aztecs must have devoted a great deal of care to both the cultivation and the preparation of cacao. They dried the beans in the sun and crushed them with a kind of rolling pin, thus obtaining a sort of fatty paste which was kneaded into cakes for use later on. When required, the cakes were ground up, mixed with water and flavoured with vanilla and spices. Sugar was then not known. Cacao beans were not only used to make *xocolatl*, they were used as currency, and a tolerably good slave could be purchased for 100 beans. In the list of tributes paid to the lords of Mexico, besides twenty bags of gold dust, some more unusual items appear, such as 'twenty chests of ground chocolate' and 'two hundred loads of chocolate'.[1]

Cortés brought the cacao bean to Spain, together with the knowledge of how to use it. In Mexico the bean was known as *cacuatl* and the beverage made from it as *chocolath*, *lath* being water and *choco* a form of *cacuatl*. The Spaniards found the Mexican word difficult to pronounce and called the bean *cacao*. 'Cocoa' became the more usual form of the word in English; this was deplored by many writers for causing the bean to be confused with coconut, but efforts to retain the earlier form of the word have been in vain. The word for chocolate has survived almost unaltered.

For nearly a century the Spaniards managed to keep their discovery a secret. They followed the method of preparation used by the Aztecs and made a souplike beverage which they flavoured with chillies and other spices. So successful were they in guarding the secret of the cacao bean that when the Dutch as well as the British sea captains like Sir Francis Drake (1545–96) and Sir Martin Frobisher (1535–94) captured treasure-laden Spanish galleons returning home on the high seas, they flung the bags of cacao beans overboard with scorn. It must be said that not everyone found chocolate an agreeable drink. José Acosta, the Spanish Jesuit historian whose book on the natural history of Mexico and Peru was translated into English in 1604, wrote, 'The chief use they make of this cocoa is in a drinke which they call chocolate, whereof they make great account, foolishly and without reason; for it is loathsome to such as are not acquainted with it, having a skumme or frothe that is very unpleasant to taste if they be not well conceited thereof . . . The Spaniards, both men and women, are very greedy of this chocolate.'

The ladies of Chiapa, a town in the south of Mexico, were obviously 'well conceited thereof'. It is told of them that they had their maids interrupt both sermon and mass by bringing them cups of hot chocolate. Their bishop, after due warning, excommunicated them for their presumption, but the ladies simply changed their church and continued as before. The bishop was poisoned for his trouble, according to Thomas Gage in his *New Survey of the West Indies*, which caused a sensation when it was published in 1648.

It is thought that chocolate was first introduced into France at the marriage of Louis XIII and Anne of Austria, daughter of Philip III of Spain. It is an engaging theory. Louis was nine when his father, Henry IV, was assassinated in 1610 and his mother, Marie of Medici, became regent. She determined to reverse her husband's policy, and instead of attacking Spain, she arranged to cement an alliance between the two countries through a double dynastic marriage. Louis was married to Philip of Spain's daughter, Anne, while his son, later to become Philip IV, married Louis's sister. The double nuptial celebration took place in 1615, notwithstanding strong opposition from the French Protestants and the nobility. If chocolate was served at this grand occasion, it must have bestowed a very special cachet on the beverage.

The truth about the way the Spanish lost the monopoly on the secret of chocolate is probably a good deal more prosaic. Travelling monks are said to have introduced it in France and Germany. By this time the Spaniards had learned to mix sugar with their chocolate, thus making the drink a great deal more palatable. Antonio de Ledesma Comenero wrote a treatise on chocolate in Spanish which was published in Madrid in 1613. During the next decade his book was translated into English, French and Latin, evidence of how interest in this novel drink was spreading. Whether Anne of Austria was the first to introduce chocolate to the court of France or not, when Maria Theresa, the infanta of Spain, married Louis XIV in 1660, her partiality for the drink certainly ensured its success at the king's court. It has been said that Maria Theresa had only two passions, the king and chocolate. It is to be hoped that she found the sweet warm drink consoling, for the king, preoccupied by affairs of state, intrigues at court and his succession of powerful mistresses, had little time for his queen.

There was much discussion in France of the digestive and medicinal qualities of chocolate. Madame de Sévigné (1626–96), whose splendidly informative letters to her daughter, Madame de Grignan, provide a fascinating and detailed account of life at the French court, fortunately included her own opinion and that of others on the merits of chocolate as a drink. In a letter she wrote that she had taken chocolate so that she could both take nourishment and yet fast until evening, for which reason she found the drink pleasant. However, this was a subject on which the church held conflicting views. Gaspar Caldera de Heredia, a Spanish doctor, argued that chocolate was a food and should not be taken during periods of fasting. On the other hand, Cardinal Brabcaccio maintained that chocolate, like wine, was one of the necessities of life and could be taken even on fast days. Whatever his views on this controversial subject, the archbishop of Lyons, Alphonse de Richelieu, the great cardinal's brother, said that he drank chocolate for its therapeutic virtues. Some time later, however, Madame de Sévigné confided to her daughter that there were as many people willing to recommend chocolate as there were to warn against the evil effects it could produce; it was said to bring on attacks of the vapours and palpitations, and although it might taste pleasant, it could also bring on fevers which could lead to death.

The chocolate that was being drunk at this period was indeed rich, for no one had yet discovered how to remove the excess cocoa butter from the cocoa bean, which must have made the drink difficult for some to digest. Brillat-Savarin (1755–1826), a politician and lawyer, today best remembered as a gastronome, had no doubts. In his *Physiologie du Goût*, a compendium on the art of dining, he wrote that he considered chocolate to be

> one of the most effective restoratives. All those who have to work while they might be sleeping, men of wit who feel temporarily deprived of their intellectual powers, those who find the weather oppressive, time dragging, the atmosphere depressing, those who are tormented by some preoccupation which deprives them of liberty of thought, let all such men imbibe half a litre of chocolate amber, using sixty to seventy-two grains of amber, and they will be amazed.

Brillat-Savarin had received advice from Madame d'Arestal, the worldly mother superior of the Convent of Visitation at Belley, on how to make his chocolate. No mean gourmand herself, she counselled him to make his chocolate the night before in a faïence pot, because, she explained, the chocolate becomes concentrated during the night and this gives it a much better consistency.

The fashion had already spread to Holland and there were several chocolate and cocoa houses in Amsterdam at that time.

It is not known when chocolate was first drunk in England, but it is first recorded as being for sale in Oxford in 1650. A notice in the *Public Advertiser* on 16 June 1657 signalled the appearance of a chocolate house in London: 'In Bishopsgate Street, in Queen Head Alley at a Frenchman's House is an excellent West Indian drink, called chocolate, to be sold, where you may have it ready at any time, and also unmade at reasonable rates.'

The eastward spread of cocoa can be paralleled by the westward spread of coffee from the Near East. Coffee houses had become popular in Constantinople and Venice before reaching London, where the first one was opened in St Michael's Alley, Cornhill, in 1652. By the early eighteenth century chocolate and coffee houses were very much part of the fashionable and social life of London. Pepys, in a much quoted passage in his diary, noted that on 24 November 1664 he had been 'to a coffee house to drink jocolatte, very good'. Pepys's brief endorsement reflects the more matter-of-fact English approach to the chocolate question. This impression is confirmed by Lewes, Baron de Pollnitz, writing of his visits to the various coffee and chocolate houses he visited during his visit to London in 1745:

> The average English gentleman starts his day with a walk in the park, afterwards he saunters to some coffee or chocolate house frequented by the persons he would see, for it is a sort of rule with the English to go once a day at least to houses of this sort, where they talk business or news, read the newspapers, and often look at each other without opening their mouths, and 'tis very well they are so mute, for if they were as talkative as the people of other nations, the coffee houses would be intolerable and there would be no hearing of what one man said, where there are so many.

The best known and most successful coffee and chocolate houses were in Pall Mall, according to John Macky, a continental traveller, writing of his journey through England in 1722. He described Pall Mall as the ordinary place of residence of all strangers 'because of its vicinity to the King's Palace, the parks, the Parliament House, the theatres and the chocolate and coffee houses where the best company frequent'. He continued, 'At twelve o'clock the Beau Monde assembles in several coffee and chocolate houses, the best of which are the Cocoa Tree, White's Chocolate House, St James's, the Smyrna and the British Coffee House, and all these are so near to one another than in less than an hour you can see the company of them all.'

Today White's Club occupies the site of White's Chocolate House, the best-known of the houses. Unlike many of the others it was not a centre for political or literary discussion, its clients preferring to gamble and amuse themselves in other ways. It opened in 1693 on the west side of St James's Street and moved to the east side in 1697. When the proprietor, Francis White, who may have been a naturalised Italian, died in 1707, his widow carried on the business under the name of Mrs White's Chocolate House. After her death, her manager, John Arthur, took it over until it was burned to the ground in a fire in 1733.[2] Nothing was saved, but Hogarth has immortalised the event in his *Rake's Progress*, which shows the gambling room at White's at the moment when the fire broke out.

Another widow, Mrs Elliott, found herself running the celebrated St James's coffee house on the other side of the street from White's after the death of her husband in 1722. For several years 'Widow Elliott' ministered to the wants of the literary world. The St James's was much frequented by Joseph Addison (1672–1719) and Richard Steele (1672–1729), the essayists and men of letters, creators of the *Tatler*, Oliver Goldsmith (1728–74), the poet and playwright, and David Garrick (1717–79) the actor and theatrical manager. For a while it became the headquarters of the Whigs, the political party of great landowners, merchants and tradesmen.

In its early years the Cocoa Tree Chocolate House was very much a centre of

Toryism and no Whig could have thought of going there, any more than a Tory would have gone to the St James's. Such distinctions seem not to have applied to men of letters and Richard Steele mentioned in *The Spectator* that his face was very well known at the Cocoa Tree. There, too, tickets for animal baiting could sometimes be had. An advertisement in the *Daily Post* in June 1721 read:

> At the Boarded House, Marylebone Fields, will be baited a large panther, at the desire of several persons of quality, to fight several bull and bear dogs for 200 guineas. Likewise, for the desire of the quality, is a green bull to be baited to death on a stage 30 ft square, and a large bear to be baited on the same stage. Tickets to be had at Will's Coffee House, Covent Garden, and at the Cocoa Tree Chocolate House in Pall Mall.

Another newspaper advertisement, two years later, recorded the sudden death of Captain Lloyd of Sackville Street, Piccadilly, who 'as he was drinking a dish of chocolate at the Cocoa Tree in Pall Mall, fell down and died'. Another gentleman felt the loss of his cane with a gold head sufficiently to advertise for its return, writing that it was lost 'in a hackney carriage coming from the Cocoa Tree in Pall Mall'.

The Cocoa Tree was considered to have a strong French connection and the names of its proprietors, among them Narsan, Cartière and Comte Soleirol, lend substance to this claim. This might explain its reputation as a centre of Jacobite intrigue at the time of the unsuccessful 1745 uprising led by Prince Charles Edward, popularly known as Bonnie Prince Charlie. The object of the uprising was to reinstate his father, James, and known as the Old Pretender, as king of England, Scotland and Ireland. England was at war with France at the time and French support for the Old Pretender represented a strategic stab in the back. In her memoirs a Mrs Pilkington mentions a young man who boasted, 'I dress and at about 12 o'clock go to the Cocoa Tree where I talk treason.' In its later years the Cocoa Tree became less seditious and more aristocratic.

It is not known whether chocolate was manufactured in England at the beginning of the eighteenth century. It seems probable that the proprietors of the chocolate houses imported manufactured chocolate since no duty was levied on the raw beans, suggesting that few if any were imported at that time. However, duty was imposed at eight shillings a gallon on manufactured chocolate, which limited its consumption by putting up the price.

Walter Churchman appears to be the first chocolate manufacturer in Britain. Since the Frys took over the Churchman business in about 1761, it is very possible that the Frys' claim to be the oldest chocolate-manufacturing firm in Britain is valid. Walter Churchman had premises in Bristol in 1728 where he manufactured chocolate. He also had a warehouse in St Paul's Churchyard, London, from which he may have supplied some of the fashionable chocolate houses.

An enterprising man, he had invested in a water engine which enabled him to grind his chocolate more finely, and in 1729 he was granted letters patent by George

II. The notice advertising the fact was carried in *Farley's Bristol Newspaper* in June 1731 and is not without interest:

> His Majesty, having been pleased to grant to Walter Churchman Letters Patent for his new invention of making chocolate without fire, to greater perfection in all respects, than will appear on Trial, by its immediate dissolving, full flavour, smoothness on the palate and intimate union with Liquids; and as it is so much finer than any other sort, so it will go much further and be less offensive to weak digestions, being by this method made free of grit and gross particles so much disliked which is referred to the fair and impartial experiment.
>
> NB. The curious may be supplied with his superfine chocolate which is as many degrees finer than the above Standard, as that exceeds the finest sold by other Makers, plain at six shillings per pound; with vanello, seven shillings per pound.
>
> To be sold for ready money only at Mr Churchman's chocolate Warehouse at Mr John Young's in St Paul's Churchyard, London.

Walter Churchman's son, Charles, carried on the business after the death of his father, while continuing to practise as a solicitor.

The Churchmans were not the only chocolate manufacturers in Bristol. Joseph Fry (1728–87) came to Bristol when he was about twenty and was admitted a freeman of the city in 1735. Three years later an announcement appeared in the local press stating simply, 'The best sorts of chocolates, made and sold wholesale and retail by Joseph Fry, Apothecary, in Small Street, Bristol.' By 1756, according to the official history of J. S. Fry & Sons, Joseph Fry had taught himself a number of recipes for chocolate. Although he is said to have been an innovator rather than an inventor and to have relied heavily on the experiments and researches of others in the development of his enterprise, there is no doubt that he had a talent for business.

Little is known about Joseph Fry's life at this time. During his apprenticeship to a Dr Henry Portsmouth of Basingstoke, whose daughter he married, he received an extensive and thorough training in the medical properties of plants and herbs and in the compounding of drugs. In the medical literature of the eighteenth century there was much discussion of the therapeutic effects of chocolate. This, added to the knowledge that chocolate was pleasant to drink, doubtless encouraged Dr Joseph Fry, as he was known, to start up in business as a chocolate manufacturer.

When Charles Churchman died in 1761 he left the patent for the water engine and his chocolate business to his executor, John Vaughan. Fry, seeing an opportunity, purchased the patent and advertised the fact in the local paper: 'Churchman's patent chocolate is now made by Joseph Fry and John Vaughan Jnr, the said Churchman's executor, the present sole proprietors of the famous water engine at Castle Mills.' Competition must have increased, for the *Public Advertiser* in 1776 emphasised that the water mill was the only one of its kind in Great Britain. The business obviously prospered because a warehouse was later established in

London under the supervision of the founder's brother, John Fry, a cheesemonger of Whitehall.[3]

Infringements of the patent must have been sufficiently numerous to cause the Bristol chocolatemaker to announce that 'only chocolate with a stamp of an oval form . . . affixed to each half pound and quarter pound, with the words "Churchman's Patent Chocolate, made only by Joseph Fry of Bristol"' was the genuine article.[4] The successful marketing of Fry's chocolate depended in part on its reputation for quality, but also in part on the fact that Joseph Fry, as a Quaker, stood for the belief in honest trading; with the introduction of the manufacturer's stamp he thus ensured both quality and standardisation, so the public would know what they were buying. He also catered for the less well-off and the less fastidious: 'Those who do not choose to go to the price of the pack may be supplied at London Prices with a very good sort of chocolate without the stamp, far superior to what is usually sold.'

Bristol was well served by hauliers and by 1750 a total of ninety-four carriers plied goods from Bristol to other towns, thus providing facilities through which Bristol manufacturers and merchants could market their goods over a wide area. On receiving an order, Fry dispatched small packets of chocolate on the scheduled services of the coach or by penny post.

Unfortunately the heavy import duty meant that only the relatively wealthy could afford to purchase the Bristol chocolate. In 1771 a pound of Fry's vanilla chocolate retailed at seven shillings and sixpence, a sum roughly equivalent to the average weekly agricultural wage. Joseph Fry addressed a 'Humble Memorial' to the Lord's Commissioner of the Treasury in 1776 pleading for a reduction in the excise duty which was now levied, not only on manufactured chocolate at two shillings and threepence, but on the raw material as well, at the rate of ten shillings per hundredweight of cocoa beans. This tax ensured that chocolate and cocoa joined the list of products which interested smugglers, and for a while there was much illicit trading. Fry had also to compete with manufacturers who used primitive methods and adulterated the product, for the public had not yet learned how to distinguish the good from the bad.

Joseph Fry was a man of parts, and although his contribution to the manufacture of chocolate is historically important, the business did not absorb all his energy. He also had an interest in Richard Champion's ceramic works in Bristol, but it is not in connection with either his chocolate or his ceramic business that he is best remembered. *The Dictionary of National Biography* rated his contribution to type founding as his most important contribution to society. He entered into partnership with William Pine, the first printer of the *Bristol Gazette,* and the new type of Messrs Fry and Pine may be traced in several eighteenth-century works.

A gentleman under the pseudonym Benevolus wrote in the *Gentleman's Magazine,* at the time of Joseph Fry's death, both prophetically and optimistically:

The manufacture of chocolate, both in his own name and as a succeeding Patentee to Churchman, was carried by his own skill and management to a degree of importance, now well known, to over a large part of Great Britain; a manufacture which is likely to remain a very considerable source of profit to his widow and family.

Anna Fry, his widow, and her son Joseph Storrs Fry I did indeed take over the business, changing its name to Anna Fry and Son. The business flourished as Benevolus had predicted, and the first advertisements stressing the healthful properties of cocoa began to appear. Anna Fry's cocoa was said to be recommended by 'the most eminent of the Faculty, in preference to every other kind of Breakfast, to such who have tender Habits, decayed Health, weak Lungs or scorbutic Tendencies, being easy of Digestion, affording a fine and light nourishment, and greatly correcting the sharp Humours in the Constitution.' This was followed by directions on how to make cocoa in the pot: 'Take an ounce of cocoa, (which is about a common Tea Cupful) boil it in a Pint and a Half of Water for Ten or Fifteen minutes, then keep it near the fire to settle and become fine, after that, decant it off into another Pot for immediate Use. It is drunk as Coffee, sweetened with a fine moist sugar, and a little cream or milk should be added.'[5]

It was Sir Hans Sloane (1660–1753),[6] another man of parts, a collector, a physician and the first doctor to be made a baronet, whose interest in chocolate had already led to a further development in its manufacture. Sloane, whose natural-history collection formed the nucleus of what has become the British Museum, had, while in South America, realised the significance of the nutritional value of the cacao bean. He was also the first person to think of combining milk with chocolate to make a nourishing drink.[7] A certain Nicholas Summer appears to have been the first to have marketed Hans Sloane's milk chocolate at his shop in Greek Street in the early eighteenth century. Like the Fry advertisement which followed it, it stressed the medical qualities of the chocolate and it was said to be recommended 'by several eminent Physicians, especially those of Sir Hans Sloane's acquaintance, for its lightness on the stomach and its great use in all consumptive cases'.

By the middle of the eighteenth century chocolate was being manufactured worldwide, but all the better-known manufacturers postdate Fry and Vaughan. Lombard of France, who claim to be 'la plus ancienne chocolaterie de France', started business in 1766; von Lippe of Germany had started the previous year, as had Dr James Baker in the United States. The next big advance was not made until the beginning of the nineteenth century, an advance which was to give the continental and particularly the French chocolate manufacturers a head start over their British counterparts.

The cocoa bean is so rich in cocoa butter that to make the drink palatable, starch and other farinaceous ingredients were regularly added to counteract the excessive fat. In 1828 Conrad van Houten, a Dutch chemist, learned to press out some of this fat and so enable cocoa powder to be sold pure and undiluted. This discovery had another important consequence, for chocolate manufacturers soon learned how to blend the extracted cocoa butter with the pure cocoa in different proportions, making possible the production of many different types of eating chocolate. The French, in particular, soon became expert at varying the proportion of cocoa butter and sugar they mixed with the cocoa, thereby creating different degrees of fluidity in the chocolate, which gave their confectioners much greater scope.

It is not known when eating chocolate was first sold in Britain. It appeared on Cadbury's price list in 1842, but the firm advertised only one brand and that appeared to have been imported from France as it was listed as 'French Eating Chocolate'. Cadbury's also sold a milk chocolate prepared after the original recipe of Dr Hans Sloane, but that was almost certainly a drinking chocolate. It was not until 1875 that the Swiss firm of Peters at Vevey discovered a way to combine milk and chocolate to make solid milk chocolate. Their example was followed by Fry in 1902 and Cadbury in 1905.

Half the cocoa imported in the early nineteenth century went to the Royal Navy. There has been a long and interesting association between the navy and cocoa, or 'kye', as it has always been affectionately known in the senior service. The origin of the word 'kye' is itself mysterious; it could be a corruption of 'cocoa' or perhaps derive from the initials of 'chocolate issue', CI in naval parlance, for cocoa has been part of the regular issue to ships for over two centuries.

The drinking of cocoa at sea goes back to the time when English Harbour in Antigua was much used by the British navy. There Captain James Ferguson, a serving officer, came to appreciate both the nutritional qualities of cocoa and its cheapness. He introduced the drink on board the ships stationed in the West Indies in about 1780.[8] The lime has been given so much credit in the fight against scurvy that the role played by cocoa in providing a more balanced diet for sailors has been almost overlooked. Surgeon Trotter, urging that the use of cocoa should be extended from the West Indies station to the Channel fleet, wrote: 'In a cold country it could be singularly beneficial. What a comfortable meal would a cup of warm cocoa or chocolate be to a sailor on a winter cruise in the Channel or North Sea in coming from a wet deck in a rainy morning watch.'[9] Many sailors must have cause to be thankful to Surgeon Trotter for those sentiments.

According to naval records it seems that the first reference to cocoa was in an instruction from 'your affectionate friends' the victualling committee, directing that her majesty's ships abroad should be supplied with cocoa and sugar in lieu of butter and cheese, in an order dated 1783. The use of cocoa only became general in June 1824, when one ounce per man per day was ordered to be issued in lieu of the breakfast issue of 'burgoo', a mixture of oatmeal boiled in water and sweetened with molasses. Cocoa was originally issued in powder form, but its keeping properties evidently left much to be desired. Many solutions to the problem of packing the cocoa so that it would not deteriorate were tried without success. When the surgeon superintendent of convict ships to the Admiralty was moved to complain that 'the cocoa is of such quality as to be rejected by the stomack', it was obvious that something had to be done.

Modifications were introduced at the Deptford victualling yard and 'kye' was produced in slab form, which was a decided improvement on what had gone before.

But the Royal Victoria Yard at Deptford took no heed of the developments in the manufacture of cocoa; not for them the refinements introduced by van Houten and copied sooner or later by all manufacturers. They continued to make cocoa as they always had, excess butter fat and all, for more than 150 years. A young midshipman recalled making his first mug of 'kye' for the officer of the watch on a rough night sailing past Harwich. He grated a small portion of the chocolate into the mug and poured on hot water, causing the yellow butter fat to gleam. Having added condensed milk, he took it to the bridge. After one gulp of the anaemic brew the officer spat out the words 'weasel water'.[10] They took their 'kye' rich and strong in the Royal Navy. It was only in 1968 that drinking chocolate in slab form was abolished and ordinary cocoa powder substituted, thus ending a long naval tradition.

The same great upsurge in demand for chocolate and cocoa that enabled the Frys, Cadburys and Rowntrees to expand into major businesses was also in evidence in the United States. In 1883 the US imported 9 million pounds of cocoa beans; in 1893 the amount imported had nearly trebled. Chicago celebrated the 400th anniversary of the discovery of America with a great exhibition called the World's Columbian Exposition in 1892. An enterprising German manufacturer, J. M. Lehmann, had shipped over his complicated chocolatemaking machinery to show at the Exposition. A successful caramel confectioner, Milton Hershey, came to Chicago, saw the machinery and was fascinated by the way it could roast, hull, grind, mix and mould the beans to produce the chocolate. His chocolate-dipped caramels were very popular with the public and he knew that imports of cocoa were increasing fast. He bought the machinery because he was certain that the future lay with chocolate rather than caramels, which he dismissed as a 'fad'; 'chocolate is a permanent thing'.[11] By 1900 Hershey had sold his caramel factory for $1 million. He had decided to build – not just a factory to manufacture his chocolate, but a whole town. What is more, he decided to build it out in the country, to buy farming land and stock it with cows so as to have a plentiful supply of milk for the chocolate he wanted to make.

Work started in 1903 and Hershey's factory was finished in 1905, 'the most complete of its kind in the world', according to the *Confectioners' Journal*. The building work on the town had started at the same time. The houses of Chocolate Avenue and Cocoa Avenue were mainly for sale, because Hershey's idea was that every man should own his own home. There were a very few houses for rent, but the rents were low. As the town grew Hershey added to it – an inn, a bank, a store and schools. He helped the churches and later founded a school for orphan boys. Hershey's brilliant idea – to concentrate on one single item, to produce it in vast quantities and to make it cheap, so that everyone could buy it – paid off. From the profits of the Hershey bar the Hershey Chocolate Corporation, the largest chocolate manufacturer in the world, has been able to finance the continued growth of the town of Hershey, and many other philanthropic undertakings.

The Food of the Gods, once the preserve of the wealthy, served in gold and silver vessels, was transformed by modern machinery and marketing methods into paper-wrapped bars which would be enjoyed by the masses. Europeans, however, eat more chocolate per head it seems than do their American cousins. And it is European names like Lindt and Sprüngli in Switzerland, Godiva Chocolatier in Belgium and Charbonnel and Walker of London that vie for the status of the makers of the best chocolates in the world. Few can resist the enticing appeal of chocolate in some form or other, be it temptingly cheap or wickedly expensive, a quick snack or a graceful gift to others.

2

Quaker Heritage

George Cadbury and Joseph Rowntree, both inheritors of small grocery businesses, were the creators and architects of the great chocolate-manufacturing concerns which today bear their names. Joseph Storrs Fry II, on the other hand, was born with a chocolate spoon in his mouth. When, in 1878, he took over the chairmanship of J. S. Fry & Sons from his uncle, Francis Fry, the Frys were by far the largest manufacturers of chocolate and cocoa in the country; their output accounted for nearly a quarter of all the chocolate sold in Britain, their sales totalled more than a quarter of a million pounds.

The families of all three chocolate manufacturers had belonged to the Society of Friends for several generations. The Frys had entertained George Fox (1624–91), the founder of the Society of Friends, at their home at Sutton Benger in Wiltshire, where they had lived since the fourteenth century.[1] The early Quakers were often persecuted by the authorities on account of their religious beliefs, and Zephania Fry (1658–1728) had the distinction of being imprisoned in 1684 as a recalcitrant Quaker.

Joseph Fry (1728–87), the son of John Fry (1701–75), was the first member of the family to leave Wiltshire. He settled in Bristol in 1748 and, as has been seen, started to manufacture chocolates, a business which was continued by his widow, Anna, assisted by their son, Joseph Storrs Fry I (1767–1835). When Anna Fry died Joseph took on a partner, a Mr Hunt. When Hunt retired in 1822 Joseph brought his three sons, Joseph (1795–1879), Francis (1803–86) and Richard (1807–78), into the firm, and the well-known name of J. S. Fry & Sons was adopted. In 1935 the firm was taken over by Cadbury, who, however, have kept the name in being. Francis was the most notable of the three brothers and the development of the business was chiefly his work.

As seems to have been traditional with the Frys, Francis Fry devoted only part of his energies to the running of the business and had many other interests and pursuits.[2] He took a major part in the introduction of the railways into the west of England and his friend Edward Pease (1767–1858), one of the moving spirits behind the Stockton and Darlington railway, described him as 'a man of talent, full of much enterprise and engagement'. He was a dynamic businessman, a scholar and, as a devout Quaker, he became a strong advocate for temperance and the abolition of slavery. Under his chairmanship Fry's first produced the Chocolate Cream bar in 1866, which was a most successful innovation. Francis Fry's claim to eminence, however, was due more to his scholarship than to his business acumen. He became one of the world's leading authorities on Bibles and, by his death in 1886, his collection of Bibles and Testaments was one of the finest in the world. His proudest achievement was to produce a facsimile of the only known copy of Tyndale's first edition of the New Testament, printed in 1525–26.

Joseph Storrs Fry II, Francis Fry's nephew, was already fifty-two when he took over the chairmanship in 1878. He directed the firm in collaboration with other members of the Fry family, including his cousin, another Francis Fry. Joseph was born on 6 August 1826 in a house which formed part of the factory complex. Little is known about his father, Joseph Fry, Francis Fry's elder brother, except that he was said to have been an omnivorous reader and to have held strong free-trade and liberal views; his interests, apart from the business, were philanthropic and religious. Joseph Storrs Fry was much attached to his mother, Mary Ann, the daughter of Edward Swaine. She was a confident and buoyant character. He never married and lived with his mother until she died, when he was well over sixty.

It is difficult to form any clear idea of the childhood influences that moulded the character of the young Joseph Storrs Fry. He and his younger brother, Edward, were such very different personalities that little can be assumed from the evidence that exists. Both Joseph and Edward were educated at home until they went to Bristol College in 1841, where they remained for a year. During their time at the college both suffered ridicule on account of their Quaker dress and speech, an experience which was never forgotten by Edward, who later tried to have the regulations concerning the plain Quaker dress modified. Although Joseph was said to have shown considerable ability in mathematics, his scholastic career was brought to an end by the sudden closure of the college. He subsequently spent a couple of years learning business management, but that and his year at college appear to have been his only outside formative experiences.

If his later life reflects the influence of his childhood, it must have been narrow and austere. Joseph was said not to be interested in art, science, gardening, nature or people; he was not interested in social intercourse and rarely if ever took a holiday or indulged in any kind of recreation. Yet Edward, who shared his upbringing, became a distinguished judge and was knighted in 1877.[3] Edward never forgot the intense love of observation instilled in him by his father and had a lifelong interest in scenery, animals and plants; so perhaps it is dangerous to push such an inference too far. Joseph was evidently a deeply introverted character and lacked the broad vision and wide range of interests that so many of his family had shown. His only interests appear to have been his own business, the affairs of the Society of Friends, where he held the highest office, as clerk of the yearly meeting, for thirteen years, and his involvement in many philanthropic undertakings and local good works.

A copy of the rules for day and piece workers promulgated in 1851, four years before Joseph Storrs Fry II joined the firm as one of the family directors, gives an immediate impression of the authoritarian and paternalistic way in which the business was run by Francis Fry, Joseph Storrs Fry's uncle. It was natural that the hours of work and the wages should be laid down, but the Frys took a strong line about the way in which their employees should conduct themselves, not only inside the factory but outside it as well; their spiritual needs were also ministered to and they were actually locked into the room where the scripture reading took place. The rules for day workers stated:

1. The Time Keeper to enter in his book every day the time at which the day worker comes to the premises, the time at which he goes to work after every meal, the time at which anyone may be absent during work hours, also the times at which the engine starts in the morning and stops at night.

2. No Day worker to leave off work, to wash, to make any other preparation to leave off work before the bell rings for that purpose.

3. No Day worker to absent himself or herself from the premises during work hours without permission from the Timekeeper.

4. Piece workers to finish their work as early as possible and not to remain on the premises after they had done their work under any pretence. They are not to leave the premises without permission.

5. All Day and Piece workers are expected to attend the scripture teaching at a quarter to 9 a.m. As soon as the bell rings for reading, every person to go immediately into the room and the Timekeeper to bolt the door five minutes after the bell has rung.

6. No person to use or eat any cocoa or chocolate, or to bring any onto the premises for that purpose or to apply to their own uses in any way any article the property of their employer.

7. No person to sing or make noises on the premises.

8. No person to go in or out of the back gates, but always through the front shop; no person to bring any basket onto the premises.

9. All girls taking dinner or tea on the premises to take it in the room provided for them.

10. It is particularly requested that every person, whether on the premises or at other places, be at all times strictly sober and that no one be in the habit of

1 A portrait of J. S. Fry, circa 1905.

1 Joseph Rowntree picknicking at
Scarborough, 1918.

3 George Cadbury, 1920.

4 *Left to right*: standing George Gillet, George Cadbury; sitting Joseph Pelvin, J. S. Rowntree, Lewis Fry. The Pavement Street apprentices, York, 1858.

frequenting Public Houses or Beer Shops; any person known to do so will not be regarded by their employer with confidence and this knowledge will at any time be considered good reason for discharging a man or a girl.

11. It is also required that all persons conduct themselves with strict order and propriety on the premises and whilst passing in or out.

12. All unnecessary conversation and familiarity between men and girls is strictly prohibited.[4]

From the wages book of the period it appears that men received about 15 shillings a week and girls half that amount. Apart from a gradual increase in wages, the conditions of employment probably altered little over the years, considering Joseph Storrs Fry's inbuilt conservatism.

Like the other cocoa and chocolate manufacturers, Frys grew in keeping with the national trend. A rapidly growing population and rising living standards contributed to increased turnover and profits. The number of employees rose from 500 in 1861 to nearly 5000 in 1913. Like the Cadburys and the Rowntrees, the Frys had increased the size and number of their factories, but instead of moving to new sites they continued to build in the cramped centre of Bristol on the site of slum tenements. As the premises were enlarged, many strange edifices were absorbed: the packing department was housed in an ancient Baptist chapel and the church of St Bartholomew was swallowed up to become part of the factory complex. These adverse working conditions contributed materially to the decline in profits which started during the last six years of Joseph Storrs Fry's chairmanship.

Joseph died in 1913, aged eighty-seven, in the room in which he had been born, blind but full of honours. He had been made a freeman of the city of Bristol in 1909 and an LL.D. of the university in 1912, and the business had made him a millionaire. He left over 200 benefactions in his long will, including one of £42,000 to be distributed among his employees.

The legacy he left to his nephews and successors was less happy. By 1910 Fry's were no longer the leading manufacturers of chocolate and cocoa; Cadbury's sales had exceeded those of Fry by £1,670,221 to £1,642,715.[5] With every passing year Cadbury increased their lead.

—— THE ROWNTREES ——

Joseph Rowntree (1836–1925), did not enter the chocolate and cocoa manufacturing business until he was thirty-three. Unlike Joseph Storrs Fry or George Cadbury, who both inherited their cocoa and chocolate businesses, Joseph Rowntree seemed destined to remain a master grocer, carrying on the business in Pavement, York that he and his elder brother, John Stevenson Rowntree, had inherited from their father. Joseph's younger brother, Henry Isaac (1838–83), became the first of the

Rowntree family to go into the cocoa and chocolate business. He had not been made a partner in the family shop with his brothers and he was probably given his patrimony in the form of capital, which enabled him to buy the cocoa, chocolate and chicory department of Tuke and Company.

Both Tukes and Rowntrees were old-established Quaker families, although the Rowntrees were fairly new to York, having come to that city in 1822. Joseph senior was the sixth son of yet another Joseph. As there had been no place for him in his father's grocery business in Scarborough, he came to York and within a very short space of time had established a grocery business in a house in Pavement.

Joseph senior would have liked to make his career at sea and have command of a ship, but his Quaker upbringing debarred him from following his true inclinations. The shop at Pavement was successful and in 1832 Joseph married Sarah Stevenson, who, although only twenty-four at the time of her marriage, took on the responsibilities of a household of over a dozen people – including the apprentices – entertained and helped her husband with his accounts. At two-yearly intervals three sons, John Stevenson, Joseph and Henry Isaac, were born to the couple, followed by two daughters.

Although devout members of the Society of Friends, the Rowntree children were brought up in a less circumscribed manner than either the Frys or the Cadburys. For one thing the apprentices, boys of thirteen and fourteen who worked in the shop, also lived in the house and teased and played with the children. For another, their father had been a member of the distinguished committee of the Quaker school at Ackworth since 1827 and was later also on the committee of the school at Bootham in York, and was alive to the importance of a good education for his children. The Ackworth general meeting drew ministering Friends like a magnet and became second in importance only to the yearly meeting as the Quaker function of the year.[6]

Quakers, like other dissenters, were barred from Oxford and Cambridge universities until 1871, and the problem of finding satisfactory teachers for the schools was one with which Joseph senior was familiar. 'Do parents bring up their most highly gifted sons for schoolmasters?' he asked on one occasion. 'It cannot be affirmed they do; hence society suffers from the lack of really able teachers and the profession fails from the same case in obtaining its right place in public estimation.' The Bootham school, nevertheless, had a number of distinguished visitors, including the philanthropic brothers Joseph John Gurney (1788–1847) and Samuel Gurney (1786–1856), sons of a wealthy Norfolk banker; Luke Howard (1772–1864), one of the founders of modern meteorology; and Samuel Tuke (1784–1857), the philanthropist.

In 1848 the Rowntree family were forced, reluctantly, to leave the house in Pavement. Besides having no wish to join the increasing band of prosperous tradesmen whose success in business had enabled them to move to more luxurious homes in the suburbs, Joseph was very concerned that the move meant he could no longer give such close supervision and care to his apprentices as he had done previously. But after the birth of a fourth child the house had become too small and the family moved to another house in York, near Bootham School.

Being apprentice to Joseph senior was no sinecure. A memorandum dated 1852 sets out plainly what was expected of the apprentices:

> The object of the Pavement establishment is business. The young men who enter it as journeymen or as apprentices are engaged to assist in this business and are expected to contribute their part in making it successful . . . It should be understood, however, that the value of the situation in Pavement mainly depends on the temper and disposition of mind of those who enter it. It presents a good opportunity for the industrious to learn, but there is little direct business teaching. The place is not suitable for the indolent and wayward.
>
> On ordinary occasions only one half of the Pavement family can take their meals together, hence much time is unavoidably occupied with meals. Without neglecting business much may be done by consideration and arrangement to prevent the needless extension of meal taking. From the frequency of meal times and the general absence of severe labour in the occupation of the family, I think about twenty minutes for each meal is as much as required. As however it is very desirable that these occasions of meeting together should be of a social and uniting character it is not designed to determine their exact duration.

Joseph was sent to Bootham School, York, when he was eleven, following in the steps of his elder brother, John. He spent five years at the school. John Ford, a scholar and a remarkable man, was the superintendent and a lifelong friend of the headmaster of Ackworth, Thomas Pumphrey. Both men were members of the Society of Friends educational committee. Under John Ford's rule there was no question the boys were forbidden to ask and no subject he would not explore. He believed Latin and Greek to be essential subjects and although the teaching of science in schools was highly controversial at that time, without discussion he made it a part of the school curriculum. This intellectually stimulating training was to reinforce the naturally enquiring minds of both John and Joseph.

When he was twenty-one, Joseph got permission from his father to go to London to broaden his experience by working for a big wholesale grocer in the City. He thoroughly enjoyed his stay in London and after work was drawn like a magnet to the House of Commons, where he listened with critical appreciation to the speeches of Gladstone and Disraeli. He was not impressed by Disraeli's performance in the budget debate on 21 February 1857. 'His utterance is hesitating, his argument not very clear – his brilliance seems only to display itself in satire – his arguments seem saturated with party feeling,' he wrote to his father.

His enthusiastic reports of the debates in the House of Commons somewhat alarmed his father, who perhaps feared that Joseph's interest in politics might take precedence over his responsibilities at the shop, but Joseph, sensing his father's concern, returned from London in 1859, maybe with some regret. It was not only the wider intellectual stimulus that attracted Joseph; from London he was also able to visit Hitchin, the home of the Seebohm family, old friends of the Rowntrees.

The interconnected lives of the Quakers are well illustrated by the links between the Rowntrees, the Seebohms and the Tukes. Benjamin Seebohm came from Germany and his family can trace their association with the Society of Friends to the visit of an Englishwoman, Sarah Hustler, daughter of William Tuke (1732–1822) of York. Sarah persuaded Benjamin Seebohm to come to England, where, as a member of the Society of Friends, he became a notable figure in the religious world of his day. He married Esther Wheeler of Hitchin, who was a granddaughter of William Tuke. Both Seebohm sons, Henry and Frederic, had been educated at Bootham School and Julia, their sister, and the main reason for Joseph's visits to Hitchin, was at the Quaker school in York which later became known as the Mount. Three years after his return to York, Joseph married Julia Seebohm, who died the following year. Joseph later married her cousin Emma Antoinette Seebohm in 1867, Antoinette Seebohm had been brought up in Germany and did not find it easy to adjust to life in York.

When Henry Isaac Rowntree acquired the Tuke family business, in 1862, he also inherited the good will of a family who had lived in York for more than three generations, whose ancestor had been one of the first to join the Society of Friends and whose services to the city of York went beyond their business interests.

It is unusual, even today, for a business to be founded by a woman, but Mary Tuke, a Quaker, the daughter of a blacksmith and orphaned young, opened a little shop in Walmgate, York, in 1725. If membership of the Society of Friends imposed limitations on its male members, it gave to women a greater freedom of movement than many of their contemporaries enjoyed. It was basic to Quaker faith that there was something of God in every man, and this applied to women also, who were thus given the same freedom to testify in meetings and to take part in the ministry as men. (For instance, Elizabeth Fry, taking advantage of her special position as a Quaker minister, was able to travel to address meetings and so came to discover for herself the appalling conditions in women's prisons in the early eighteenth century which she did so much to ameliorate.) Mary Tuke was also obviously a woman of great determination, and being a member of the Society of Friends no doubt strengthened her resolve to do battle with the Merchant Adventurers' Company, who never succeeded in getting her to pay the fine they had imposed on her for trading without a licence. The shop moved to Castlegate in Mary's lifetime and, as Tuke and Company, dealt first in tea, then became a manufacturer of chocolate and cocoa. From small beginnings the business grew and the Tukes prospered. Mary Tuke died in 1752 childless, and under the direction of her nephew, William Tuke, the shop became more specialised. But, like so many Friends, William Tuke had time for more than just his business.

Treatment of the insane was little short of barbaric in the eighteenth century. Fear and lack of understanding made forcible restraint the only treatment given, if that word may be used to describe the brutal and humiliating regime under which most of the insane lived in asylums. When a member of the Society of Friends died in the York asylum in 1791 under suspicious circumstances, the plight of these unfortunates incarcerated in the asylum was brought to the attention of William

Tuke. He saw that change could only be brought about by example and, writing that there was need 'for an institution for the care and proper treatment of those labouring under that most afflictive dispensation, the loss of reason', he brought the need to revolutionise the care of the insane before the Friends' monthly meeting in York.

Four years later an institution known as the Retreat was opened, where thirty people could be treated on humane and enlightened principles. All unnecessary restraints were abolished, the place was run on quiet and orderly lines and, for those able to work, industrial employment was provided. It has been rightly said that William Tuke struck the chains from lunatics and laid the foundations of all modern, humane treatment for the mentally ill. This was not William Tuke's only contribution to the wellbeing of his fellow Quakers; he was the instigator of the Trinity Lane Girls' school, which became known as the Mount, and he was also concerned for the 'education of children whose parents were not in affluence'.

For three generations the Tuke business had descended from father to son, but when Samuel Tuke realised that neither of his sons was interested in his business, he sold the business to Henry Isaac, the younger son of his old friend Joseph Rowntree. The change of ownership was announced formally:

> We have to inform you that we have relinquished the manufacture of cocoa, chocolate and chicory in favour of our friend H. I. Rowntree, who has been for some time practically engaged in the concern, and whose knowledge of the business and its several departments enables us with confidence to recommend him to the notice of our connection.
>
> We remain very respectfully,
>
> Tuke and Company, York, 1st of seventh month, 1862

Henry Isaac was a light-hearted, witty young man, perhaps the only Rowntree with a bubbling sense of humour. When he took over the business it manufactured products with exotic names like Iceland Moss Cocoa, Hexagon Cocoa and Pearl Cocoa, as well as Flake Cocoa, Farinaceous Cocoa and Tuke's Superior Rock Cocoa, names that must represent the many different ways in which cocoa was blended with other products to make it palatable. When Tuke's Superior Rock Cocoa won a local prize, Henry Isaac renamed it Rowntree's Prize Medal Rock Cocoa and liked to quote a verse from Deuteronomy in its praise, 'For their Rock is not our Rock, even our enemies themselves being judges.'

Total sales, at the time of Henry's purchase, were estimated at only £3000 a year. Nevertheless Henry Isaac splashed out and bought a 'wonderful new machine for grinding cocoa' and a collection of buildings costing £1000, which consisted of an old iron foundry, several cottages and a tavern bounded by a river on one side and a little street called Tanners Moat on the other. Out of this strange jumble of buildings Henry Isaac created his new factory, which was always known as Tanners Moat.

By 1869 Henry Isaac was in grave financial difficulties, at the very time when

Cadbury's were exploiting their new product, Cocoa Essence. Was this cause and effect? There is insufficient evidence to say for certain. The situation was serious; bankruptcy brought shame and expulsion to members of the Society of Friends, and it may well have been to avert such a disaster that Joseph, after seventeen happy and successful years as a master grocer, unversed in the art of cocoa and chocolate manufacture, took his capital out of the shop in Pavement and joined his brother.

Joseph left the manufacturing side to his brother and concentrated on the accounts. The regime at Tanners Moat had been very unsystematic, with office staff expected to hump a heavy sack like the factory employees when necessary. The work force at that time numbered fewer than a dozen. Joseph began to study the production costs with meticulous attention to detail, to see how the business could be made more profitable. Both brothers worked on the principle that sales depended on the quality of their goods, and they saw little advantage in advertising.[7] Joseph may well not have expected to stay long at Tanners Moat once he had helped make the business profitable, for he continued to enter his profession on the birth certificates of his children as master grocer until the birth of his third son, in 1875, when he called himself a cocoa manufacturer.

Joseph had much to contend with during those years. The Cadburys were pressing the view that only pure cocoa should be called cocoa and advertising their new product expensively on a national scale. Although Henry Isaac had bought the new grinding machine, the Rowntrees could not afford the Dutch machine which would have enabled them to extract the cocoa butter from their cocoa products and compete on equal terms with Cadbury's and Fry's. They had, perforce, to continue to market their own brands, although they sometimes sold their cocoa to shops who then retailed it under their own name.

Joseph was extremely sensitive to the way in which his products were described, even when sold under someone else's brand name, particularly since the Cadburys had made the whole question of the adulteration of cocoa a live issue. Joseph wrote, complaining of one of his retailers, 'About Blank's Homeopathic Label. I extremely dislike the wording of this label and will be no party to supplying a new man with a similar one. It is *not* pure ground cocoa. It is *not* produced from the finest Trinidad Nuts. It is *not* the "best for family use". In fact the whole thing is a sham, not very creditable for anyone concerned with it.'[8]

Joseph's insistence that there should be no advertising was a serious business miscalculation, although his reasons for the ban were certainly taken for personal rather than business considerations. Families now had more money to spend and could choose how to spend it; food and drink were the most heavily advertised products[9] and those entrepreneurs who were prepared to spend large amounts on advertising campaigns benefited. At the end of the 1880s Thomas Lipton had an advertising budget of over £40,000 a year. The development of chromolithography in the 1870s made it possible to produce cheaply large numbers of illustrated posters in colour. Neither the Frys nor the Cadburys were backward in making use of advertisements, so it was hardly surprising that the Rowntrees, relying on dignified letters to wholesale customers to promote sales, and lacking any outstandingly successful product, found their business making only very modest profits.

The Rowntree business was too small to have even a *mélangeur* department (the technical term for a department where chocolate is produced and mixed) and all the chocolate was made by seven men who took turns in 'grinding, roasting, rubbing and fetching the sugar, while two small machines did the "melanging" and eight hundredweight of chocolate was a very good day's work'. Joseph went to see George Cadbury in 1875 and spent a holiday with him, as well as going alone to Holland, but he still does not appear to have felt that the firm could afford the Dutch cocoa-press machine.

It was not cocoa but Crystallized Gum Pastilles that finally brought success to the business. A Frenchman called Claude Gaget called on the Rowntree brothers in 1879, bringing with him some samples. Nothing like these gums was produced in England at that time and when Joseph and Henry Isaac, thinking one boy and a boiling pot a less expensive investment than a cocoa press, started to retail the gums at a penny an ounce in four-pound wooden boxes, the business doubled in size between 1880 and 1883. Crystallized Gums notwithstanding, the trade slump of the early eighties resulted in the firm making a loss in 1883 of £385. In that year, too, Henry Isaac died, leaving Joseph on his own. Even during the very difficult years that followed, Joseph managed to go abroad for his annual holiday, his one luxury.

THE CADBURYS

When George Cadbury was born, on 19 September 1839, his family, unlike the Frys in Bristol, had not long been established in Birmingham. His grandfather, Richard Tapper Cadbury, had left the West Country only thirty-five years previously to set up in business as a silk merchant and draper with one Joshua Rutter. Richard Cadbury set up his third son, John, George's father, as a tea and coffee dealer at 93 Bull Street, close to his own business. Birmingham in the early years of the nineteenth century was developing at an unparalleled rate and the Cadburys from the start involved themselves in the life of the city. Richard Cadbury became first an overseer of the poor and then a poor-law guardian. He was a member and subsequently chairman of the board of commissioners for Birmingham. He was followed by his son, John, who became the influential chairman of the committee appointed to secure the passage of the bill through Parliament which transferred the duties of the old board of commissioners to the new city corporation. It is said that John Cadbury was responsible, in large measure, for the character of Birmingham's civil development.

Besides taking a leading part in public life, John Cadbury was also a champion of the underprivileged. As an overseer of the poor he found himself attending one of the regular dinners at which choice food was served while outside the forlorn paupers stood waiting for relief. He had the dinners declared illegal.

Although Charles Kingsley and Lord Shaftesbury, between them, share most of the credit for outlawing the barbarous practice of using climbing boys to sweep chimneys, John Cadbury's contribution to the fight to rescue children from this inhumane treatment combined the practical with an appeal to man's better instincts, a characteristic approach which his son George inherited. John Cadbury not only gave demonstrations to show the practicality of using machines rather than boys, he bought machines and set up master sweeps to use them. His efforts in this direction, incredible as it may seem, were strongly opposed by the old sweeps, as is shown in the letter he wrote to the duke of Sutherland, chairman of the select committee of the House of Lords set up to investigate the scandal:

> I beg respectfully to state that the progress of the use of machines for sweeping chimneys in this town has been for the last six years gradually on the increase . . . the old sweeps who keep climbing boys have found it necessary to obtain machines to satisfy some of their employers who were determined no longer to use children – but I regret to say that out of this circumstance much prejudice against the machine has been raised owing to these masters of the boys having very improperly worked the minds of servants against them. I rejoice to say, nevertheless, that our cause is still progressing onward. The public buildings in this Town, which are not very numerous, are generally swept with a machine, such for instance as the hospital, asylum, deaf and dumb asylum, Oscott College, banks and the principal hotels.

The letter is signed John Cadbury, Tea Dealer.[10] In his original advertisement in the local newspaper, the *Aris Gazette*, on 1 March 1824, John Cadbury had described himself as a tea dealer and coffee roaster. He announced that he intended starting business in that line, 'Having had the advantages of residing a considerable time in a wholesale tea warehouse of the first eminence in London and of examining the teas in the East India Company's warehouse and attending sales, likewise of frequenting the coffee market'. But it is the last paragraph of the modest announcement of John Cadbury's credentials that is of special significance. It read, 'JC is desirous of introducing to particular notice Cocoa Nibs, prepared by himself, an article affording a most nutritious beverage for breakfast.'[11]

This is the very first intimation that Cadbury was toying with the idea of dealing in cocoa. His apparatus for roasting coffee beans was doubtless also used for cocoa beans. After roasting, the kernels have to be freed from their shells and the remaining broken fragments are called nibs. Cadbury had only a pestle and mortar with which to grind his nibs, in contrast to the sophisticated water mill used by the Frys, but he too was excited by the possibilities of the cocoa bean. So confident did he feel about the future of the trade that in 1836 he rented a warehouse in Crooked Lane where he tried different ways of preparing chocolate from the beans he roasted and ground.

The Cadburys links with the Society of Friends, like those of the Frys, went back to the earliest days when John's great-grandfather, Richard Tapper, was one of George Fox's companions in persecution. Candia Barrow, his wife, came from as devout a Quaker family as John himself, and Candia had an ancestor burned at the stake for his religious beliefs. John and Candia Cadbury moved from Bull Street three years after acquiring Crooked Lane and took a house in Edgbaston, then a pleasant suburb, with neighbouring Ladywood still unspoiled country. It was here that George Cadbury was born.

The atmosphere at Edgbaston was spiritually highly charged, the daily regime strict, spartan severity the rule and any self-indulgent propensities crushed. John Cadbury had even given up the simple joy of playing the flute in obedience to his father's wishes and not even a piano was to be seen in the house almost to the end of his days. The only music available to the young Cadburys was that provided by musical boxes, which, perhaps because it was unalterable, was felt not to offer any temptation. A. G. Gardiner, George Cadbury's biographer, had no doubt that it was 'this stern martyrdom of the senses, physical and intellectual' that left an abiding impress on George Cadbury's character. 'It drove all the energy of his nature into certain swift deep channels, and left large spaces of life – the world's pleasures and aesthetic emotion, wholly unexplored.' These were Quaker restraints that John Stevenson Rowntree, Joseph's brother, was to point out, in an important essay entitled 'Quakerism Past and Present', as being inimical to the future health of the Society of Friends.

The children were encouraged to run a mile before breakfast by their parents, but the lawn at Edgbaston was small. To run the distance the children had to circle the lawn twenty-one times with their hoops, which they did daily before sitting down to breakfast. The only secular books they were allowed were Bunyan's *Pilgrim's Progress* and Foxe's *Book of Martyrs* until the advent of Harriet Beecher Stowe's *Uncle Tom's Cabin* and *The Wide, Wide World* by Elizabeth Wetherell opened the door to other aspects of literature. Although their parents had no carriage, the boys were allowed ponies and, to the consternation and sorrow of the household, were once reported for furious riding. It is good to know that the children could occasionally break free from the unnaturally tight reins which their parents kept on their development, for there is no hint of rebelliousness or chafing at the limitations imposed on them. Maria, the only daughter, wrote, 'Our home was one of sunshine. Our parents doing all they could to make us happy, and the consistency of their own lives was a great help in forming the characters and the tastes of the children. Home was the centre of attraction to us all, and simple home pleasures our greatest joy.'[12]

George Cadbury's mother died when he was fourteen. She had been a woman of great firmness of mind and character. She devoted her life to the training of her children and her death signalled the end of George's childhood. A year later his brief school days came to an end. He became an apprentice and two years later, aged seventeen, he was sent to complete his apprenticeship at the Rowntrees' shop in York. The Rowntree family themselves no longer lived over the shop as they had done in earlier days, but the elder Joseph Rowntree always lunched with his apprentices. He had a natural gift for conversation and expected the apprentices at lunchtime to take part in any discussion. George Cadbury did not find the atmosphere as congenial as he might have expected. He did not think much of his fellow apprentices, as he makes clear in a letter home to his sister Maria, written soon after he arrived; he also missed the garden around which he had so often run.

> Our dining room, which is about the size of our drawing room at home, is the only one in which the young men may sit. It has two windows looking out onto brick walls, in one of which is an aquarium, an interesting object indeed, the only thing we have to take the place of a garden, except two old raisin boxes at the bottom of the yard with a few little plants in them . . . The business of the shop is divided between two bodies of young men who are nearly separate from each other, each taking one counter and one class of work. On the one side, which it has fallen to my lot to work on, there are some rather foolish young men who talk a good deal of nonsense, but I have told them I much prefer sensible conversation and I think I have been enabled pretty much to keep clear of nonsense.

But it would seem that George's unremittingly serious attitude to life did not endear him to his fellow apprentices, for he continues:

> As regards friendship I think that the spirit most congenial to my own is G. Gillett, he has treated me with much kindness, indeed he is, I think, the only young man on our side who has shown me how to do anything. The others delight to keep me in drudgery saying apprentices ought not to attempt wrapping at first, but I care little for them and am very much improved in wrapping [13]

The dates would suggest that George Cadbury came to the Rowntree shop while Joseph Rowntree was in London. Had they worked alongside each other at this time, George would surely have mentioned it in his letter.

John Cadbury never recovered from the death of his wife in 1853. Although as a cocoa and chocolate manufacturer he had received a royal warrant in 1853 and the cleanliness of his factory and his care for his workers had been singled out for praise, after 1855 poor health deprived him of his drive and vigour and when George and his elder brother Richard took over the business in 1861 it was near collapse. Of the dozen employees working at Bridge Street, half were girls who were earning five shillings or less a week and the goods they made were of very inferior quality. Had the Trade Descriptions Act been in force, the label on the packet would have revealed that potato starch, sago, flour and treacle had been added to the cocoa, which represented only one fifth of the contents.

George was twenty-one and his brother Richard twenty-five when they took over the business and between them they disposed of capital worth £10,000. George, in later life, often referred to the desperate struggle they had in their early days to save the firm. Working extremely long hours, Saturdays included, they fought to keep going. Although as Quakers they could have borrowed capital to invest in the business, they decided to manage on their own. Had they not succeeded, Richard planned to become a land surveyor and George had ideas of becoming a tea planter in India, where doubtless he would have made a name for himself.

Self-denial was habitual to George and with total single-mindedness he applied himself to saving the business, cancelling his newspaper to save money and to avoid being distracted from work, walking home to a midday meal of bread, butter and water and often not leaving work until nine at night. He wrote in 1914, 'I was spending at that time for travelling, clothing, charities, and everything else about £25 a year. My brother had married, and at the end of five years had only £150. If I had been married there would have been no Bournville today – it was just the money that I saved by living so sparely that carried us over the crisis.'[14]

By 1864 the business was solvent, but it was the introduction of the revolutionary Cocoa Essence that really turned the tide.

The story of how the firm came to make Cocoa Essence and the way in which the discovery was used, ostensibly for the public good but consequentially for private gain, accurately reflects the sometimes ambiguous moral stance that George Cadbury was to adopt at times during his life and which involved him in a series of controversies. The story is worth telling at some length.

For almost forty years, following van Houten's invention of a machine to press out the excess cocoa butter, the Dutch and, soon after, the French had been able to market pure cocoa and, by blending cocoa and cocoa butter, greatly to improve the quality of their chocolate. Some time in 1866 George Cadbury learned of the machine press used by van Houten and, realising the potential of the machine, went to Holland. 'I went off,' he later wrote, 'to Holland without knowing a word of Dutch, saw the manufacturer with whom I had to talk entirely by signs and a dictionary and bought the machine. It was by prompt action such as this that my brother and I made our business.'[15]

The new machine meant that Cadbury's could now produce a pure cocoa. With all the cocoa butter removed, there was no need to mix the cocoa with any other ingredients, like starch or treacle, to make it palatable. It was George Cadbury's good fortune to be marketing his new, pure cocoa at time when abuses connected with the adulteration of food were much in the public mind. George Cadbury had been consulted by the government on matters associated with the Adulteration of Food Act in 1872, and Cadbury's were not slow to point up the difference between their cocoa and those of their competitors.

The medicinal benefits that the old cocoa mixtures were said to provide had long been used as part of the stock in trade to promote the different types of cocoa; it was not so long ago that Cadbury's themselves had been among the ranks of those who sold heavily adulterated cocoa. Now all was changed. Cadbury's could be more specific and quotations from the *Lancet* were used to back up their claim that their new Cocoa Essence being 'absolutely pure was therefore best'. Full-page advertisements were placed to back up this claim, showing an earnest bearded gentleman, not unlike Richard Cadbury himself, surrounded by test tubes, microscopes and other scientific impedimenta, gravely gazing at a beaker of Cocoa Essence. The caption under the advertisement indicated that the analyst was comparing the 'flesh-forming' ('body-building' in today's language) ingredients in cocoa. Not surprisingly he came to the conclusion that the best commercial cocoas on the market, with added starch and sugar, only supplied 6 per cent of the necessary ingredients, while Cadbury's pure cocoa supplied 21 per cent.

Had George Cadbury merely been content to promote his new product through an advertising campaign, there would have been no controversy. But, riding on the back of public disquiet over the adulteration of food, Cadbury sought to claim that all cocoa which had anything added to it was 'adulterated' and should not be called cocoa, but labelled chocolate or chocolate powder. The Royal Society of Arts, founded in 1754 for the encouragement of manufacturers and commerce, published a letter from George Cadbury to that effect in 1873. It was soon answered. Cadbury was, in effect, trying to put all the other cocoa manufacturers out of business, including Rowntree and Fry, although Fry's acquired a Dutch machine of their own soon afterward.

John Holm, a member of the firm of Dunn and Hewitt, read a paper on cocoa and its manufacture to the Royal Society later the same year. He argued that the words 'cacao' ('cacoa', 'cocoa') and 'chocolate' were identical terms and that both had been used for manufactured goods. 'Chocolate' was used to describe chocolate in cake form, fancy chocolate and the finer preparations in powder; 'cocoa' was applied to all the commoner preparations. It would therefore be a misrepresentation to call commoner kinds of cocoa that retailed at sixpence or eight pence a pound chocolate. If, he said, the term 'adulteration' meant an injurious addition, his firm were justified in repelling the term as applied to their products.

The controversy was further fuelled by a prosecution, brought under the new act, against a grocer, a Mr Kirby, for selling Dunn and Hewitt's cocoa which was alleged to be adulterated by a mixture of sugar and farina. The case was dismissed by the Marylebone magistrate Mr D'Eyncourt, but a second case, brought by the inspector appointed by St Pancras Vestry, brought renewed claims and counter-claims.

George Cadbury wrote again to the trade magazine, the *Grocer*, pointing out that the present trial going on in London showed the necessity for some radical change in the way the trade was conducted. 'It is no surprise,' he wrote, 'that grocers ask what is the difference between cocoa and chocolate – and no surprise that manufacturers cannot answer as they supply precisely the same kind of article in one to four-pound tins as chocolate powder and smaller packets of cocoa.' He claimed the public were pleased with the way in which Cadbury's now labelled their products, calling the genuine article 'cocoa' and all admixtures 'chocolate' or 'chocolate powder'.

A week later the *Grocer* printed a letter from J. S. Fry explaining their views on the Adulteration of Food Act. Not unnaturally they were annoyed at the assumptions being promulgated by George Cadbury and politely said they were unable to see any impropriety in continuing to use the name 'cocoa' for their products.

It would only confuse the public rather than serve any other purpose to change it. For if it is said that cocoa with the addition of sugar and arrowroot is not longer cocoa, may it not with equal justice be affirmed that cocoa which has been deprived of a portion of its natural ingredients, in order to render it comparatively soluble, is no longer cocoa? If it is said that the word cocoa means cocoa and nothing else, the same may be said of the word chocolate. But all that is beside the point. The Adulteration Act was not intended to interfere with such articles as we manufacture. The real question is whether the purchaser gets what is sound and wholesome and that which he expects to get. All the important cases that have been tried before the magistrate sustain the view we have taken – one of common sense and justice.

The public correspondence continued. The Cadburys replied to both J. S. Fry and Dunn and Hewitt, provoking from the latter a letter which roundly accused the Cadburys of making misleading statements in order to push their own product.

Messrs Cadbury Bros, in reply to the letters of Messrs Fry and ourselves, are kind enough to say they do not want to cast any stigma upon their fellow manufacturers, although they had previously stated that our evidence was misleading. We are under the impression that Messrs Fry, after a hundred years, and ourselves after nearly seventy years of honourable business as cocoa manufacturers might possibly be able to survive any stigma that Messrs Cadbury might endeavour to cast upon our respective houses.

But what is far more significant is that Messrs Cadbury, in order to push a speciality of their own, have not hesitated to cast a stigma upon all cocoa manufacturers in the country by their misleading statement. 'Caution: when cocoa thickens in the cup it proves the addition of starch', knowing full well by that term 'starch' is conveyed to the general public only the substance used by laundresses, which as far as we know is never used in the manufacture of cocoa. They made a 'suggestio falsi'.

Dunn and Hewitt went on to weaken their case, however, by saying that mixed cocoa powders were the only possible form in which cocoa could be used as a national beverage for the masses, a statement that would later be disproved. They also tried to pretend that pure cocoa was analogous to skimmed milk, and used any argument, relevant or otherwise, such as that it was expensive and required boiling, to prove that Cadbury's were not playing fair. They ended by saying that if Cadbury's meant what they said, they should give up using all their other cocoas.

The controversy rumbled on for years. As late as 1891, the food and drugs inspector brought a test prosecution relating to Rowntree's Rock Cocoa, the lowest grade of cocoa they then produced, containing 40 per cent cocoa, 16 per cent sugar and 44 per cent starch.[16] The magistrate dismissed the case, accepting that Rock Cocoa was a well-understood trade description for a cocoa admixture and that there was no possibility of confusion with pure cocoa. He added for good measure that his family liked it. In 1904 the prosecution of another product, containing 30 per cent cocoa and 70 per cent sugar and sago, failed. Cadbury's did not succeed in manipulating the market in this way in their favour, but certainly their attempt to do so made Joseph Rowntree extremely cautious about any claims he made for his products, and probably was a one of the reasons that made him so reluctant to advertise. Only when public demand for the cocoa mixtures ceased did the controversy finally end.

3

The Society of Friends

The beliefs of the early seventeenth-century Quakers, proclaimed by George Fox and his fellow missionaries in the first flush of their religious enthusiasm when they were hoping to convert the world, differ greatly from Quakerism as it is understood and practised today. Already by the beginning of the nineteenth century there had been many changes. Early members of the Society of Friends had made themselves conspicuous by their unorthodox behaviour and in so doing had cut themselves off from other religious groups. By the 1850s there was a groundswell of opinion in favour of removing barriers which had given rise to the concept of the Quakers as a 'peculiar people'. Members of the Rowntree, Fry and Cadbury families all played a part in bringing about this change, certain members of the Rowntree family being particularly active. It is well known that the Victorian Quakers, though few in number, exerted a quite disproportionate influence on the economic and social development of their time. Victorian Quakerism differed as much from present-day practice as it did from its seventeenth-century beginnings.

George Fox, the founder of the Society of Friends, was born in 1624, the son of an undistinguished Lincolnshire weaver, and received but little schooling in his youth. At the age of nineteen he left home in a state of spiritual conflict and the next four years were spent on a pilgrimage in search of truth. He was both prophet and mystic and during those years passed through a succession of mystical experiences. He started preaching in 1647, at a time of great unrest. The Civil War, which would end with the execution of Charles I and the establishment of the Commonwealth under Oliver Cromwell, had divided the country, and many people were unsettled in their religious beliefs. Fox gathered round him a devout band of followers, mainly from the middle and lower classes, who were soon to be numbered in thousands.

The central doctrine of the new movement was the belief that in every man there was the seed of God and that knowledge of God came through direct communication with his spirit. Friends believed that Christianity was neither a matter of conformity to doctrine nor mere observance of form, but came from an overwhelming sense of the nearness of God to them through the indwelling spirit of Christ. This reliance on the inward authority of the spirit, the doctrine of the inner light, together with the Quakers' disregard for the tradition and authority of the established churches, inevitably brought them into conflict with the religious establishment.

Like other dissenters, the Quakers resented the fact that they were expected to pay church rates and many were fined, had their goods distrained and were imprisoned for refusing to pay tithes, an obligation on all which was only lifted in 1868. As dissenters they were barred from entering English universities and their opposition to all war meant that they served neither in the army nor navy and could not take part in any enterprise which could be said to have military implications. Their peculiar form of silent public worship increased their separateness from other Christian groups. The form of austere Puritanism adopted by Fox and his followers also had the effect of increasing the isolation of the Friends. They adopted a manner of speech and dress which marked them as 'peculiar'; they addressed each other as 'thee' or 'thou' and the men wore broad-brimmed hats and collarless coats, the women bonnets and plain dresses in sombre colours with little or no trimming. Any sign of ornamentation, the unnecessary bow or touch of colour, was frowned upon.

Such was the vigour and fervour of Fox's ministry that by 1680, roughly thirty years after his vision on Pendle Hill, which some Friends take as the starting point of the Society, there were not 'fewer than sixty thousand persons in England and Wales of the persuasion of people called Quakers'.[1] Fox's idealism was not only that of the visionary, it was strongly rooted in realism. He strove, in his unconventional way, to get at the core of things; his ability to impose order on the thousands who joined him from the fringes of many sects was a mark of his inward power. The erratic behaviour of some of his followers, not to mention his own zeal and extravagances, led to Macaulay's well-known epigram, 'too much order for liberty and not sufficiently disordered for Bedlam.' But Fox's discipline of silence had a sobering influence and the growth of a systematic network of meetings induced a sense of corporate responsibility. Marsden, in his *History of the Later Puritans*, gave great weight to the intellectual merit of Fox's doctrine of the inner light.[2]

William Penn (1644–1718) the English Quaker and founder of Pennsylvania, has left a powerful and moving description of George Fox, written, as he said, 'by knowledge and not by report, he having been with him for weeks and months together'. This first-hand evidence adds to our understanding of a man whose spiritual legacy has affected the lives of so many. Penn wrote:

And truly I must say though God has visibly clothed him with a divine preference and authority, and indeed his very presence expressed a religious majesty, yet he never abused it; but held his place in the Church of God with meekness and a most engaging humility and moderation. For upon all occasions, like his blessed Master, he was servant to all; holding and exercising his eldership in the invisible power that had gathered them with reverence to the Head, and care over the Body; and was received only in that Spirit and Power of Christ, as the first chief elder of the age; who as he was therefore worthy of the double honour, so for the same reason it was given by the faithful of his day; because his authority was inward and not outward and he got it and kept it by the love of God and power of an endless life.[3]

Fox was responding to a widespread need, as was evident from the way his message was received by independent congregations and small communities, composed mainly of yeomen and small craftsmen. It was no easy message that he and his fellow missionaries preached throughout the land. The central theme of the Quaker teaching invited retaliation from the established churches, for the concept of the inner light meant that the church itself was seen by the early Quakers as nothing more than a great, idolatrous temple. Baptism and communion became no more than external rites and had no place in Quaker worship. The scriptures lost their pre-eminence in the order of things. Since, however, most of the early Quakers were imbued with the Puritan spirit, they had, as a natural consequence, a deep knowledge of the Bible.

Just as the rejection of the church led inexorably to the refusal to pay tithes, so social and hierarchical distinctions were seen as equally unacceptable since Quakers believed that all men were equal in the sight of God because 'the seed of God dwelt in all men's hearts'. The way in which Fox and his followers gave practical expression to this truth was by refusing to doff their hats to anyone. Since the swearing of oaths was forbidden to Christians in the New Testament, Quakers refused to take the oath even in a court of law, a demand which to them was clearly unscriptural. Because of their uncompromising stand over such matters, together with their success in recruiting followers, Quakers soon became known as being against both magistry and ministry. Their uncompromising attitude to both inspired fear, which led to their becoming a persecuted minority. Many went to prison for their beliefs, while others suffered economic and financial hardship. The Meeting for Sufferings came into being in 1675, a representative body responsible for recording the sufferings of Friends under persecution and for seeking redress when practicable. Fox died in 1691.

By Victorian times the early Friends' belief that they held a monopoly of the truth and that all other religions had been corrupted had vanished. Their missionary zeal, the result of their revolutionary vision, had given way to a form of quietism. Prosperity and respectability had softened their attitudes, and their early antagonism to established religious and civil authority seldom led to open conflict. Keeping to many of their traditional practices, the Quakers, in effect, turned in on themselves.

This change in attitude, while easing some of their early difficulties, created problems of its own. The Society of Friends had some idea of the startling effect their chosen way of life had had on their numbers from the unofficial census of 1840, which showed that from 60,000 in 1680 the Society's membership had fallen to just over 16,000.[4] But it was probably the religious census taken one Sunday in 1851, when a count was made of everyone who attended a religious service on that day, that really brought home to the Society of Friends just how rapidly their numbers had declined. The census was widely read and commented on because it showed that it was not only the Quakers who had lost support; it revealed the shocking fact that in a supposedly Christian Britain, less than half the population attended church on Sunday.

Among its many merits, the census gives an admirably concise description of the main features of the system that bound the Friends together, which had not changed since it was introduced by George Fox himself:

> The whole community of Friends is modelled somewhat on the Presbyterian system of gradations of meetings or synods – monthly, quarterly and yearly, to administer the affairs of the Society, including in their supervision matters both of spiritual discipline and secular policy. The monthly meetings, composed of all the congregations within a definite circuit, judge of the fitness of new candidates for membership, supply certificates for such as move to other districts, choose fit persons to be elders, to watch over the ministry, attempt the reformation or pronounce expulsion of all such as walk disorderly and generally seek to stimulate the members to religious duty. They also make provision for the poor of the Society and secure the education of their children. Overseers are also appointed to assist in the promotion of these objects. At monthly meetings also marriages are sanctioned previous to their solemnisation at a meeting for worship. Several monthly meetings compose a quarterly meeting, to which they forward general reports of their decisions. The yearly meeting, which holds the same relative position to the quarterly meeting that the latter do to the monthly meetings, has general superintendence of the Society in a particular society.[5]

The formal structure of a church and the spirit that animates its followers combined give it the characteristic qualities which differentiate it from other sects and churches. The formal structure remained, but the spirit of the Society had dramatically altered and the lives of its members reflected a very different understanding of its beliefs and practices from those of Fox and his early followers. The missionary fervour had all but disappeared, and numbers had fallen so dramatically that at the time of the census, the Society of Friends, at just over 14,000 members, had less than a quarter of the membership of 1680. Yet these Victorian Quakers, in spite of their small numbers, smaller even than the obscure sect called 'the Countess of Huntingdon's Connection', were able to exert a considerable influence on the conscience of the nation through the example they set.

The year 1859 has been taken as a turning point in the Victorian age. The population was growing fast, industry and commerce were creating vast new wealth, and a network of railways spreading throughout the country brought increased mobility. The new industries, which brought wealth to some, also brought intolerable working conditions, bad housing and poverty to others. A hundred years earlier, two thirds of the population lived and worked in the country. In the words of G. M. Young, the new manufacturing towns grew up 'outside the orbit of the old ruling class, neglected by their natural leaders, the industrial territories were growing up as best they might, undrained, unpoliced, ungoverned and unschooled'.

Slums, a word which only came into the English language in 1812, appeared in every large city, including Bristol, York and Birmingham where the Frys, Rowntrees and Cadburys had their businesses.

With the changes came new ideas. It was in 1859 that Charles Darwin (1809–82) published his controversial work on the theory of evolution, the *Origin of Species*, which was to threaten the pre-eminent place held until then by revealed religion. John Stuart Mill (1806–73) wrote his essay *On Liberty* in the same year, which gave a jolt to established political thought. A third publication, an essay written by a young unknown Yorkshire Quaker, John Stevenson Rowntree, was also published that year and opened the way for the spread of a more liberal theology.

John Stevenson Rowntree wrote his essay a year before his father Joseph died and he and his brother, another Joseph, took over their father's grocery business. The elder Joseph Rowntree had been disturbed by some modern aspects of Quakerism and had been campaigning to get the regulations governing marriage altered. The rule was that any Friend who married anyone of another religious denomination was automatically disowned by the Society. John Bright, an outspoken Member of Parliament, a friend of Joseph's and a not infrequent visitor to the shop, lent his support to the campaign. But even with such a vigorous champion as Bright, Joseph was unable to overcome the strong conservative obstinacy of his fellow Quakers. When he first brought forward proposals to modify the regulations to the London yearly meeting, 'not at any great length, but sufficiently, so I should have thought, to convince every truth seeker',[6] as his elder son recorded, he failed to convince the Society. Since Joseph had spent three years preparing this recommendation, the subject must have been frequently discussed round the family table. It is not surprising, therefore, that John Stevenson Rowntree seized the opportunity to make known his own views when occasion presented itself. The essay was written in answer to a printed announcement which appeared in 1858 as follows:

> A gentleman who laments, that notwithstanding the population of the United Kingdom has more than doubled itself in the last fifty years, the Society of Friends is less in number than at the beginning of the Century; who believes that the Society at one time bore powerful witness to the world concerning some of the errors to which it is most prone and some of the truths which are most necessary to it; and that this witness has been gradually becoming more and more feeble, is anxious to obtain light respecting the causes of this change.

John Stevenson Rowntree was twenty-five years old when his lucid review and succinct analysis of the causes of the decline of the Society of Friends won him his prize in an essay he called 'Quakerism Past and Present'. The essay, together with that of the runner up, Thomas Hancock, which was entitled 'The Peculium', was published in 1859. It is interesting that the year that saw an upturn in the spiritual awareness among evangelical Christians, remembered as the second evangelical revival, should also have been the year when the fortunes of the Society of Friends were at their lowest ebb. There was unrest among the members. Joseph Rowntree was not alone in asking for change; Edward Fry, remembering the ridicule he and his brother Joseph had suffered at school on account of their plain Quaker clothes, wrote a pamphlet asking that regulations concerning dress should be relaxed. This too was refused.

The monthly and quarterly meetings of the Friends in York were part of the very fabric of the Rowntrees' lives, and possibly the only quarterly York meeting they ever missed was the one in 1847, after the death of John's four-year-old sister from whooping cough, when the family went to Scarborough to recuperate, thankful for once to 'escape the bustle of the winter quarterly meeting'.[7] It was therefore as an involved and knowledgeable young Quaker that John Rowntree showed how certain weaknesses, which had been relatively unimportant in the early days, had become major difficulties by the mid-nineteenth century.

According to Rowntree it was the dual nature of the Society in the early years of the seventeenth century, when the country was both licentious and puritanical, that accounted for the rise of Quakerism, which can be seen as a protest against both extremes. The English Reformation, the long struggle between monarchical and popular authority, was partly political and partly religious. The polemical controversies of the times were incessant and embraced a wide theological area. From 1600 to 1660 the central Christian mysteries of free will, predestination, election and rejection were under constant discussion. It was natural, under these circumstances, that little companies of people, given leadership, would react against the lofty pretensions of high-class clergymen and the rigid religion of the Puritans. George Fox provided that leadership.

John Rowntree argued that Fox's radical idea, that a measure of divine light is given to all men and that only through the testimony of heart and conscience can the true knowledge of God be revealed to man, contained both the strength and the weakness of Quakerism. Although in the early days persecution for refusal to pay tithes had strengthened the resolve of the Quakers, and the courage and fortitude of those early Friends in the face of their sufferings was an inspiration, the same did not apply now. Rowntree believed that attempting to enforce compliance with modes of action not immediately connected with moral duties was injurious to the Society; it should not have made the refusal to pay church tithes an essential of church fellowship, a ruling which now accounted, in large measure, for the loss of that same fellowship.

Denied entry to the universities and barred from a career in the army or navy, many Quakers had gone into business. Their sober way of life, industry and single-minded sense of purpose made them disproportionately successful. To cripple their businesses by forcing them to pay large fines for nonpayment of church rates or tithes seemed to many unnecessary, particularly since to fail in business and become bankrupt could lead to disownment. Expulsion of bankrupts was justified by the argument that it was a form of dishonesty, and the sanction certainly helped to reinforce the Friends' reputation for integrity and reliability in business.

Rowntree bravely went to the very heart of Quakerism in suggesting that by giving central importance to the doctrine of the indwelling word, although the doctrine illuminated a previously slighted truth, Friends had given it an undue place and this unbalanced the symmetry of the Christian truth. He considered the theology that had grown up round the doctrine of the inner light to be defective, exalting the inward Christ and denying Jesus of Nazareth his atonement for sin and oneness with the Father, and ultimately landing many of its authors in virtual infidelity.

He considered that the disuse of symbolic rites, baptism and communion, Friends' views on preaching and prayer, and the idea that silence is and must be a special and principal part of God's worship, although suited to early Friends, were not fitted for later congregations. He pointed out that the early Friends brought with them their Puritan heritage of biblical knowledge, but that recent neglect of Bible teaching meant that there were fewer teachers of eloquence and ability and that religious meetings over the last 150 years had all too often had a passive quality about them which drove younger Friends from the Society. In addition, Friends, had been disowned for having undergone the rite of baptism, and this was not only a sign of decadence, but, Rowntree said forthrightly, a grave infringement on religious liberty.

Simplicity of dress and truthfulness of language lay behind observance of plainness of speech, behaviour and apparel, but the extent of the importance attached to the observance of these 'peculiarities', as they were known, was hardly to be credited. The minds of the young were filled with 'ideas of gloom and unreasonableness, to use no stronger words' and this attitude contributed to the defections from the Society. Rowntree was also critical of the failure of Quakers to realise the importance of love and of the beautiful in art and music, and upbraided them for their neglect of science and liberal literature. He ascribed this failure to Fox's Puritan upbringing and wrote that the attitude of the Friends toward the fine arts constituted evidence of their imperfect understanding of the dignity of all feelings and emotions implanted in man by his creator. He said this narrow and inelastic quality in Quakerism was one of the main reasons why it had not spread, and, in a particularly perceptive passage, pointed out that although Quakers had been in the forefront of the struggle to abolish the slave trade, the Society of Friends was 'without the elastic, adaptive qualities which fitted Christianity for every tribe from the impassive, matter-of-fact Dutchman to the sensuous, impulsive Negro, and it was for that reason that it had not spread among those for whose liberties it had struggled so hard'.

Rowntree's analysis of the Quaker attitude to poverty and the poor is of particular interest because of the light it throws on the class structure of the Society of Friends. Since one of the duties of the Friends was to make provision for the poor of the Society – overseers were appointed to assist in the promotion of this object – there were few poor Quakers. But, by a curious inversion, neither did the poor apply for membership, because of the association of temporal advantage with admission to the Society. He argued that the Society had, in fact, acted prejudicially and repelled the poor, who did not want to be charged with joining for 'interested motives'. The importance attached to the education of their children was another reason why few Quakers were to be found among the 'labouring class'. By 1672 fifteen boarding schools were in operation and in 1799 one of the most famous Quaker

Schools, Ackworth, near Pontefract in West Yorkshire, had been founded. Although in one sense the education provided was narrow, nevertheless basic education was something still denied the generality of the poor. Thus even the poorest Quaker children started life better equipped to make their way in trade or industry than were their contemporaries, whose future prospects were bounded by mine, factory or domestic service if they were lucky, the casual labour market or destitution if they were not.

John Rowntree, working alongside his father and younger brother Joseph in the grocery shop in Pavement, York, was not unaware of the paradox that business success created for the Society of Friends. The problem had already been identified as early as 1697 by the author of a publication entitled *Snake in the Grass*, who wrote: 'Though Quakers at first left their houses and their families to shift for themselves, to run about and preach, and cried down riches when they had none, yet since that time they have gripped mammon as hard as any of their neighbours and now call riches a gift and a blessing from God.' Is it merely coincidence, asked the author, that 'lofty professions of spirituality made by the Friends has gone hand in hand with shrewdness and tact in the transaction of mundane affairs'? It can be argued that if the early Quaker view had continued to dominate society there would have been a social revolution far greater than any so far accomplished. Victorian Quakerism, however, sanctioned and encouraged the pursuit of wealth and rich philanthropists were given an honoured place in society. A writer to the *Friend,* a Quaker periodical, put the case for the pursuit of wealth in 1844: 'Whatever else we do or do not do, I suspect we shall only be lightly esteemed by the Church if we do not succeed in providing for ourselves . . . the poor man's wisdom is very apt to be despised . . . and to get rich is one important part toward a "good degree in Society".'

It is no surprise that Rowntree concurred and robustly stated that real piety favours the success of the trader whose habits of prudence and forethought gave him an important advantage in gaining credit in the commercial world. Another advantage, which Rowntree did not mention, was that brought about by the closely knit structure of the Quaker business community. The isolation of Friends from general society and the binding together of families through the yearly, quarterly and monthly meetings, along with their refusal to allow any of their number to marry outside the Society, meant that Quaker families were mostly known to one another. This extended family system not only engendered a feeling of trust between them which made it easier for them to do business among themselves, it also helped with the problem of raising capital and made the dissemination of commercial information relatively easy. This sense of fellowship gave stability and strength to the small businesses as well as to the larger ones.

There was one grave disadvantage to this system which Rowntree recognised and highlighted in his essay. He considered the disowning of Quakers who married out as the 'most influential proximate cause of the decline of the Society' and quoted Elizabeth Fry's opinion, 'It is the most undue and unchristian restraint as far as I can judge.' In what Rowntree called a 'deliberate act of suicide' about 4000 Friends who had married outside the Society between 1800 and 1855 had all been disowned. Jesus' first miracle, he wrote, should have taught Friends that a church should be simple, indulgent and attractive rather than harsh, complex and repelling. In 1857 there had been an excess of disownments over admissions of 2400, of deaths over births of 2336 and losses of 700 owing to emigration. Giving figures nearer to home, he showed at the largest monthly meeting in England, the West Yorkshire meeting, that although 113 Friends had been married according to the rules, sixty-one had married out and all sixty-one had been disowned.

Not even Ackworth, the school which might be regarded as the flag ship among Quaker schools, could inspire and hold its scholars. Of the 850 boys who had passed through it, 304 had left the Society of Friends. Why, demanded Rowntree, was there this indifference to diminishing numbers? The Society was as unsuited to evangelism of the heathen as of the ignorant masses of the population, and even those who shared some of the Quaker fundamental beliefs joined other movements, like the Peace Society and the Society for the Liberation of Religion from State Patronage. It was no use relying on the argument that the Quakers are not a proselytising people, or to excuse the facts by saying that the condition of the Society resulted from individual unfaithfulness. It was not even enough, said Rowntree, to say that numbers were not a correct test of strength. Rowntree was implicitly acknowledging that the influence of Quaker businessmen and bankers in the early part of the nineteenth century had been disproportionate to their numbers, but would not allow that fact to excuse the Society of Friends' lack of vision for the future.

Some of the weaknesses John Rowntree identified were being recognised. His father, the elder Joseph Rowntree, had been a moving spirit in the struggle to get the marriage regulations changed, and six months before his death, in 1858, the proposition of the Yorkshire quarterly meeting concerning the marriage regulations was adopted. In the same year the regulations concerning dress were also discussed and three years later they too were amended. What Rowntree had not anticipated was the problems the increasing number of influential and successful businessmen and bankers would face in reconciling the power and status that their wealth conferred with their obligations as Quakers. He did not foresee that a large number of prominent businessmen would resign from the Society in the next fifty years. Of the fifty wealthy Quaker businessmen listed by T. A. B. Corley who were active between 1860 and 1914, only half remained 'plain', living simply and attending to their business and philanthropic interests; a handful, though considered 'worldly', by which was meant dressing more extravagantly, going out in society and to the theatre, perhaps even riding to hounds, remained within the Society; the rest resigned their membership.[8]

At one end of the spectrum J. S. Fry remained as the very model of the pre-1860 Quaker, with his plain dress a relic of the past and a reflection of his narrow conservative approach to both religion and business. For several years he held office as clerk of the yearly meetings, a demanding job, for he had to record the 'sense of the meeting', a procedure which sometimes led to long delays before a decision was reached. Chosen annually, the clerk had to be a man of discretion and standing within the Society, for in effect he ran the meetings and needed a minute knowledge of the meeting's affairs. If, as Elizabeth Isichei writes in her book, *Victorian Quakers*, unwearying diligence and self-effacing devotion were typical of the Victorian clerk, then J. S. Fry would be a good example of the type. In spite of becoming the richest industrialist of his time, he and William White, chairman of the firm of White and Pike of Birmingham, both weakened their businesses by giving a disproportionate amount of their time to outside religious activities.

At the other end of the spectrum were those who, having become wealthy, resigned from the Society for mainly social reasons. This was nothing new; the often quoted saying 'a carriage and pair does not long continue to drive to the Meeting House' applied as much to Quakers as to other nondenominational sects. The wealthy Henry Ashworth warned his brother-in-law as early as 1832 that 'with very few exceptions the third generation of the rich leave our society'.[9]

Those successful and prosperous businessmen who remained members of the Society of Friends had, in effect, to make their own decisions on how the ethics of Quaker social thinking applied to them. All were individualists by nature, and their individuality was further enhanced by their Quaker reliance on an inner spiritual light to inform their actions, so their responses were many and varied. There is little evidence that the Society of Friends itself offered any guidance before 1906, when the conflict between business needs and the idea that mutual service should be the principle upon which life is organised began to be discussed at the London yearly meetings. It was only after the First World War that the question of the grave ethical responsibilities that ownership and control of substantial industrial wealth had given to certain Quaker businessmen began to impinge on the thoughts of other Quakers. But by that time both George Cadbury and Joseph Rowntree had worked out many of the answers for themselves. Their sons, Edward Cadbury and Seebohm Rowntree, in their respective books, *Experiments in Industrial Organisation* (1912) and *The Human Factor in Business* (1921), both further analysed the question of industrial efficiency in the light of their Quaker beliefs. The overall impression left by the first conference of Quaker employers, held in 1918, was one of benevolent paternalistic control coupled with a keen sense of moral duty. But by the end of the Second World War Quaker influence in the business world had further declined. Among those companies passing out of Quaker ownership, Fry's had disappeared, being taken over by Cadbury, and Rowntree's chairman was not a member of the family.

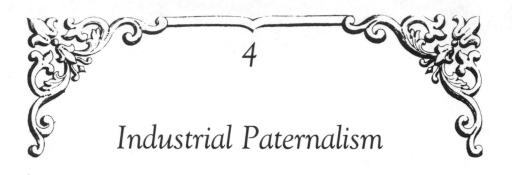

Industrial Paternalism

The significance and the complexities of a paternalist ethos in the factory have often been dismissed as irrelevant because the nineteenth-century factory system has usually been associated with class consciousness and conflict. Industrial paternalism has been branded as merely a paying proposition, its economic value as well as its social benefits being paid for by low wages and long hours. Yet in many cases there was a genuine warmth between employer and employee, even though for the employer the provision of reading rooms, day and night schools and trips to the countryside and to the employer's own home all played a role in establishing cohesiveness and stability among the workforce. But that said, underneath the mateyness there was an element of obedience and deference on the part of the worker which was inherent in the relationship. How could it be otherwise when the employer was the all-powerful provider of the vital weekly wage?

Employer paternalist regimes broadly speaking divided themselves into two fairly representative forms, Tory Anglican and Liberal Nonconformist.[1] While the former might be more relaxedly expansive, the latter had about them a moral restrictiveness which was certainly apparent in the management style of Joseph Fry, George Cadbury and Joseph Rowntree. All three chocolate manufacturers devoted a considerable amount of thought and time to the physical and spiritual wellbeing of their employees. Their working conditions, opportunities for education, facilities for recreation, the provision of pensions and in some cases housing were matters which concerned them and when such developments became financially possible, the chocolate manufacturers were among the most enlightened employers. To Joseph Rowntree, who had shared his house with his apprentices, the idea of continuing to take part in an act of daily worship with his work force was the most natural thing in the world. Joseph Fry, who had not had this close relationship with his workers, regarded the morning service not only as a matter of duty, but something to be enforced. As his firm expanded, a hall that would accommodate 2000, comfortably seated, was set aside for the daily religious service held at 9 a.m. George Cadbury is known to have consulted Joseph Fry about the form such a service should take when he was thinking of instituting the practice. The reply is

5 The croquet lesson: the girls' recreation ground at Cadbury's 1896.

6 A chance to read in the girls' recreation area at Rowntree's, York.

7 Tanner's Moat factory, the earliest Rowntree's cocoa works, 1892 (time lapse photography).

8 The outgrown Cadbury's premises at Bridge Street.

illuminating and shows that even attention to the spiritual needs of the workers had managerial advantages. George Cadbury received a detailed account of the methods and benefits of the system, about arrangements for light and ventilation, the separate entrances for men and girls and the manner in which the service might be conducted. The postscript revealed a less exalted benefit. 'I would remark,' wrote Joseph Fry, 'that in addition to the religious benefit that may be looked for, I think there is a great advantage in bringing the workpeople once a day under review. It is often a means of observing their conduct and checking any tendency to impropriety.'[2] The daily service at the Cadbury works continued for thirty years, nearly always conducted by George Cadbury himself or, in his absence, by his brother Richard and occasionally by his nephew, Barrow, Richard's son. The impossibility of gathering the rapidly expanding work force together in one place eventually brought to an end the practice of daily services.

Increased business meant that all three firms had to solve the problem of how and where to expand their premises. Joseph Fry took the uninspired option of continuing to build in the centre of Bristol. During the 1880s the company acquired slum tenements in what is now the Broadmead shopping centre of Bristol and razed them to the ground so that further factory buildings could be erected. They were described as being 'solid blocks of iron, steel, red and white bricks, Cornish granite and concrete; they are built as substantially as the mason's art and lavish expenditure can make them . . . Under their tremendous loads of machinery they stand as firm as the everlasting rock.'[3] The Frys may have meant them to seem everlasting but to the Cadburys, when the two firms merged in 1918, the buildings must have appeared like a millstone around their necks, and it was they who forced J. S. Fry to move in 1921 to Somerdale, midway between Bath and Bristol. The last of the three great manufacturers to acquire modern premises, Frys had finally to accept that transporting goods between eight factories and sixteen subsidiaries, all within the confines of the city of Bristol, was proving counterproductive.

An interesting account of the manufacturing process at Fry's appeared in the *Grocer* in 1908. The article described how the bags of beans were taken up on lifts from the basement storage to the top floor, when the various manufacturing operations proceeded in a descending order from floor to floor. On the upper floor the hard beans were roasted in revolving cylinders heated by coke fires. The roasted beans were then shot down to the floor below into machines which broke them into cocoa nibs and winnowed the light, dry husks away by fans. The nibs were cocoa as it was originally used, when it was possible only to skim off some of the fat. Powerful rollers of granite in pans of granite then crushed the nibs with the aid of heat into a paste, and a large proportion of oil was drained off. The cocoa paste was then put into stout canvas bags and these were placed in a cylinder, which, under pressure of more than half a ton acting on every square inch, squeezed out the remaining oil, leaving the cocoa dry, its flavour dry and not very palatable. The cocoa butter thus extracted was extremely valuable and had many commercial uses. The various cocoas were prepared from the dry cocoa.

Chocolate was prepared by adding loaf sugar, ground very finely and sifted, to the cocoa paste. Afterwards it was sent down to the floor beneath to be ground between horizontal granite stones until it had been reduced to a still finer paste. This was moulded into large blocks, and stored for future use. To make their chocolate creams, Fry's boiled the sugar, then beat it on stone slabs until it assumed a creamlike consistency; it was then flavoured and poured into starch moulds, which were made and filled by machines. When dried and coated, the chocolate creams were packed into fancy boxes.

Visitors seem to have been more impressed by the packing and labelling of the products than by the manufacturing process. At that time Fry's used sixty-four different machines only to make boxes in which to pack their cocoa. Tins and the fancy cardboard boxes had their own departments and there was also a special department for the manufacture of show cards. One of the most successful was that of the boy whose face changed from sobs to sulks to smiles when he got a Fry's chocolate.

George and Richard Cadbury took a very different line, when at the end of the 1870s they had outgrown their premises at Bridge Street. In eighteen years their work force had increased tenfold, to 230, and there was every reason to expect that it would continue to grow. They realised that in a crowded city centre they would never be able to give their employees healthy or attractive conditions of work, so for both commercial and philanthropic reasons they took the momentous decision to move out of Birmingham. In 1878 they bought 14.5 acres of land by the river Bourn in open country, four miles to the southwest of the city. The following year they were able to move their workers to the new factory, where they had built sixteen cottages to house their foremen. These cottages, built for purely practical reasons, were to enable the foremen to be on the spot. There are no records to suggest that at this time George and Richard had any intention of creating anything other than a modern factory in a healthy environment.

The new factory was a rectangular block, 330 feet long, with other buildings tacked on. Besides the store room, packing room, moulding room, saw mill, grinding room, roasting room, engine house and drying room, there was also a reading room. The work force, which had increased to 300 in number, also discovered that a cricket field had been provided for the men, while for the girls there was a garden where swings and seats had been installed. This rather charming provision was all of a piece with the way in which George and Richard cared for their predominantly young female workers. An old employee remembered how George Cadbury would go round on rainy days to enquire of the forewomen whether all the girls under their charge had changed their shoes. There was, of course, no question of any girl being employed once she married. The Cadbury brothers had strong views on the role of women and believed that the place of a wife and mother was in the home.

Getting the work force to and from the factory was a major problem in the early days. The site was bordered on the east by what was then the Birmingham West Suburban railway and an arrangement had been made with the railways to provide cheap fares, but the trouble was that the trains did not always run at convenient times. The problem was solved in 1884, when the Midland Railway, which had

9 An aerial view of the J. S. Fry & Sons factory showing how the factory walls followed the course of the winding streets, after 1907.

10 An early view of Bournville which shows the siding constructed by Midland Railing leading right into the factory, 1884.

11 The girls' dining room at Cadbury's, 1902.

12 The rest room at Rowntree's.

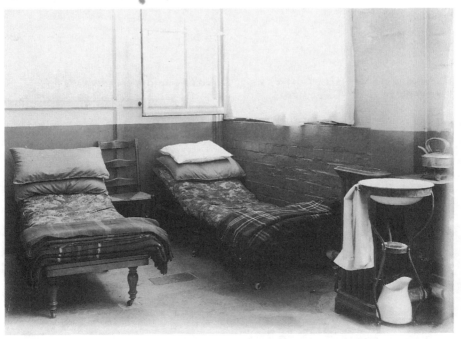

taken over the West Suburban line, constructed a railway siding leading right into the factory. A second line was built in 1901. A characteristic story is told of Richard Cadbury in those early days.[4] He was much bothered by the fact that the girls had no waiting room at the station. On wet nights he would stand outside himself and, when the train was signalled, blow a whistle, so that the girls could run straight from the changing room to the train. For those who lived locally it was arranged that a man carrying a lantern should escort them across the fields.

A print, probably an architect's drawing, made before the new factory was finished, showed that the original name was to have been Cadbury's Cocoa and Chocolate Manufactory, Bournbrook. A little stream, the Bourn, ran along the north side of the property, Bournbrook Hall stood just across Oak Lane and Bournbrook Cottage, the only building actually on the site, was close by the river. In choosing the name Bournville it is unlikely that the Cadbury brothers even knew of the small village of that name in Normandy, but they thought the French association important. All the best chocolate was made in France and to reinforce the tenuous idea that they had some link with things French they even went so far as to open a depot in Paris, which always traded at a loss but enabled them to include a French address on their publicity material.

George Cadbury had married Mary Tyler in 1872, when he felt he could afford to bring up a family. They had started their married life living very simply, in George Road, Birmingham, and employing only one servant. Soon after moving the factory to Bournville George bought Woodbrooke, a spacious, graceful house in Selly Oak, lying in large wooded grounds which overlooked a lake. Three years later, in 1884, his mother-in-law came to stay and left an account of life at Woodbrooke. She noted that George looked well and Mary 'stout and strong and in excellent health'. Although five servants were employed at that time, Mary's life was much taken up with her four children. One evening an expedition to go over to Bournville was arranged, to see the two new factory blocks, recently built, which Mary herself had not even seen. The brothers had expected the new factory to answer all their needs for the next twenty years, but within four years they were adding to it. Mrs Tyler was duly impressed by everything, noting that 'there seemed to be machines for almost every part of the work where they can possibly be brought into use . . . And now they are building again, this time a large reading room and kitchens etc. Whereunto will it grow? But George says it is impossible to stand still these days.'[5]

Another account, written many years later by H. E. Johnson, head of the general office for many years, described how George and his brother Richard divided the work between them in 1881. It shows how well suited they were to working together.

Mr Richard Cadbury used to come into the office regularly at least three times a day to give his personal decision on matters connected with the accounts, and to sign letters. His decisions were prompt and judicious and the traditions he set up for dealing with important matters in the office have had much influence during the succeeding years. The partners were in and around the works and offices continually. They had literally made the business, and were acquainted with every detail. Without any clear demarcation, it might be said that Mr Richard gave most of his time to the Sales side whilst Mr George did the same for the Buying and Manufacturing side, but they consulted one another so much that no definite line seems to have existed. One has a vision of Mr George, with a row of small tins on a counter in front of him, the tins filled with roasted 'beans' just brought in from the factory, and Mr George, with unerring skill, testing them and pronouncing judgement. At other times it would be samples of sugar or flavourings, etc., that would come under investigation. Mr Richard used often to take part in these tests, and indeed the two brothers, in touch with all sides of the business, were the centre round which everything moved. It was a kindly duocracy which they exercised, and those who served under it, a continually diminishing number, have nothing but happy recollections of those early days at the Bournville works.[6]

Richard Cadbury, who unlike his brother, loved travelling abroad and had developed a special interest in Egyptology, took some of his family for a trip up the Nile in 1899. While there he developed a sore throat, but, advised that it was not serious, he continued to Jerusalem where he died four days later from diphtheria, bringing to an end a close and fruitful relationship. Apart from their common concern with the business, Richard and George Cadbury shared two main interests, education and religion. Both devoted a great deal of their spare time to the adult-education movement, teaching their fellow men, and this made them aware of the conditions under which the working class lived and worked. Their interpretation of the religious life, however, showed a marked difference. For Richard the teaching and propagation of the gospel played an important role in his life; George Cadbury, acting under a deeply held religious belief, took upon himself, as a duty, the need to seek continuously to improve the material conditions of men.

Only a few weeks before Richard's death, by one of those strange coincidences of timing, George and Richard had entered into an agreement that in the event of the death of either one, his executors and the survivor would convert the business into a limited company. Already two of Richard's sons, Barrow and William, and two of George's sons by his first marriage, Edward and George, were in the firm.

George Cadbury's first wife, Mary, had died in 1887, giving birth to a son who died the same day. The following year George married Elizabeth Taylor (later Dame Elizabeth Cadbury) known by everyone in the family as Elsie. She was a strong-minded woman, a perfect partner to George. While caring for her children and stepchildren she found time for an active public life, campaigning for the improvement of conditions for working girls and women. She took a lively interest in the development of Bournville village and shared all George's interests outside business. Laurence and Egbert, sons of this second marriage, were children at the time of Richard's death but would both, in due course, become directors of the new company.

The first meeting of the board of the new limited-liability company, Cadbury Brothers Ltd, met on 5 July 1899 under the chairmanship of George Cadbury, and the four managing directors were his sons and nephews. Barrow Cadbury became secretary of the new company, which was capitalised at £950,000, divided equally into 6 per cent preference shares and ordinary shares. No shares were held by outsiders.

The seeds of many of the social developments which were to be implemented by George Cadbury had been sown in his brother's lifetime. The thirty-three alms-houses, built some 300 yards to the west of the cocoa works, were Richard's own contribution to the wellbeing of the work force. The houses that form part of the Bournville Village Trust are quite independent of the other two groups of houses – the almshouses and the sixteen foremen's houses – built at Bournville; they are the creation of George Cadbury and are not connected with the firm although built on land adjoining the factory and sharing the same name.

George Cadbury had been buying parcels of land to the north and west of the firm since 1893, and in 1899 he acquired another large area known as the Hay Green estate to the southwest, about a mile from the works. Adding together all his various holdings, by 1900 George Cadbury had acquired over 330 acres of land, on part of which he had built about 300 homes.

The Cadburys were by no means the first or only manufacturers to think in terms of a rural location for their factory and village. More than twenty years before, Sir Titus Salt had built his enormous wool-stapling factory away from Bradford and over the next twenty years had methodically developed what became the town of Saltaire. The first great British manufacturer to recognise that the requirements of their employees should be the first charge on the profits from the firm, Salt built 800 model dwellings. The houses were followed by the construction of a Congregational church, factory schools, baths, a public wash house, alms houses, an infirmary and a club house. In 1871 Salt presented the inhabitants of Saltaire, by then the most complete model manufacturing town in the world, with a park.

George Cadbury's purpose in building his village differed from those of both Titus Salt and William Lever, another industrialist, who created the village of Port Sunlight alongside his soap factory outside Liverpool. An equally paternalistic employer, William Lever saw his village as a form of profit sharing. He made no bones about what he thought of his employees would do if he gave them extra money. He said:

Frankly, £8 is soon spent, and will not do you much good if you send it down your throats in the form of bottles of whiskey, bags of sweets, or fat geese for Christmas. On the other hand, if you leave this money with me, I shall provide for you everything that makes life pleasant – viz, nice houses, comfortable homes and healthy recreation. Besides I am disposed to allow profit sharing in no other form.[7]

William Houldsworth was yet another manufacturer who took seriously his responsibilities as an employer. Seeking to provide his work force with the best possible conditions, he moved his cotton mills from Manchester to rural Redditch, where he hoped to create a factory community. His mill was a model of architecture and arrangement. He provided his work force with houses, a school and a recreation ground, and engaged Alfred Waterhouse, the leading Manchester architect of the day, to build a working men's club, a parsonage and, in 1883, the Church of St Elisabeth. Since one mill was unionised and the other was not, friction developed between the two work forces, and this probably accounted for the fact that they did not take advantage of the facilities provided 'with the degree of commitment Houldsworth looked for'.[8] But Houldsworth persisted, providing treats and inviting the work force for picnics to his Cheshire home, Norbury Booth Hall, and by 1887 the community was reported to be united and his 'Philanthropic Venture' can be said to have been a qualified success.

George Cadbury was thinking more widely than merely providing for his own employees. His experience as an Adult School teacher and his knowledge of the slum conditions under which the poorest families in Birmingham lived made him want to attempt something more radical, the creation of a residential community. As the numbers working at the Bournville factory increased, it was obvious that speculative builders would move in to build yet another set of slums close by unless action were taken to prevent them. George Cadbury could just have bought the land – instead he chose to build. When he handed over 300 houses to a charitable trust on 14 December 1900, he had some very clear ideas in mind. He was hoping to create a model which could be copied anywhere in the country and would be for the direct benefit of the working class. The Bournville Village Trust deed stated:

> The amelioration of the conditions of the working class and labouring population in and around Birmingham and elsewhere in Great Britain, by the provision of improved dwellings, with gardens, and open spaces to be enjoyed therewith, and by giving them facilities, should the Trustees think it desirable to do so, for purchasing the necessaries of life, and by such other means as the Trustees may in their uncontrolled discretion think fit.[9]

The trustees were all members of the family, initially George Cadbury and his wife and two of their sons. The only definite prohibition was that no property of the trust nor any building erected on it could be used for the 'manufacture, or sale, or co-operative distribution of any beer, wine, spirits or intoxicating liquor', unless by unanimous consent in writing of all the trustees. Without legally binding his trustees, George Cadbury desired that the buildings should occupy one quarter of the sites on which they stood and that the remaining part should be used as a garden or open space. If factories were built he hoped that at least one tenth of the land on which they were built would be laid out as recreation grounds or parks.

George Cadbury wanted primarily to provide better housing for the working classes, but he did not want to create just a new type of working-class housing scheme. From the start Cadbury wanted Bournville to be a mixed community, 'a home for workers of many types, employers and employed, managers and operatives, tradesmen and clerks,'[10] and the mix applied to character and income as well as interests and social class. There were social advantages inherent in the idea of a balanced community, and Cadbury was one of the first to recognise also the importance of dwelling mix. No two blocks of houses were similar in appearance and diversity of building was insisted on from the start. Nor was George Cadbury merely content just to create a model village, he wanted to publicise his achievement, and in this he succeeded brilliantly. Visitors came from all over the world to admire, and indeed enticing the poor to Bournville was a remarkable achievement, for only 50 per cent of the tenants were Cadbury employees.

But Cadbury's plans to house the poor and better-paid workers together were not without problems. By 1911 the press was only too pleased to make an issue out of the question of high rents. And it is probably true to say that no more of the real poor were to be found in Bournville than of the relatively wealthy. Cadbury's experiment was never meant to mirror true social divisions in society, but was more in the nature of an attempt to encourage by example the lower socio-economic group to emulate their 'betters'.

He took an intense interest in the village and left the imprint of his personality on all aspects of its development. Tenants moving in found that their gardens were already dug, the creepers and fruit trees already planted, the paths, hedges and lawns were made. Many of the amenities of the village were the direct gift of George Cadbury and his wife. The Friends' meeting house, the church hall and Ruskin Hall, planned as a centre for the intellectual life of the village, were followed in 1906 by two schools. George Cadbury had to struggle hard with the King's Norton education committee to get permission to build classrooms designed to accommodate only forty-five children as against the more normal fifty-five, which of course, meant greater expenditure on teachers' salaries. The clock tower with a carillon of bells became the most salient feature of the village, but no visitor could help being deeply impressed by the overall effect of the model houses, the planned open spaces and the provision of community amenities.

This was not just commercial philanthropy, it was one individual's attempt to provide a model solution to the housing problems of the working class. Health statistics provided the most immediate and measurable results of the success of the experiment. Tests made in 1919 showed that not only were children from Bournville heavier and taller than their counterparts in Floodgate Street, a poor district of Birmingham,[11] but the infant death rate was 7.2 per thousand for babies born in Bournville, as against 12.1 for England and Wales and 11.7 for Birmingham, figures which speak for themselves.[12]

Large though Woodbrooke had seemed, by 1895, after the birth of five children in quick succession, George and Elsie found that they needed more space. George moved his family to the Manor House, Northfield, a mile further down the Bristol road, where Elsie proceeded to make a series of alterations to a house which had already been considerably added to. There was a lodge at the gates, and the tree-lined drive which led to the house was a quarter of a mile long, with a branch leading off to the stables. The sweep of the lawn crossed the drive to the lake, which had an island and a pair of swans. There were several separate gardens in the grounds, and the stream which fed the lake came down through a rock garden over a series of waterfalls. There was even a dairy farm on the property.[13] To look after them and their family the Cadburys employed a staff of between twenty and thirty; nurses and governesses were employed to look after the children, so Elsie no longer needed to spend all her time exclusively occupied with domestic duties, and she developed a very active public life.

Although George Cadbury himself doubtless lived a life of personal simplicity, he was no longer a simple Quaker businessman. With the acquisition of the Manor House he had taken on the outward status of a rich and prosperous industrialist, albeit of benevolent and generous disposition. Soon after their move to Northfield, George Cadbury erected what was called The Barn, a large building capable of seating 700 people, where the Cadbury's could continue and extend their habit of entertaining children from Birmingham and other visitors who would appreciate the magnificent grounds. These personal acts of kindness were a source of great joy to George Cadbury, and Gardiner talks of him 'moving about among his guests, the picture of delighted benevolence'.[14]

Among their many acts of generosity, the Cadburys built a house in Bournville Village called the Beeches which was used in winter as a convalescent home for officers of the Salvation Army, and in summer to give children from the poorest families in Birmingham a holiday in rural surroundings.

In an attempt to lessen the difference between George Cadbury's way of life and traditional Quaker ideals, Gardiner was at pains to present George Cadbury as free from any sense of social distinction. George Cadbury certainly had an ease and freedom in his relationships with his fellow men, and there was genuine warmth between employer and worker. Gardiner's attempt to minimise the social gulf between George Cadbury and his employees was, however, misleading. The reality that inescapably underlay the relationship was the fact that poverty created dependence. George Cadbury was the all-powerful employer, and outside the factory he stood in the relation of teacher to scholar or benevolent host to those who enjoyed his hospitality. He was very much the ruler of his little kingdom of Bournville.

The Quakers came late to the idea of Sunday Schools, and the First Day schools, as they called them, only came into being in the 1840s. After Joseph Sturge (1793–1859), the Quaker philanthropist, had founded the first school in Birmingham, the movement spread under the vigorous advocacy of William White, a Birmingham printer who ruined his own business by his devotion to the cause of Friends' First Day Schools. An association was formed, run by a committee of Bristol Friends under the chairmanship of J. S. Fry. All three cocoa manufacturers played a very active role as teachers, so much so that the Adult School paper, *One and All*, even went so far once as to urge its readers to drink cocoa, in gratitude for benefits received.[15] George and Richard Cadbury could almost be said to have inherited the responsibility from their father, Richard Tapper Cadbury, an early enthusiast for the schools. Joseph Rowntree was twenty-one when he first took charge of a class of nine men, nearly all older than himself. He taught for forty years, and it was no easy task. He once wrote to a friend, 'You cannot enter into this work with less qualification that I had when I began. To prepare a bright and practical address once a week may be of immense educational value to oneself, but it is an onerous task . . . However, it becomes a little easier with practice.'[16]

Why did they do it? Quakers, having come late to Sunday-school teaching, found that the other religious denominations were already catering for the needs of children, so they turned their attention to poor and illiterate adults. Many of the schools' promoters tended to be teetotallers, but it was not only a wish to promote temperance; there was a feeling of distress at the irreligion of the poor, a desire to help them to improve their material condition and an unformulated feeling of duty: 'We had a vague notion that First-day school teaching was a good thing – that a Christian ought to be useful.'[17] By the turn of the century the Adult School movement had been weakened by competition from libraries, recreational clubs, savings banks and the advent of the Pleasant Sunday Afternoon movement. The paternalism of the movement was becoming counterproductive. The severe judgement of two Marxist critics was not entirely unmerited. They wrote, 'We emerge from a perusal of the Adult School literature with the feeling that we have been plunged in a bath of Uplift, of Earnestness, of Undenominational Goodness. But our minds have been given no direction whatever.'[18] The First Day schools were never seen as recruiting grounds for Quaker converts, although a few scholars did join. It might have been an embarrassment had they done so in large numbers, for Friends were bound to help their poorer members and subscribe to their children's education. It could then have been argued as has been noted, that in seeking to become members of the Society of Friends, converts were solely seeking material advantage. A more probable reason for the Adult School scholars' lack of enthusiasm for Quakerism was the form of worship itself; silent meetings are not easy for the uninitiated. As Elizabeth Isichei noted, 'Scholars discovered the difference between benevolence and equality, and the cheerful bonhomie of the schools was replaced by a kind of exclusiveness which was not present in the Adult School work.'[19]

The movement, however, was important to the Society itself, although it had little impact on the history of mainstream education. It gave to younger Friends a feeling of doing something constructive. But the most lasting result of the movement was that it gave to those who taught in the schools a real understanding of the way the poor lived. George Cadbury and Joseph Rowntree both had first-hand knowledge of the effects of slum conditions and what poverty really meant.

There were some surprising similarities about the lives of George Cadbury and Joseph Rowntree, some fortuitous, others less so: both lost their brothers who were also their business partners before the days of their great success; both had sons and nephews willing to play their part in the family business and both were to make two sons and two nephews directors when the businesses became limited-liability companies; both lost their first wives and both remarried, but their second partners were ladies of very different character.

Joseph's first wife, Julia Seebohm, a delicate girl, had been his childhood sweetheart and when they married the young couple set up house in part of his

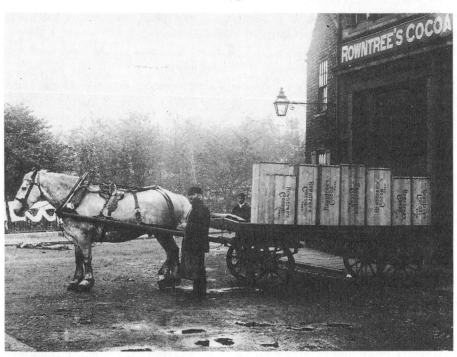

13 Laycock and his rulley at Tanner's Moat with a day's production.

14 A Rowntree's van advertising Elect Cocoa, circa 1902.

15 The Thorneycroft Steam Wagon, 1904. Cadbury's first motor van.

16 Cadbury's steam boilers, 1905.

mother Sarah's house at the corner of Bootham and St Mary's, York. There were connecting doors to Sarah's house on every floor, but at least the young couple had their own front door. The divided house meant that Julia had the vast original kitchen in the basement, which also housed the coal cellar, larder and scullery. Their sitting room was on the ground floor, two bedrooms occupied the first floor and there were bedrooms for three servants on the top floor. Their happiness together was short-lived, for within months of the birth of their daughter, Julia was dead.

During the ensuing four years Joseph spent much of his time at the Pavement shop. In 1867 he married Antoinette Seebohm, who had been born and brought up in Germany. Tonie, as she was known to the family, was not only a stranger in a strange land, she had not been brought up as a Friend and joined the Society only after she was married. Joseph did not move out of the house he shared with his mother until Antoinette was expecting their fourth child. Joseph's biographer, Anne Vernon, thinks that those early difficult years probably accounted for much of the quirkiness of her character and it is very understandable.[20] Antoinette appears to have been one of those women who would never find life easy, and even after the move to number 19 Bootham, a graceful eighteenth-century house with well-proportioned rooms, next to the Bootham School, Antoinette's life must have been dull. Social life consisted chiefly of entertaining travelling Friends, and Antoinette's interest in the Society of Friends was not sufficient to compensate for the loss of such ordinary pleasures as the wearing of fashionable clothes and a social life which might include the enjoyment of music and dancing.

It was not until 1905, with thoughts of retirement in mind, that Joseph and Antoinette moved out of York, to Clifton Lodge, a Regency house, standing in several acres of ground and with two cottages attached to it, on the outskirts of York. It had belonged to the Honourable Reginald Parker, who had enjoyed hunting and entertaining on the grand scale, and who filled the house with guests for the York races. Joseph does not appear to have used the spacious grounds for the lavish dispensation of hospitality to the less fortunate that George Cadbury found so enjoyable. He was able to house adequately the large library he had acquired and he found great satisfaction in working in the library, reading and writing about the political and social problems which concerned him and to which he devoted much time and thought.

George Cadbury had already established his factory at Bournville ten years before Joseph Rowntree was able to think of moving. In 1890 Joseph bought twenty-nine acres on the Haxby Road on the outskirts of York and started to build his factory. Bournville Village was already under construction in 1901 when Joseph bought more land, some distance from the factory, to start his new model village at New Earswick. The Rowntrees appeared to be following closely in the footsteps of the Cadburys, and one reason for this was that commercial success came later to the York cocoa manufacturers. The Cadburys had the psychological advantage of being the first to move and build.

When a family business became a limited company, the change often marked the sundering of the bond between master and man, and the paternalism of the family firm was replaced by a kind of anonymous and rational organisation. In the case of the Cadburys and the Rowntrees this did not happen for a long time, because of the strong and continuing involvement of so many members of the second generation of the family.

As the Rowntree work force increased in numbers – it went from 200 in 1883 to 894 in 1894 and twelve years later there were 4000 employees[21] – Joseph found himself unable to take the same paternal and personal interest in each individual employee as had been his wont. Joseph did not get unalloyed satisfaction from the growth of numbers and only gave up his erstwhile autocratic practices with a certain reluctance. In 1885, while the firm was still struggling, Joseph gave £10 from his own purse to match a grant by the Pure Literature Society to purchase books described as suitable for young people for the works library. But at the same time he deducted a penny from the wages of every single employee for the upkeep of the library, and although no one complained, the imposition amounted to a 2 per cent cut in salary for some.[22] There is no record of how much use was made of the library, but another innovation, the Cocoa Works Debating Society, was effectively given the thumbs down by the work force, who voted with their feet by not attending, and the idea was quietly dropped.

One of the most popular events in the Victorian era was the annual outing, when employers took their employees for a day by the sea and a good meal. Joseph's attempt at this form of entertainment ended in a spectacular failure. Joseph himself was very fond of walking, and his regular recreation was to take the train to Scarborough on a Saturday and walk for several hours before returning to York. On this occasion a special train had been hired to take all the employees to Whitby and, to increase the day's pleasure for some, the train was to stop at Goathland so that those who wished could walk the rest of the way to Whitby. Unfortunately no account had been taken of the weather, and the walking party arrived in Whitby soaked to the skin, and not unnaturally repaired at once to the warm and inviting public houses in the town. Joseph was mortified to learn that at the end of the day the police had to be called to escort some of the decidedly inebriated employees to the train, and for a good many years after that there were no more outings for the Rowntree work force.

A description of Joseph Rowntree given by one of his workers might equally well have applied to George Cadbury. ''E was very kind and very nice but ye couldn't get familiar with him. And if ye didn't give him a straight talc he made you feel like a little boy put under a table – but very nice and kind like.''[23]

Not until the late 1880s did Rowntrees begin to make significant profits. The fruit gums had been the first step along the road to success, but there had also been failures. Joseph had tried to break into the premium cocoa market in 1880 with a product he called Elect Cocoa, hoping it would prove to be the answer to the pure cocoas which both Fry and Cadbury had been aggressively marketing for some years. His refusal to advertise, for both ethical and financial reasons, meant that his salesmen had little incentive to push the product, and the first Elect Cocoa had to be rapidly withdrawn, to Joseph's chagrin. But Joseph was not defeated. He went to Stollwercks in Cologne to buy technical equipment, and he hired a Dutchman, Cornelius Hollander, for five pounds a week to make cocoa powder like that of van Houten. In conditions of the utmost secrecy, Hollander started to work behind locked doors. Joseph considered five pounds an enormous wage – 'It means we are paying three pounds a week for a secret,' he noted.[24] Hollander's appointment turned out to be something of a disaster, but Rowntree's own workers two years later, satisfied Joseph that at last Rowntree had a quality cocoa to market.

But even then Joseph's problems were only beginning. Fry and Cadbury had long dominated the market Rowntree's were trying to break into. It was fortunate for Joseph that he now had his sons and nephews in the business. His two older sons, John Wilhelm and Benjamin Seebohm, joined the business in 1885 and 1889 respectively, and spent time in every department. Arnold Rowntree, son of Joseph's brother John, came to work at Tanners Moat in 1892 and Frank, Henry Isaac's son, followed in 1893.

It was probably due to their influence, in particular to that of Arnold Rowntree, that Joseph's reluctance to use advertisements to promote his products was at last overcome. The new policy, announced to the Rowntree travelling salesmen in 1891, must have come as something of a surprise. The memorandum read:

In connection with our Advertising, we are considering the question of making an important forward move in the coming year (1892), and of entering upon National Advertisements, as distinguished from the localised advertisements, which are all that we have hitherto attempted.

We have not yet definitely fixed in which papers our advertisements shall appear, but it will most likely be in the direction of respectable weeklies of large circulation and wide distribution . . . In order that the advertising may be a success and so encourage us bit by bit to extend the area of our advertisements, we wish to invite your co-operation not only in the matter of extending sales, but of helping us to get the most effective advertisements in the spaces at our disposal. We believe it will be necessary to change the character of our advertisements pretty frequently, and to this end shall be glad of any suggestion which will assist us in drawing up new advertisement matter. It will also help us materially, if from time to time as you come across or have brought to your notice any particularly taking advertisement (either newspaper, handbill, or any other kind), that you will send us copies . . . Although we obviously may not be able to carry out every suggestion which may reach us, we assure you that every suggestion which you submit will receive careful consideration at our hands.[25]

This letter from the cocoa works was signed Rowntree and Co., and its formalised signature became the company logo and was registered as a trademark the following year. The travellers, as the salesmen were called, must have been somewhat surprised by the letter, but probably realised that this request for their co-operation was not some new advance in democratic management, but reflected the practical common sense of the Rowntrees. The salesmen would be aware of their customers reactions and alive to the effects of existing competition.

Four years after this letter, the sales of Elect Cocoa had not made the hoped-for dramatic breakthrough, although sales of other Rowntree products were increasing satisfactorily. But Rowntree's wanted to make Elect Cocoa the focus of their advertising campaign. Possibly only Arnold Rowntree could have persuaded his uncle to sanction the stunt which was used to inaugurate the campaign. For the price of a motor car and the cost of mounting a gigantic replica Elect Cocoa tin behind the driver, Rowntree's hit the headlines. Motor cars were still a novelty and the one Rowntree's bought was the first to be seen in York. For three months at a stately pace it toured the north of England, attracting crowds wherever it went. The climax to this public-relations exercise came when the car broke down in the busiest street in Sheffield. The driver was summonsed and only released on condition that he did not drive at more than three miles an hour which, as he pointed out, was anyway impossible with such a car. Arnold's next venture was equally eye-catching; spectators at the Oxford and Cambridge boat race in 1897 were startled to see a barge covered with advertisements for Elect Cocoa floating down the Thames, drawn by two mechanically propelled swans. But these one-off publicity exploits did not produce the hoped-for results, and Rowntrees appointed S. H. Benson to handle their advertising that same year.

Also in 1897, the business of H. I. Rowntree was converted into a limited company, Rowntree and Co. Ltd, with an authorised capital of £300,000. Joseph became chairman, the two sons and the two nephews already working in the business became directors, and a third nephew, Theodore Rowntree, Arnold's younger brother, became the secretary. J. B. Morrell, a director of the North of England Newspaper Company, was also made a director, the first to come from outside the family. The most dramatic expansion of both Cadbury Brothers and Rowntree and Co. Ltd occurred after they had become limited companies. One reason for their success must surely be that there were a sufficient number of young Cadbury and Rowntree males willing and able to provide continuity of management during the period of change.

Joseph's son, Seebohm Rowntree, gained national acclaim for his book, published in 1901, *Poverty, a Study of Town Life.* It was written with the family's characteristic dedication to factual accuracy, and remains an important landmark in social investigation. Joseph both influenced and was influenced by his son's work. At twenty-eight, the same age as Seebohm was when he started to work on his survey into the causes of poverty, Joseph had written a thoughtful paper entitled 'British Civilisation'. Joseph senior had taken his two sons to Ireland for a holiday in their youth, and some of the conclusions Joseph reached in his paper may have been coloured by his memories of the scenes he had witnessed during that holiday, when the famine was at its height. The paper was designed to be read to a conference of Adult School teachers, but Joseph Storrs Fry thought it too provocative and the language 'a little too strong in places'.[26] In making this comment, Joseph Fry, as always anxious not to cause offence, was also being true to his conservative nature.

A second essay, on 'Pauperism in England and Wales', written two years later, based on facts and figures that Joseph had been assembling for many years, suffered similar censorship before being publicly delivered. Quoting the medical officer of the Board of Health as saying that 'one-fifth of our population have not a sufficiency of food and clothing', he concluded: 'It is a monstrous thing that in this land, rich in natural wealth and now rich beyond all precedent, millions of its inhabitants, made in the image of their Creator, should spend their days in a struggle for existence so severe as to blight (where it does not destroy) the higher parts of their nature.'[27]

The questions to which Seebohm Rowntree wanted factual answers were basic ones. 'What was the true measure of poverty in the city both in extent and depth? How much of it was due to insufficiency of income and how much to improvidence? How many families were sunk in poverty so acute that its members suffered from a chronic insufficiency of food and clothing?'[28] *Poverty* underlines how similar in thought and style were the writings of father and son: 'The dark shadow of the Malthusian philosophy has passed away and no view of the ultimate scheme of things would now be accepted under which multitudes of men and women are doomed by inevitable law to struggle for existence so severe as necessarily to cripple or destroy the higher parts of their nature.'[29]

Ebenezer Howard (1850–1928) had written *To-morrow, a Peaceful Path to Real Reform*, which was reissued four years later, in 1902, as *Garden Cities of Tomorrow*. Port Sunlight and Bournville both reflected some aspects of Ebenezer Howard's teaching. The New Garden City Association, which was his creation, held its first conference in Birmingham and a visit to Bournville helped to give the movement the impetus to carry out the idea in founding Letchworth and Welwyn Garden City.

When Joseph Rowntree began to realise that his rapidly increasing personal wealth gave him the opportunity of making his contribution towards a fairer Britain, he therefore saw the model village as a means of putting his ideas into practice. When thinking of and planning for New Earswick, Joseph was influenced by both the revelations and the suggested remedies contained in Seebohm's work. New Earswick was no philanthropic venture, it was a social experiment, designed to show that it was possible to create decent housing for a socially mixed community. Joseph sought to create a village community which was to have nothing charitable about it, where the tenants would pay rents which would give a practical return. He realised that to do this there must be variety in the planning and in this respect he was a pioneer. He wrote that the houses should be 'artistic in appearance, sanitary and thoroughly well built, and yet within the means of a working man earning twenty-five shillings a week'.[30]

It is unlikely that he asked William Lever for advice. That flamboyant autocrat, although a Liberal and a Nonconformist (he was a Congregationalist although he never joined the church), had such a different outlook on life. His huge estates made him one of Britain's greatest landowners and his art collection put him on a par with Henry Clay Frick, the American industrialist, as a collector, but his model

17 Girls packing coronation tins for Edward VII at the Rowntree's factory, 1902.

18 The staff at Manor House, the Cadburys' family home, 1901.

19 The bustling Sycamore Road shops in Bournville village, 1914.

20 Houses in New Earswick, Joseph Rowntree's model village, 1910.

village, for all its imaginative conception, was seen by some of its inhabitants as no more than a 'rich man's plaything'. The secretary of the Bolton branch of the engineers' union wrote, 'No man of an independent turn of mind can breathe for long the atmosphere of Port Sunlight. That might be news to your Lordship, but we have tried it.'[31]

If Lever's attempts at social engineering did not interest Joseph Rowntree, George Cadbury's experiments at Bournville most certainly did. Joseph was interested in the possibility of almost indefinite expansion which George Cadbury's scheme seemed to imply, and turned to him for help and advice on the setting up of a trust similar to that of the Bournville Village. His reply to a letter from Cadbury shows the high hopes both men had for the benefits that might flow from the creation of model villages: 'Thy letter is most interesting. It is a great pleasure to think of Bournville village as a happy home for many generations of children where they will be brought up amid surroundings that will benefit them spiritually, mentally and physically . . .'[32]

The New Earswick site was not an easy one to develop; the land was flat and uninteresting and there was little industry nearby to attract people from York. Joseph persevered and thirty houses were built before the creation of the trust. Raymond Unwin, whose abilities had been recognised by Seebohm Rowntree, was the first architect chosen to develop the village. Unwin was later to be involved in the planning of Letchworth. The lessons learned at New Earswick had an important influence on housing policy and its planning at the time and during the postwar period.

Although Joseph sought George Cadbury's advice and used the same counsel to draw up the trust deed, there were important differences in the way the trusts operated. Determined not to create another 'cocoa works village', Joseph had included in the trust deed of 1904 a clause which specifically stated that he was 'especially desirous that nothing may be done under the powers hereby conferred which may prevent the growth of civic responsibility amongst those who may live in any community existing on the property of the Trust'. The trustees were enjoined to avoid any hint of paternalism. But there were difficulties, in that the trustees were not only the landlords but also controlled the services which would normally have been controlled by the local authorities. It proved impossible to separate financial responsibility and management, and this has militated against the concept of the village as a self-governing community, although the spirit of partnership between the trustees and tenants of the village has been excellent. The most obvious failure is that the trust was unable to provide housing to the standard required and still obtain a commercial return. All housing in the village is now subsidised and has been for many years.

The great success of New Earswick, apart from its value as an experiment in community housing, is that it demonstrated that the new principle in planning, the grouping of neighbourhood units, was not only successful at the time, but has proved infinitely adaptable. New experiments have been carried out, with different buildings grouped together in different ways, without at all spoiling the overall aesthetic effect of the village. On the contrary, the diversity of the buildings and the contrast in styles are a delight to the visitor. Older buildings have been altered and modified to meet modern requirements and so the village has been able constantly to renew itself. If the Folk Hall, which was a gift in 1935, has now lost its appeal, the recently built old people's home is one of the most attractive and inviting buildings.

Seebohm Rowntree's words at the Warburton lecture on housing, which he gave in 1914, testify to the success of the idea: 'There is a little village outside York, two and a half miles from the middle of the city, with no means of transit except walking or bicycling along a muddy road, yet the houses could be let over and over again.' New Earswick can now be approached by car; its well-planned environment is an equally strong attraction today.

5

The Power to Influence

Newspapers were at the turn of the century the most potent political force available, outside the ballot box, to oppose war; at least their proprietors and editors and the politicians they supported believed them to be of crucial importance.

Alfred Harmsworth, the proprietor of the *Daily Mail*, had during the Boer War hired special trains to dispatch the paper, which was strongly in favour of the war, throughout the country.[1] The British press as a whole was pro-war and the only newspapers not to indulge in the current jingoistic frenzy, so popular with the people, were the *Morning Leader*, the *Daily Chronicle* and the *Manchester Guardian*. When the *Daily Chronicle* changed its attitude in 1900 and H. W. Massingham, the editor, resigned with a number of his staff, the *Morning Leader* in the metropolis and the *Manchester Guardian* in the north were the only two newspapers that expressed the point of view of those opposed to the war and denounced the concentration camps and other evils.

This development deeply concerned George Cadbury, and following Harmsworth's example, he too arranged to pay for a special train, as a temporary expedient, to take the *Morning Leader* to Northampton, Birmingham, Leicester, Nottingham and Sheffield[2] so that it might be delivered early. Until that time, Cadbury's only involvement with the world of newspapers had been local. In 1891 he had bought a group of four weekly papers with a large circulation in the suburbs of Birmingham; his aim was to raise the civic and moral standards of public life by bringing an enlightened and public-spirited criticism to bear on public affairs, and to use his influence for good in an area where he was known and respected. The Boer War presented George Cadbury with a quite different challenge. As a Quaker he was against militarism and war, and the war in South Africa and the events leading up to it particularly outraged his sense of what was just or fair. A supporter of the Liberal cause, he was opposed to Liberal statesmen like Sir Alfred Milner (1854–1925), high commissioner in South Africa since 1897, and later Viscount Milner, and Lord Rosebery (1847–1929), whose imperial ambitions he regarded with the utmost suspicion.

The Jameson Raid in 1895, an attempt led by Dr L. S. Jameson to precipitate an uprising and overthrow the Boer government by invading the Transvaal with a small force, failed dismally. Instead of alerting the country to the dangers of slipping into a war, it inflamed public opinion again the Boers. Cadbury himself was convinced that the future of South Africa depended on the British and the Boers living amicably together, with the Transvaal and the Orange Free State eventually becoming self-governing colonies like Australia and Canada, and he wrote to Lord Rosebery putting forward his views.[3]

David Lloyd George (1863–1945), a Liberal politician who well knew how to use the press to his advantage, wanted the benefit of a newspaper more in tune with his own ideas than most of the press at that time. The *Daily News* had been in financial difficulties and it was not surprising that Lloyd George should approach George Cadbury, as one of two rich Liberal businessmen who might be persuaded to take over control of the paper. In a careful letter George Cadbury and Franklin Thomasson, son and heir of a Bolton textile manufacturer, were asked to put up £20,000 each, which would enable the paper to be acquired by a syndicate. Cadbury and Thomasson agreed. However, when E. T. Cook, who was editor, heard who the new owners were to be, he wrote in his diary that he could not on any account change the policy of the paper for men whom he considered the agents of all that was most mischievous. On 10 January 1901, in his farewell leader, he declared that the object of the *Daily News* under his editorship had been 'to keep steadily in view the larger interests and duties of the country as an imperial power, and to sink, in some measure, mere party considerations in the face of national emergencies'.[4]

Only Cadbury's particular sense of duty made him put up the money in the first place. Soon afterwards, Thomasson indicated that he did not want to put in more money as not only had the circulation failed to rise sufficiently but the paper was also taking a more socialistic line than he could support. Thomasson wrote that he did not believe 'the State has anything to do with old-age pensions or housing the people . . . politicians think the state should be *generous* whereas I think its business is simply to be just'.[5] Cadbury had now either to let the paper revert to its former attitude to the war or to be solely responsible for it. In a letter to C. P. Scott, editor of the *Manchester Guardian*, Cadbury revealed that he was quite aware just what a burden he would be taking on:

> Of course my personal comfort would be served by selling out my shares and getting out of the concern for which, as far as I can see as a man of business, there is little or no chance of success and I believe we could sell the paper at the present time . . . but this seems to me a terrible responsibility, as the *Daily News* ought to be a power for peace in the south of England as the *Manchester Guardian* is in the north . . . I believe the only chance for the *Daily News* would be for one individual practically to have unlimited control. It is a tremendous responsibility, but I am not sure it is not my duty to endeavour to effect this.[6]

In taking over full control of the *Daily News*, which he did in 1902, Cadbury differed from most Liberal industrialists and businessmen who entered the field of newspaper proprietorship. They found it more convenient to serve their party simply by writing a cheque. Sir George Newnes, publisher and MP for Swansea, wrote to remind Gladstone that for ten years he had lost £10,000 per annum and 'never asked anyone in the party for help. I believed it is admitted that the *Westminster Gazette* has supplied an effective weapon to the Liberal party, and has been a powerful influence for the principles we advocate. This could not have been achieved unless I had personally taken upon myself a great responsibility.'[7]

Andrew Carnegie (1835–1919) was also for a time a newspaper proprietor and as such can be seen as a forerunner of George Cadbury, in that having already by 1884 amassed a fortune from steel, he acquired a two-thirds interest in the London *Echo* and, by the end of the year, he owned or held a controlling interest in seven daily newspapers and ten weeklies in the Midlands and the north of England.[8] His object was to reawaken the old Chartist movement he had known as a child in Dunfermline. His papers called for the abolition of the monarchy and the House of Lords and the disestablishment of the Church of England. But he lost on his investment and his losses dulled his enthusiasm. He surrendered his final shares in the London *Echo* in 1902.

Charles Dickens had been the first editor of the *Daily News*, a London daily paper founded in 1864. Though he only remained editor for twenty-six days, he regarded even that time as a mistake. Nevertheless in his first edition he laid down guidelines for the *Daily News* which were to be 'Principles of Progress and Improvement, of Education, Civil and Religious Liberty and Equal Legislation . . . It will be no part of our function to widen any breach between employers and employed; but it will rather be our effort to show . . . their mutual dependence.'[9] It was a tradition worthy of the new proprietor.

George Cadbury's first job was to appoint a business manager and he chose a fervent primitive Methodist, T. P. Ritzema, a former proprietor of the *Daily News* who had only just been stopped from advertising the paper with a card which bore the compelling legend, 'Get right with God and the *Daily News*.'[10] Ritzema's moral fervour was even more extreme than George Cadbury's and although Cadbury had made it a condition that the paper should carry not only no betting forecasts, but no racing news at all. Ritzema wanted to ban all liquor advertisements as well. Cadbury agreed, though demurring that 'millions of good people drink intoxicating drink, but I know of no earnest Christian worker who gives way to betting'.[11] Financially these decisions were disastrous for the paper, and the change of policy had caused many other advertisers to boycott the paper. Cadbury confided to Harold Spender that the early months of his chairmanship had cost him £10,000. When Spender consoled him with the thought that his efforts had probably 'saved ten thousand lives . . . his face brightened with a beautiful smile. "Ah, in that case," he said, "I willingly bear the loss."'[12]

The one service that Ritzema had performed for George Cadbury was to advise him to appoint A. G. Gardiner as editor. Gardiner was relatively unknown in London, but he had worked for Ritzema when the latter was owner-manager of the successful *Daily Telegraph* in Blackburn, and Ritzema had a high opinion of his abilities. It was, however, due in large part to Ritzema's mismanagement that the

Daily News was losing money at such an alarming rate. George's son Edward, too, thought 'that rascal Ritzema' was to blame[13] but he had no time to deal with the problem, so Henry, his younger brother, was called in to take over as managing director, one of the strangest appointments ever made in Fleet Street.

The relationship between the Cadburys and Fleet Street seem always to have been uneasy. Confident and secure in Birmingham, where their business went from strength to strength, they never really came to terms with the newspaper world with which they involved themselves. A letter from George Cadbury, writing about his eldest son Edward and his wife, is revealing:

> Edward and Dorothy have very nobly determined to go up to London for the whole of November so that Edward may give up the whole month to the *Daily News*. You know how early they go to bed at home, but probably Edward will many nights not go to bed until three or four o'clock in the morning and it was a lonely time for Dorothy sitting through these midnight hours waiting for him . . .[14]

Thought to be delicate, Henry had had a sadly overprotected childhood, often living apart from the rest of the family so as to avoid undue noise and excitement. He grew up shy and lacking in confidence, and no wonder. He was only taught to read when he was eleven and went to school at twelve, where he stayed until he was eighteen, reaching only the fourth form. His form master, however, detected ability and wrote, 'His thoroughness will bring its own rewards.'[15] While he was at Leighton Park, a Quaker school near Reading, he met Bertram Crossfield, later to become his brother-in-law, who, like Henry, was to go on to Cambridge. Once at Cambridge, Henry struggled to take the entrance examinations so that he was eventually able to take an examination known as the Agricultural Special. After Cambridge Henry bought a farm and, with the help of a manager, ran it for three years until in 1907 he received a very unexpected, and perhaps unwelcome, letter from his father, asking him to go to London and look after the Cadbury interests at the *Daily News*. After deliberating for a fortnight, Henry accepted. Henry's own description of his first day at the newspaper's offices in Bouverie Street shows just how much, in personal terms, it cost him to take on the job:

> I knew nobody at Bouverie Street except Mr Gardiner, whom I had met once at the Manor House and for whom I had a sense of great respect and a distinct feeling of awe. I stayed at the parent's flat at Whitehall Court, and I remember the first day walking to Bouverie Street, getting to the door of the office, and turning back again and back to Whitehall Court; however, I made up my mind that that wouldn't do, so at the second time I went into the office . . . To begin with I had no status and while everyone was more or less studiously polite my coming was not welcome and I found myself in a somewhat equivocal position . . .[16]

Edward, understanding the difficulty in which Henry found himself, sent up a man called Tom Curtis from Bournville to act as secretary and friend. But Henry did not take long to find his feet, and a few months later his surprised father was writing, 'His brothers and I had no idea he was such a first-class man of business, but it is such a relief to Edward and me that you can hardly realise.'[17] Henry had thought his position at Bouverie Street 'pretty hopeless' as Ritzema was under contract for ten years. However, once he had been made a director, Henry decided to query the very large amount of Ritzema's expenses and the following day had Ritzema's resignation in his hands, which was accepted with alacrity. Having achieved that, he wrote to his father suggesting that his school friend, Bertram Crosfield, should be invited to join him at the *Daily News*, a most successful appointment.

Henry became managing director and lived and worked in London. Both his father and his brother sent him directives from Birmingham on how the paper should be managed. One characteristic piece of advice from George Cadbury read, 'Even religious people hate a paper that poses and I would advise giving up the religious column, this will save Mann's salary. It is difficult to get quit of him without giving up the column and he will never do it efficiently – there is too much of the parson about him.'

Two years after George Cadbury had acquired the *Daily News* it was Joseph Rowntree's turn to be approached and asked to help save a newspaper. Charles Starmar, the managing editor of the *Northern Echo*, asked for help and Joseph responded by buying the paper in 1903. At the same time he also purchased weekly papers in County Durham and in York. He created the North of England Newspaper Company with himself as director and his nephew, Arnold Rowntree, who became Liberal MP for York, as chairman. In the following year he set up the Joseph Rowntree Social Services Trust, which was non-charitable and given the powers to buy and control newspapers. In the memorandum to his trustees, then all members of his own family, he wrote:

> Perhaps the greatest danger to our national life arises from the power of selfish and unscrupulous wealth which influences public opinion largely through the press (e.g. the Opium and Drink traffic, and the South African War). If the funds permitted, and the Directors of the Social Service Trust were equal to the task, it would be quite in accordance with my wish that they should control, by purchase of or otherwise, a newspaper or newspapers, conducting them not with a primary view to profit but with the object of influencing public thought in the right channels.

Joseph Rowntree meant to attack what, in his view, were the great scourges of humanity, especially war, slavery, intemperance, the opium traffic, impurity and gambling. His political objectives were less detailed than Cadbury's but included religious liberty, free trade and economical government.

In 1910 two more papers came on the market, the *Star* and the *Morning Leader*. The possibility of the papers falling into Conservative hands led George Cadbury and Joseph Rowntree, after much hesitation, to agree to buy out the proprietors. Together the papers had a circulation of half a million, and the two cocoa manufacturers feared that the papers might be used to promote war with Germany and to oppose measures of social reform.

Both realised the moral dilemma they were creating for themselves by publishing papers that gave betting news, and George Cadbury already knew from personal experience something of the financial cost of excluding it. His first paper, the *Echo*, had failed within six months because he suppressed the betting page. In a letter to his son Laurence, he wrote that he had consented to the purchase with the idea that in course of years it might be possible to do without betting forecasts, but to change the character of the *Star* immediately was impossible, as no halfpenny evening paper could do without betting news.[18]

It is unlikely, however, that George Cadbury or Joseph Rowntree foresaw the extent of the moral controversy that the decision not to ban racing news would bring in its train. There had been those who had welcomed the stand Cadbury had taken over racing in the *Daily News*, but others felt that his decision implied an unwarrantable censorship of public morals. So when he and Joseph Rowntree negotiated a bilateral agreement to take over the *Star* and the *Morning Leader* and then failed to ban not only racing news but racing tips as well, their opponents took full advantage of the anomaly. The May edition of the *National Review*, a monthly journal owned and edited by Leo Maxse, a Liberal Unionist and a supporter of Joseph Chamberlain's campaign for imperial trade protection, contained a vehement attack on the cocoa manufacturers entitled 'The Cocoa Press and its Masters'.

> Fine professions of purity come very oddly from people who derive profit from circulating betting news. When Messrs. Cadbury took control of the *Daily News* it was pompously announced that they would 'cleanse Fleet Street'. There is no betting news in the *Daily News*, it is true, but it is guilty at one remove. 'Captain Coe's betting notes appear daily in the *Star*, and, we believe, sell that paper largely. Why not Captain Cocoa? Both it and the *Morning Leader* devote much space to betting and racing. And the *Daily News*, we have seen, owns some 9000 shares in these two journals. Notwithstanding this, it has not been above attacking Archdeacon Sinclair bitterly because he has a small investment in a brewery company. If it is wrong for the archdeacon to draw a modest revenue from brewing, it is equally wrong for a Quaker organ to draw dividends by encouraging betting. 'Physician, heal thyself' has here a distinct application.

In an article headed 'Superior Virtue' *The Spectator*, taking its cue from the *National Review*, launched into an attack.

> We had long noted with astonishment the manner in which the *Morning Leader* and the *Star*, but especially the *Star*, turned themselves into public gaming tables. The *Star* publishes tipsters' prophecies in a specially alluring way, and thus incites the kind of people who buy it – for the most part poor men – to risk their money in gambling on horse races . . . We fully realise, however, that there are a great many people, including probably the mass of newspaper proprietors, Liberal and

Conservative, who . . . hold, we presume, that the desire to gamble will find vent somewhere in every community and that it is better that it should result in honest betting than in hole-and-corner or house betting. Now whether we agree with this view or not, [*The Spectator* was careful to hedge its bets] those who hold it cannot be called hypocrites. Those who do not hold it . . . and actually regard betting as a vice, have certainly no right to have anything to do with newspapers which lend themselves to the encouragement of betting . . . What in others is at worst an error of opinion in them becomes cant and hypocrisy, or to use the language of theology, sinning against the light.

The Spectator quoted against the Rowntrees a passage from Seebohm Rowntree's book, *Poverty*:

'Until comparatively recent years, betting and gambling were largely confined in this country to the wealthy few. Now, however, the practice has spread so widely among all classes of the community that those who know the facts name gambling and drinking as national evils of almost equal magnitude. There is no doubt that the social conscience is as yet only very partially awakened to the widespread character of the gambling evil and to its grievous consequences. Like a cancer the evil thing has spread poisonous roots throughout the length and breadth of the land, carrying with them, where they strike, misery, poverty, weakened character and crime.'

The following week *The Spectator* carried a harsh letter from Sir Edward Fry. He was not the only member of the Society of Friends to deplore the action of the Cadburys and Rowntrees, but because he was a judge and the brother of Joseph Storrs Fry, his words must have caused distress to both families.

I have waited, in the hope that some member of the incriminated families would write and disprove some of the facts very circumstantially alleged by you; but not a word has been said in contradiction. As it is highly improbable that your charges should be unknown to the persons in question, I am driven to conclude that the facts are as stated in your paper, and that the persons accused prefer to allow judgement to go by default. And surely, on the facts thus set forth, the judgement must be one of the severest condemnation possible . . . In my efforts to find some reason for conduct so unintelligible as to be almost incredible, I thought that perhaps the *Star* might in the main be devoted to the promotion of temperance and peace and other good things . . . I find in them nothing to promote any good work, nothing to refine or elevate. But I do find in them, not only numerous articles on betting and racing but advertisements of worthless quack medicines, and of dry gin . . . and an air of utter vulgarity pervading almost every column of the paper.

Sir Edward Fry went further and in a pamphlet addressed to members of the Society of Friends said flatly that the 'National Anti-gambling League is largely supported by members of the Rowntree and Cadbury families, these very men who are themselves among the principal owners of the sporting press'.

George and Joseph produced a pamphlet of their own with the uninspired title of 'Friends against whom Sir Edward Fry's Criticisms have been Directed' in which they expressed their fears that the *Star*, which had always supported campaigns for social reform, had helped to expose the horrors of the opium trade and had worked for peace and the reduction of armaments, would pass into the hands of those who would have reversed its policies. With more than a hint of superior virtue they wrote, 'There are not so many daily newspapers willing to take the unpopular side and to make a brave fight for national righteousness even to the extent of opposing the leaders of their own political party, that the country can lightly dispense with one of them.'

There were calls from members of Society of Friends that Quakers in a corporate capacity should condemn the action of the Cadburys and Rowntrees, and regret was expressed that the days of disownment were over. However, another Friend, writing in *The Spectator* on 18 June, noted, 'It is no part of the work of a body whose functions should be spiritual to act as censor in matters which are not primarily breaches of moral law, and which should be, therefore, left to the individual consciences of its members.' Another correspondence recalled the old Spanish proverb which says, 'No one pelts a tree unless it has fruit upon it,' and wrote:

This saying is called to mind by *The Spectator*'s attack on the Cadburys and Rowntrees. The very bitterness of the attack betrays its origin. Moral indignation on any question is expressed very differently . . . Personal abuse is the last refuge of disappointed politicians and disappointed newspapers . . . The future will do full justice and full honour to the moral uplifting and progress Great Britain owes to these two great families, but when history is written their grandest record will always be that they incurred this misunderstanding and bitter antagonism in an attempt to save their country's honour, the only form of patriotism of any permanent value to a nation.

The final word must come from a Mr H. M. Paull, writing from the Cocoa Tree, St James's Street, whose letter to *The Spectator* put the matter in perspective:

Sir, The upshot of the correspondence on the above subject seems to prove (1) that the publication of the betting news is detrimental to the public interest; (2) that it is exceedingly difficult to omit from a morning paper, and practically impossible to do so from an evening one. The conclusion reached is that when a proprietor shows by his action that he has the courage to risk loss by omitting the objectionable feature, and this proves his desire to elevate the Press, he alone of all men is barred from having an interest in any other paper, unless he is a 'canting hypocrite'. The conclusion seems a strange one. I fear it is very improbable any of our newspaper proprietors will have the courage to omit betting news in the future, seeing that should they own other papers (as some do) they must never try the experiment with one paper unless they can face the accusation of hypocrisy because they do not at once abolish it in all and so ruin themselves inevitably. But only if they are content to do nothing will they be safe from abuse; and, in fact, if they wish, may point out the inconsistency and cant of their rival proprietors.

The attacks were not without effect. The Rowntrees had found the original decision an agonising one to make, as the minutes of the Social Services Trust make clear. They might have withstood attacks with a purely political bias, but the disapprobation of the Quaker community was too much. Besides all the difficulties inherent in the moral controversy, there was the added problem that the Rowntree trust was a non-profitmaking organisation, unlike the Cadburys' Daily News Trust, which was run as a business. So when the Cadburys wanted to merge the Morning Leader with the Daily News and print the new paper together with the Star in one building, they met with considerable resistance from Arnold Rowntree. The final upshot was that the Rowntrees' controlling interests in the Morning Leader and Star were handed over to the Cadburys without consideration. Joseph Rowntree was said to be particularly pleased that the papers would continue to support policies with which he was in sympathy, but he must also have been relieved no longer to be involved with two such controversial papers.

But even after the problem of the Morning Leader and the Star was solved, the Rowntrees' troubles were not over. By 1910 the Northern Echo wanted permission to resume publication of sporting predictions, and the trustees only arrived at their decision to sanction betting tips with 'deep reluctance'. They insisted that the paper carry, both in its leaders and in its correspondence columns, tactful and judicious references to the disastrous effects betting and gambling had both on the individual character and on society generally.[19] Joseph Rowntree went further, and by 1913, whenever sporting predictions were published, he wanted the paper to carry a statement, rather like a government health warning on a packet of cigarettes, that 'persons who followed these predictions would in the long run be likely to incur a loss'.[20] In spite of these precautions the Rowntrees came in for renewed criticism from the Society of Friends, so much that they feared that the work they were doing to forward the movement of the Society might be hampered by their connection with Northern Newspapers.

Henry Cadbury, as managing director of the Star, came in for a lot of criticism from St Loe Strachey, the editor of The Spectator. He chided the Cadburys about the general vulgarity of the Star and reminded them that in a leader in 1902 the Daily News had reaffirmed its refusal to publish information or news of any kind which might lead to the papers assisting, however slightly, in the traffic of waste and greed which has grown up in connection with the turf; all that time the paper had been convinced that if its example were followed, the principal apparatus of this kind of gambling would be destroyed. But Henry Cadbury, no doubt under instructions from his father, stood firm. In a biting pen portrait of Henry Cadbury in his dual capacity as managing director of the Daily News and the Star, Strachey wrote, 'I have little doubt that at heart he is quite a good young man, but he appeared to me to be wrapped in a rhinoceros hide of self-righteousness which made him think he could do no wrong, and that he need not in the very least fear the charge of inconsistency as long as his own conscience told him he was doing right.'[21]

Although he continued to buy provincial newspapers in Sheffield, Birmingham, Lincoln and Lancaster, as a result of the betting controversy, Joseph came round to the view that opinion-forming periodicals were perhaps a better medium for advancing his ideas. The *Speaker*, a weekly periodical, was acquired in 1906 and relaunched as the *Nation*. H. W. Massingham the former editor of the *Daily Chronicle*, was appointed editor. At an interview at the cocoa works he agreed to the general lines of policy expressed in Joseph's memorandum of 1904, and left in no doubt about the Rowntrees' expectations of the general tone and content of the paper.[22] There were frequent conferences between him and the trustees, who were all members of the Rowntree family, to ensure that their policy line was being carried out.

Massingham clearly did not live up to Joseph's expectations for the religious side of the paper. Massingham argued that it was hard to get well-written articles on religious questions in an age when thought on the whole was critical rather than constructive. A list of possible contributors was reluctantly accepted by Massingham. This was not the only area where his editorial freedom was curbed. A canvass had shown that readers enjoyed Massingham's signed articles on 'persons and politics', but the Rowntrees wanted no such display of independence and the articles were discontinued.

Gardiner had inherited a talented group of contributors to the *Daily News*. Among the most eminent was G. K. Chesterton, a notable literary figure on the London scene; Harold Spender and Herbert Paul, a former MP wrote for the paper; and Gardiner recruited two experienced journalists, H. N. Brailsford and H. W. Nevinson, as leader writers. Gardiner, like Massingham, had his difficulties with his employers. Herbert Paul was the first to fall foul of the Cadburys. A vitriolic obituary of Cecil Rhodes brought about his dismissal, but H. W. Nevinson, commenting later about the incident wrote that he was 'sure that Gardiner himself had nothing to do with it, but there was a power on that paper behind the editor as I was myself to discover in 1909'.[23] Nevinson's suspicions were shared by Harold Spender, who confirmed that Paul had proved 'too much' for George Cadbury, 'the simple moral person who holds the reins',[24] and his brother J. A. Spender thought it a shame that an anti-imperialist paper like the *News* could not find a place for Paul.

Another conflict of interests arose over the question of women's suffrage, a cause Nevinson had taken up with all the fiery passion that was his hallmark when defending the rights of the oppressed. George Cadbury was an ardent supporter of Lloyd George, and Lloyd George was, on this subject, not unsympathetic, but had warned against the adoption of extreme tactics by the militants. Matters between Nevinson and Gardiner on this issue came to a head after a particularly violent meeting at the Royal Albert Hall on 5 December 1908, when Lloyd George was addressing a gathering of Liberal women on the emotive subject of women's suffrage.

Suddenly a group of militant suffragettes threw off their cloaks to reveal prison garb (they had all been imprisoned) and another group of suffragettes started to shout from one of the boxes, 'Deeds not words', and all was suddenly chaos. Nevinson's description of what then happened catches the flavour of his style:

> The crowd of Liberal stewards went mad with political fury. They rushed upon the Union women with what the *Manchester Guardian* (no friend of the militants) rightly called 'nauseating brutality'. They seized them like savage dogs. They bumped them down the steps of the orchestra. They dragged them over chairs by the hair. They assaulted them with obvious indecency. Still, one after another the women rose in their places to utter the defiant cry.[25]

Nevinson himself shouted at Lloyd George and found himself unceremoniously dumped outside the hall, but remained enough of a journalist to notice 'that each of the women, as one by one they were flung out after me, no matter how horribly hurt and torn, first put her hat straight, if any hat was left'. When Nevinson got home he found a note from Gardiner, who had been sitting behind Lloyd George, suspending him from service. The suspension was lifted by the board of directors, but when Gardiner hesitated to condemn too strongly in print the practice of forcible feeding, of which he privately disapproved, for fear of offending the Cadburys, both Brailsford and Nevinson tendered their resignation 'so that G. might use it to coerce the Cadburys if he liked'.

Gardiner, like Massingham was in effect riding two horses. His primary responsibility was to serve the interests of the Cadburys, his employers, but as editor of a prominent Liberal daily he had, of necessity, to promote party policy, not all of which he necessarily agreed with. Although immersed in his business and philanthropic interests, George Cadbury still found time and energy to make endless comments and suggestions to Gardiner, which were supplemented by letters from his wife on subjects as varied as literary criticism and the content of the religious articles. After Ritzema retired in 1907, Gardiner is said to have found the 'niggling criticisms' levelled by Henry Cadbury intolerable.[26]

Apart from Bertram Crossfield, Henry Cadbury's other appointment was Wilson Harris, chosen because he was by upbringing a Quaker and Henry Cadbury had known him as an undergraduate, but his journalistic experience was nil. Gardiner accepted him on to his staff and told him he would be taught journalism and given an approximation of a living wage. Fortunately the experiment turned out well. Harris recorded in his memoirs, 'I might be a Cambridge graduate, I might have been President of the Union, but in the sub-editor's room of a London daily I was precisely nothing at all. Fortunately I had the sense to realise that and behave accordingly.'[27] Wilson Harris went on to become the editor of *The Spectator* in 1932, a post he held for more than twenty years.

The curious behaviour of G. K. Chesterton, which eventually led to his resignation, provided yet another example of the difficult path Gardiner had to tread. By that date Liberal support had been eroded to such a degree that any criticism of government policy could be seen as an attack on the government itself and might have had devastating consequences. Chesterton chafed under the restrictions that Gardiner imposed. 'If I have to follow the Liberal Government, I cannot write for the paper: nor could Massingham. But if I can attack it as he does, I will go on attacking it as he does . . . I would rather write for the *News* than anything; if I can leave on record that I wrote on the right side.'[28] Chesterton clearly understood the dilemma he faced and perhaps it was his own sense of inner frustration that impelled him to resolve the problem in an odd manner. He published his 'Song of Strange Drinks' with its controversial attack on cocoa, which was understood by most people as an attack on the Cadbury's, in the middle stanza:

> Tea, although an Oriental,
> Is a gentleman at least.
> Cocoa is a cad and coward,
> Cocoa is a vulgar beast,
> Cocoa is a crawling, cringing,
> Lying, loathsome swine and clown,
> And may very well be grateful
> To the fool that put him down.

Gardiner, seeking to allow Chesterton the option of disowning the 'outrage on those with whom you have been associated in journalism for years', called on him to correct the impression his poem had created. Chesterton denied that he had intended anything personal, but finally cut the Gordian knot by writing, 'It is quite impossible for me to continue taking the money of a man who may think I have insulted him. There is no other course but to surrender my position quite finally.'[29] So ended a very curious episode.

George Cadbury set up the Daily News Trust in 1912, when he felt personally unable to cope with all the stress involved in newspaper ownership and wanted to surrender his interest to the younger members of his family. The wording of the trust deed demonstrates how strongly both writers were actuated by religious motives, encapsulates what he had wanted to achieve through his ownership of the *Daily News* and embodied his intentions for the future, although without seeking to bind his successors.

> I desire in forming the Daily News Trust that it may be of service in bringing in the ethical teaching of Jesus Christ to bear upon National questions, and in promoting National righteousness; for example that Arbitration should take the place of war, and that the spirit of the Sermon on the Mount – especially the Beatitudes – should take the place of the military spirit which is contrary to Christ's teaching; that Love is the badge by which the Christian should be known.

He went on to say that he hoped the *Daily News* would be unsectarian. He saw much current philanthropic effort as remedying superficial evils and desired that the *Daily News* should help those who were seeking to remove their underlying causes. He went into detail about some of the controversial policies he wanted to see implemented, such as the taxation of land values, the appropriation by the nation of unearned income, land laws to increase the number of smallholdings, the cutting down of military expenditure, fewer opportunities for the accumulation of wealth in a few hands and the gradual nationalisation of all minerals below the surface. George Cadbury claimed that these policies were in the spirit of Christ's teaching, which is unchangeable, and by using a biblical quotation, 'The words that I speak to you, they are the spirit and they are life,' he used the highest authority to validate his point.

Gardiner's forced resignation in 1921 brought home to many just how great was the power and influence the Cadburys could and did exert over the policies of the *Daily News*. Gardiner, who at the time of the 1910 election had been one of Lloyd George's most fervent admirers, had by 1916 become deeply disillusioned. Lloyd George had supported conscription, to which Gardiner was opposed, but far worse, he believed that it was due to Lloyd George's machinations that the Liberal government had fallen, to be replaced by a coalition. On 22 April Gardiner published 'A letter to Mr Lloyd George' in the *Daily News*. 'Your friends have been silent long. They have turned a deaf ear and a blind eye to many things that have happened. They have pretended not to know what they knew only too well. They have refused to see your figure flitting about behind the scenes, touching the strings, prompting the actors, directing the game . . .' Joseph Rowntree thought Gardiner's letter painful to read and wrote that it must have been written under great irritation and in lamentable forgetfulness of the splendid service to freedom which Lloyd George had given in the past. But Rowntree admitted that there was no doubt that Lloyd George had allied himself with those who were against reform and he went on to say that Gardiner's words 'will meet with a general response from thoughtful people'.[30]

Gardiner returned to the attack on 3 May and 6 May, provoking Lloyd George, in a speech to his constituents in Conway, to refer to 'a cloudy discharge of poison gas' released by an 'assassin' in Fleet Street – 'I seek neither his friendship nor his support.' The next day, Gardiner answered:

> You said I was an assassin, you spoke of poison gas, you talked darkly of invented conversations, you dismissed me from the charmed circle of your friendship – But though you replied you did not answer the letter, nor did I expect you to. Like the Minister in the story you say, 'This, my brethren, is a very knotty problem. Let us look at it straight in the face and pass on.' It is much easier to say 'assassin' than to meet the accusation which you know to be true and to which you have no answer. The cuttle fish, I am told, discolours the water with an inky substance in order to conceal its movements. It is an artifice which no politician employs with a skill greater than your own. You must excuse me if I cleanse this rather dirty water and leave your evolutions visible.

During the run-up to the so-called 'khaki' election of 1918, Gardiner's dislike and distrust of Lloyd George were given full rein. In a letter to the voters on polling day, 14 December, he wrote, 'has Mr Lloyd George come to you and told you honourably what he means on any of the great questions on which he claims your mandate? . . . He does not mean that you shall know what he intends. For he does not want your mandate, he wants your blank cheque.'

The Liberal defeat was a bitter blow for George Cadbury, who must have wondered whether all the time and money that he had poured out over the years to make the *Daily News* a voice in the land had been worth the effort. Inevitably he blamed Gardiner. In a letter to Gardiner he said that the paper 'had lost influence in the country because it never acknowledged the good work that Lloyd George had done'. – 'Constant nagging at an individual very largely diminished the influence of the paper.'[31] Gardiner did not believe that the difference between himself and the Cadburys was profound, so apart from vigorously denying that the paper had lost influence, he contented himself with the reply that it would be painful to quarrel with 'one whose love and esteem I respect so much . . . We have the same spirit and the same objects, what we disagree about is the interpretation of events and the reading of men.'[32] But the circulation figures told their own story, down from over a million in 1917 to 350,000 in 1919.

Yet Gardiner could not desist from berating the prime minister, and one of the worst of Lloyd George's blunders, in Gardiner's opinion, was the appointment to the war office of 'Generalissimo' Winston Churchill. With the publication of the peace terms Gardiner attacked Lloyd George even more bitterly, writing, 'If the Peace Terms are the last word we have to say to Germany, let us make up our minds for the inevitable consequences . . . and prepare for the next war in whatsoever quarter it may break.'

This was the final breaking point for the Cadburys. After long discussions with Henry Cadbury, Edward Cadbury wrote suggesting that Gardiner should resign the editorship and executive control of the. *Daily News* and *Star*. He added, 'I think you should understand my personal feeling toward yourself which will remain unchanged, and if you can see your way to continue with us without quite such a heavy burden as you have had hitherto, we should only feel that it is in some measure meeting the debt we owe to you, particularly in the early days of our connection.'[33] The terms the Cadburys offered to Gardiner were generous, the parting as friendly as such an abrupt severance of a long-standing association made possible.

When the news became public on 10 September 1919, the outside world was puzzled. Massingham in the *Nation* asked rhetorically 'Is it that Mr Gardiner was too fond of liberty and not fond enough of Lloyd George?' Two years later, reflecting on Gardiner's dismissal, Massingham, who was himself to resign as editor of the *Nation* over the same issue in 1922, wrote, 'What is extraordinary is that a newspaper with such a past should drop its missionary side as if it were a stale sandwich thrown out of a railway carriage. The *Daily News* has accumulated readers who do not want a thinner feebler paper, and they will go elsewhere for their accustomed diet.'[34]

Henry Cadbury did not find it easy to replace Gardiner. There was a lot of suspicion about the true status of the editor. Wilson Harris fleetingly believed he could have been offered the editorship himself. A dinner in Gardiner's honour was held at the National Liberal Club with Asquith in the chair. J. A. Spender had delivered a rousing speech on the virtue of political independence in journalism. Since there was a dearth of subjects for the leading article that evening, Harris suggested making use of Spender's speech to fill the gap. Because the subject matter was delicate, Harris took the proof to the night editor, H. W. Smith, and to Hodgson, who was *in loco editoris*, and both approved it. Two days later Henry Cadbury came to Harris's room and told him he had not trusted himself to speak till he had had time to govern his feelings. 'He then expressed himself in terms which might have preluded immediate expulsion,' wrote Harris later, 'after which I realised that I could as well aspire to the Archbishopric of Canterbury as to the editorship of the Daily News.'[35]

Arthur Greenwood, one of those approached, wrote, 'People don't give up the editorship of a daily paper, or proprietors get rid of editors for nothing. I suspect, therefore, the "hidden hand". I may, of course, be all wrong in this, but if there is any truth in it I wouldn't touch the *DN* with a long stick.'[36]

Henry Cadbury also approached W. P. Crozier, the news editor of the *Manchester Guardian*, through the editor, C. P. Scott. The danger for Crozier, as Scott saw it, was that Henry Cadbury was so desperate that he would promise anything without strictly meaning to perform. 'Henry is a weak and rather shuffling person and would be a broken reed', incapable of sustaining an editor in conflict with a board of directors. Edward Cadbury he valued as a real person, but he was not in day-to-day control. Crozier did not accept, and finally Stuart Hodgson was given the post of editor.

Gardiner was not alone in finding Lloyd George's policies impossible to support. In letters to Joseph Rowntree, Massingham made clear his increasing unhappiness at the situation in which he found himself. By 1922 his opposition to Lloyd George was such that if the Liberals were reunited under his leadership, Massingham wrote that he would go over to the Labour Party. He continued, 'I think him impossible and I doubt whether my tactics of uncompromising opposition are of much avail to stay the movement in his favour.' He was tired of editorship and overcome by self-doubts. He referred to differences of opinion among the proprietors. 'I think the effort to put the *Nation* on its legs will need greater union among the proprietors than now exists and it will not be furthered by my personality. Everyone has a right to his opinions, mine may be wrong . . . Seebohm may be quite right . . .'

By this time the *Nation* was losing £4000 a year and the Rowntrees urgently needed to find a purchaser. Massingham resigned, and the Rowntrees sold the paper shortly afterwards.

6

A Time of Trial

The furore over the acquisition of the *Star* by the Cadburys and Rowntrees might not have been so violent had the Cadburys not been involved in an even more controversial matter in 1908, which culminated in a spectacular trial.

The *Daily News* had played a very active part in the run-up to the election of 1906, when the Liberals swept to power. The paper lost four members of staff to politics. C. F. G. Masterman, a leader writer, P. W. Wilson, the labour columnist, and L. G. Chiozza Money all exchanged their seats behind desks for seats in Parliament, and Vaughan Nash, another member of staff, became private secretary to Sir Henry Campbell-Bannerman (1836–1908), the prime minister. Masterman entered the government. This showed how close the links were between the *Daily News* and the Liberal Party at that time.

The paper had come out strongly in favour of social and land reform; it had attacked what it regarded as the fallacies of protectionism and it had campaigned vigorously against the importation of Chinese labour to work in the mines of South Africa. Millions of pamphlets and leaflets were circulated by the *Daily News* championing these views. George Cadbury's contemporary and fellow citizen, Joseph Chamberlain (1836–1914), Liberal statesman and leading advocate for the Campaign for Tariff Reford, was provoked into attacking the *Daily News* leaflets. At a campaign meeting Chamberlain dramatically produced two loaves of almost identical size and argued that the trifling difference between them represented the true effect of the corn tax.

Chamberlain was three years older than George Cadbury, and although different in character and outlook, they had a surprising amount in common. Both had made their fortunes as Birmingham manufacturers. Chamberlain was so successful that he and his brothers sold half their screw-manufacturing enterprise to Nettlefolds, their partners, for £600,000 in 1874.[1] The civic genius of Birmingham had depended on the large number of its small manufacturers who contributed greatly to its social and commercial prosperity. Great mills and factories like the ones he and George Cadbury built to further their business interests put that system at risk. Yet, like Cadbury, Chamberlain could see the advantages of the new system – healthier workplaces, regularity of hours, economy of labour, increased demand, lower prices and at the same time higher wages. Chamberlain brought in the nine-hour day as early as 1872 and set up the Smethwick Working Men's Club, Institute and Benefit Society, to demonstrate just how advantageous the new system could be.

Unlike Cadbury, whose life remained centred on his business and whose influence came through his success at Bournville, Chamberlain wanted further outlets for his talents. He first joined the town council, and, making use of his successful business methods, municipalised the gas company, which almost immediately returned a profit to the taxpayers. By simultaneously bringing down the cost of good water he dazzled the town council and gave Birmingham a reputation as the best-governed city in the world. His attempts to deal with some of the worst slums in Birmingham by pulling them down and transforming Corporation Street into a handsome thoroughfare for prosperous commercial and professional interests were more controversial. Not only did he make inadequate provision for the displaced slum dwellers, but the costs of the transformation of Corporation Street threatened to be disproportionate to its supposed benefits.

Nonetheless Chamberlain, when he entered Parliament in 1876, representing a mainly working-class constituency in west Birmingham, took with him a solid reputation, and his influence and political dominance over Birmingham was unchallenged. Until that time George Cadbury probably did not find much reason to disagree with Chamberlain's actions. However, when Chamberlain became colonial secretary in 1895, his equivocal actions at the time of the Dr Jameson's abortive raid into the territory of the Transvaal republic and his support for the Boer War aroused Cadbury's opposition. Cadbury fought, through the *Daily News*, not only the aims of the Liberal imperialists but also Chamberlain's campaign for imperial tariff protection.

The *Daily News* as an active political campaigning newspaper was bound to attract opposition, not just from those Liberals who supported Chamberlain, but chiefly from newspapers representing the Conservative interest. In this the *World*, a gossipy weekly with snob appeal which Northcliffe, who already owned the *Daily Mail* but not yet *The Times*, had bought because he thought it would bring him 'social prestige and influence',[2] was the leader. The *World* coined the term 'the cocoa press' to describe the papers owned by the Cadburys and Rowntrees, a lead which was eagerly followed by Horatio Bottomley, promoter of companies and dubious speculations is his weekly paper *John Bull*. His paper was lively, aggressive, frequently libellous, but sometimes hit the nail on the head with uncomfortable revelations, its readers being left to judge for themselves whether the paper was unmasking some wrongdoing or chastising an innocent victim.

The attacks on the Cadburys and Rowntrees were not confined to the newspapers. A small anomaly in the tax on imported cocoa gave Andrew Bonar Law (1858–1923) – the Conservative MP for Dulwich, who was to be prime minister for a brief period in the year he died – the opportunity to attack the cocoa manufacturers in Parliament, during the debate on the budget in 1907. Under the law as it stood, import duty was levied at one penny a pound of raw cocoa powder and at tuppence a pound on processed cocoa powder, from which the cocoa butter had been removed. Cocoa butter was used in the manufacture of chocolate, thus giving the manufacturers who imported raw cocoa the advantage over their competitors who imported the processed cocoa. 'I think it very unreasonable and most unfair that the large fortunes which are made in this country of these [cocoa] industries should be used as they are to subsidise newspapers and to help to finance Members of Parliament whose influence is used to prevent other people getting precisely the same advantages as they enjoy, and without which advantages there would be none of the money to spend in this way.' There were cries of 'Cadbury' in the House while Bonar Law was speaking, which shows how strong the feeling against Cadbury was at that time. Apart from the newspapers owned by the Cadburys, George Cadbury was known to be giving financial help to certain Members of Parliament whose views he approved of. The extent of George Cadbury's political patronage was and remains one about which little is known, except that it was considerable.

The ownership of the *Daily News* did not bring only trouble, and perhaps one of George Cadbury's chief satisfactions came when the paper organised an exhibition of sweated industries to expose the wretchedly low wages paid to the home workers. The six-week exhibition at Queen's Hall drew 30,000 spectators who could see for themselves that 'button roses made at 1s. 4d. a gross, with buds thrown in; . . . cardboard boxes at a wage which worked out at 1s. 3d. for twelve hours; hook and eye carding at 1s. 4d. for 384 hooks and 384 eyes; . . . a heavy day's work at eleven hours at chain-making which gave an average wage of 6s. to 8s. a week . . . did not make goods cheap: it only made human life cheap'.[3] The National Anti-Sweating League was founded to press for a minimum wage for home workers and Cadbury became the president; among the vice presidents were Beatrice and Sydney Webb, the social reformers, Keir Hardie and Herbert Gladstone, respectively Labour and Liberal Members of Parliament, and H. G. Wells, the novelist. The League's primary objective became the promotion of Charles Dilke's (1843–1911) Sweated Industries Bill. When the Trade Board's Bill, introduced by Winston Churchill (1874–1965) then president of the Board of Trade, based largely on Dilke's proposals, became law it coincided with the League's third and final session. The success of this campaign afforded Cadbury great satisfaction, and he would be saddened to know that in spite of legislation, the problem is still with us. It also brought very great credit to A. G. Gardiner and won respect for the *Daily News*.[4]

The Cadburys and nearly all the other cocoa manufacturers in the country were in the habit of importing some of their best cocoa from the equatorial islands of São Tomé and Principe, which lie in the Gulf of Guinea about 150 miles from the coast of West Africa. There had been reports and rumours that conditions of virtual slavery existed on the islands, and H. W. Nevinson's book, *A Modern Slavery*, published in 1906, gave the matter wide publicity. Nevinson, who was then still working for the *Daily News*, had heard that the Cadburys were looking for someone to send out to the Portuguese province of Angola in west central Africa and to the islands to make an on-the-spot report, and he offered to undertake the investigation.

But the Cadburys wanted whoever took on the assignment to spend six months in Portugal learning the language before going, and this Nevinson was unwilling to do. Instead he went out to West Africa and visited the islands, commissioned by *Harper's Monthly Magazine* to do a series of articles for them, which he later made into a book.

The cocoa planters of São Tomé and Principe had found an area where cocoa trees flourished in a climate where the heat was constant and the torrential rains, which lasted from October to April, meant that the *servicaes*, as the workers were called, laboured under clouds of dripping mist during the rainy season. Only by compulsion could anyone be made to work on these rich but deadly islands. In his book Nevinson described the way in which the natives were rounded up in Angola and driven down to the coast under conditions of appalling hardship by the traders. The death rate in São Tomé and Principe was very high, running at 12 per cent to 14 per cent a year, so that it was almost impossible to keep up with the demand for labour on the islands. Even on a good plantation, child mortality was over 25 per cent.

Nevinson's most severe censure was reserved for the ceremony which transformed the helpless natives into *servicaes*:

A day or two before the steamer is due to depart a kind of ripple passes over the town. Early one morning the Curador arrives and takes his seat representing the Portuguese Government. The slaves are herded into his presence in gangs by the official agent. They are ranged up and, in accordance with the decree of 29 January 1903, they are asked if they go willingly as labourers to São Tomé. No attention of any kind is paid to their answer. In most cases no answer is given. The legal contract for five years labour on the island of São Tomé or Principe is then drawn out, each slave receives a tin disc with his number and a tin cylinder with a copy of his register containing the year of contract, his name, birthplace, chief's name and the agent's name. The climax of the farce has now been reached. The deed of pitiless hypocrisy has been consummated – the requirements of legalised slavery have been satisfied. The Government have redeemed the slaves which its own agents have so diligently and so profitably collected. They went to the tribunal as slaves, they have come out as contracted labourers or *servicaes*.[5]

No *servicaes* who reached São Tomé or Principe alive ever returned home.

The slaves were delivered into the hands of the traders for many different reasons; some had broken native customs or Portuguese laws; some had been charged with witchcraft by the medicine man because a relation had died; some were wiping out an ancestral debt; others were sold by their families; yet others served as indemnity for village wars or had been raided on the Congo frontier; and there were those who had been purchased for a gun or a few cartridges.

The doctors told Nevinson that if they could keep a slave alive through the melancholy and homesickness of the first year or two, he or she sometimes lived for some years longer.[6] According to law, the labour contract lasted only five years. The planters from time to time collected some fifty slaves who had been with him for five years, sent for the Curador and paraded the fifty in front of him. In the presence of two witnesses and his secretary, the Curador then announced that their contract was renewed for five years more, and the slaves were dismissed to their labours. One planter told Nevinson that some of his slaves counted the years for the first five, but never after that.

Nevinson was deeply disappointed that his revelation about the slave traffic had so little immediate effect. He had imagined that there would be an outcry in the newspapers, the government would make representations to Portugal – in his view a gunboat could have stopped the traffic – and the Quaker firms would at once boycott the raw material derived from such an abominable source. None of this happened and almost the only support Nevinson got was from St Loe Strachey, editor of *The Spectator*, who helped Nevinson organise a meeting at Caxton Hall, wrote leading articles on the subject and allowed Nevinson the freedom of the paper.

Nevinson later wrote that when urging the cocoa firms to boycott the slave-grown cocoa, both for the sake of the slaves and for their own reputation, he was met by 'that peculiar hesitation which often characterises Quakers when action is called for. Perhaps a boycott seemed to them too violent as being resistance of evil . . . perhaps, as in fact they pleaded, they relied on Sir Edward Grey's official advice to keep quiet lest a boycott should impede diplomacy's artful aid.'[7] In collaboration with the other cocoa firms, the Cadburys had sent their own man, Joseph Burtt, to West Africa to make a report for them on the conditions obtaining in São Tomé and Principe. When the Cadburys heard that Nevinson was going to publish an article in the *Fortnightly* on slavery, they actually sent their solicitor to dissuade him, without success.[8] They also attempted to prevent Brailsford writing on the subject in the *Daily News*.

Nevinson had met Burtt in Principe and gave a pen portrait of him at that time. 'There was all the attraction of youth about his appearance and manner – so handsome he was, clean, and secure in the health of Quaker temperance. His mind was youthful too, being full of theories upon life – theories often contradictory but fine.' Nevinson reported Burtt as telling him, 'The Portuguese are certainly doing a marvellous work for Angola and these islands. Call it slavery if you like. Names and systems don't matter. The sum of human happiness is being infinitely increased. And, after all, are we not all slaves?' Nevinson recognised Burtt as a man of transparent honesty, but feared that he had been sent out in the hope that he would report well of the labour system he had come to investigate. He analysed his reactions to the Quaker characteristics he recognised in Burtt:

[Burtt] was imbued with that admirable Quaker quality which has often maddened my impatient and unregenerate soul. It is a capacity to obey the precept, 'Resist not evil, but overcome evil with good.' It is the character which, upon encountering evil, instead of violently striking at it as we heathens are inclined to do, surveys it calmly, engages in silent prayer, and walks around to discover some way of taking it in the rear by persuasion or appeal to a sense of virtue always latent in the heart of evil men. To indignation the process is irritating in its quietude, its deliberation, and perhaps in its success. But I acknowledge that the success is almost invariable, and Joseph Burtt's subsequent service to the cause that I had most at heart was only one more example of it.

But in 1908 Burtt's report had only been privately printed. It ended:

> Now that I have to state my conclusions, I must use the words which most nearly portray actual facts. I am satisfied that under the servical system, as it exists at present, thousands of black men and women are, against their will, and often under circumstances of great cruelty, taken away every year from their homes and transported across the sea to work on unhealthy islands, from which they never return. If this is not slavery, I know of no word in the English language which correctly characterises it.[9]

The reactions of the cocoa firms who had been involved with sending him out were unknown and Nevinson's attempts to create a climate of opinion that would force the Portuguese to alter the system of slave labour had been of no avail.

H. A. Gwynne, who had been recommended for the editorship of the *Standard* by Chamberlain, was a strong imperialist. His links with Alfred Milner (1854–1925), who had been governor general in South Africa from 1897 to 1905, dated from his time as the Reuters war correspondent in South Africa, where he had been a colleague of Nevinson's. When he came to read Nevinson's book, *A Modern Slavery*, he evidently saw that by making use of the revelations it contained of the conditions in São Tomé and Principe he had a useful weapon with which to attack the *Daily News* for its long campaign against Milner's policy of importing Chinese labour to work in the South African mines as well as for its opposition to Chamberlain's tariff-reform policies.

William Cadbury had made several journeys to Lisbon in an attempt to get the Portuguese government to take some action to improve the conditions of the *servicaes*, but to no effect. In 1908 it was therefore decided that he should go to West Africa himself and investigate.

The *Standard* used William Cadbury's impending journey as the peg on which to hang their attack. It is unlikely that an experienced journalist like Gwynne could have written such a sustained piece of satirical invective and not been aware of the risk he ran of involving both himself and his proprietor, Sir W. D. Pearson, in a libel action. He began his article by congratulating William Cadbury on his journey:

> We learn with profound interest from Lisbon that Mr Cadbury, the head of the famous firm of cocoa manufacturers, is about to go to Angola, where he will investigate for himself the manner in which 'labourers' are recruited for the plantations of islands which supply Messrs Cadbury with the raw material for their justly celebrated products . . . One might have supposed that Messrs Cadbury would have long ago ascertained the condition and circumstances of those 'labourers' of the west coast of Africa and the islands adjacent who provide them with raw material. That precaution does not seem to have been taken.

It was the ironic passage in the article, contrasting the joys of Bournville with the miseries of the African *servicaes*, that really left the Cadbury's with little alternative but to sue for libel:

In his model village and factories of Bournville the welfare of the workpeople is studied as closely as the quality of the goods manufactured. There are lecture rooms and gymnasia, and no public houses; the young ladies in the firm's employ visit the swimming bath weekly, and they have prayers every morning before beginning their honourable task of supplying the British public with wholesome food. But in this latter useful process they are not the only agents. The white hands of the Bournville chocolate makers are helped by other unseen hands some thousands of miles away, black and brown hands, toiling in plantations, or hauling loads through swamp and forest. In the plenitude of his solicitude for his fellow creatures Mr Cadbury might have been expected to take some interest in the owners of those same grimed African hands, whose toil also is so essential to the beneficent and lucrative operations of Bournville.

The article then continued with a brief summary of Nevinson's book and a eulogy of his character and powers of observation. It ended with the words:

Such is the terrible indictment, made as we have said by a writer of high character and reputation on the evidence of his own eyesight. There is only one thing more amazing than his statements, and that is the strange tranquillity with which they were received by those virtuous people in England whom they intimately concerned.[10]

It was impossible for the Cadburys not to answer an accusation which contained so many damaging inaccuracies. They had started making enquiries into the true situation as long ago as 1901; they had sent out Joseph Burtt; William Cadbury had two or three times gone to Lisbon to protest to the Portuguese authorities; they had asked Lord Grey, the foreign secretary, for advice and had been enjoined not to do anything that would make negotiations more difficult between HM Government and the Portuguese government; and now, finally, William Cadbury was himself going to Angola and the islands.

More than a year passed before the case came up for trial. No expense was spared on either side. Rufus Isaacs and John Simon, both brilliant lawyers, appeared for the plaintiffs, as well as two more lawyers, Norman Craig, KC, and H. Joy. Sir Edward Carson, equally brilliant, passionate, satiric, and deadly in cross-examination, was retained as defence counsel by the *Standard*, together with four more lawyers. The case came before Mr Justice Pickford and a special jury, and at the request of the Cadburys the trial was held in Birmingham. It started on 29 November 1909 in a crowded courtroom with several members of the Cadbury family in the ladies' gallery.[11]

William Cadbury was in the witness box for three days. Under cross-examination by the clever and astute Carson, who well knew how to apply pressure, he proved calm and composed.

21 This girls' PT lesson is an example of George Cadbury's concern for the health and fitness of his workers, 1903.

22 Mixed doubles on the Rowntree's tennis courts: an unusual view of men and girls relaxing together.

23 Men using adding machines in the Cadbury's accounts department, 1905.

24 Coolies sorting cocoa for Rowntree's in Ortinola, Trinidad, 1896.

Carson: Would you say it was slavery of an atrocious character?
Cadbury: Generally speaking, as far as the collection of labour in Africa that is true.
Carson: Then the men who were producing the cocoa in São Tomé which you were buying were procured by atrocious methods of slavery?
Cadbury: Yes.
Carson: And not only men, but women and children?
Cadbury: Yes.
Carson: Men, women and children had been forcibly taken away from their homes against their will?
Cadbury: Yes.
Carson: Marched away, labelled like cattle, down to the coast for embarkation to São Tome?
Cadbury: They were marched under force to the coast. They were not labelled on the march.
Carson: Were they labelled when they went on board ship?
Cadbury: Yes.
Carson: How far had they to march?
Cadbury: Various distances. Some came from more than a thousand miles, some from quite near the coast.
Carson: And never to return again? From the information you procured, did they come down in shackles?
Cadbury: There is a usual custom, I think, to shackle them at night on the march.
Carson: And those who could not keep up with the march were murdered?
Cadbury: I have seen statements to that effect.
Carson: You don't doubt them?
Cadbury: I don't doubt it has been so in some cases.

Given the slightest ambiguity in any answer by William Cadbury, Carson drove home his advantage.

Carson: Men, women and children openly and freely bought and sold?
Cadbury: I don't believe, as far as I know, that there is anything that corresponded to the slave market of fifty years ago. It is done now by subtle trickery and arrangements of that kind. I don't think it is fair to say that in Angola there is any open slave market.
Carson: You don't suggest that because it is done by subtle trickery that makes it better?
Cadbury: I do not.
Carson: But in some cases they are bought and sold?
Cadbury: In some cases they are bought and sold.

The Cadburys had not denied that conditions of virtual slavery existed in Principe and São Tomé since Burrt's report, and Carson, step by step, made William Cadbury spell out in court just what that slavery meant. William had to admit that the children of the *servicaes* were owned by the planters, that the *servicaes* had no days of freedom, except part of Sunday, and were never repatriated. In answer to Carson's questions concerning their wages, William said they were paid ten shillings a month, and added that in parts of the eastern hemisphere even free labour is not remunerated any higher. He went on to add that they received housing, clothing, food and medical care. When Carson commented that their clothing needs were few, the court laughed.

Carson then began a different line of questioning, aimed at eliciting the extent of Cadbury's commercial involvement in São Tomé and Principe. Cadbury's had begun to buy cocoa from the islands in 1886, and between 1902 and 1908, when they knew that conditions of slavery existed, they had imported the main portion of their cocoa from São Tomé and Principe. They stopped in 1908 and it became official policy in 1909. Carson produced evidence to show that over £1336 million had been paid for the cocoa and that considerable profits had been made from it, and went on to ask if 'it was not against the principles of Cadbury Brothers to make a considerable profit out of slave-produced cocoa?' William replied steadily, 'Not under the circumstances.'

There was laughter in court again when Carson referred to the way in which Bournville was used in advertisements with headings like 'Bournville Garden City', 'Simple and happy life', 'Comfort for workers in beautiful Bournville' and 'Girl workers in Paradise', but noted that nothing was said about conditions in São Tomé. This was ruled inadmissible by Rufus Isaacs for the plaintiffs, as the advertisement had appeared after Cadbury's had given up buying cocoa from São Tomé. An advertisement to the effect that 'Cadbury's cocoa is made under ideal conditions . . . the cocoa beans are specially selected and produce the purest and most delicious cocoa' appeared that day in the *Birmingham Daily Post*, which was reporting the trial in great detail; it differed little from those that had appeared before the Cadburys gave up buying São Tomé cocoa.

Carson then tried to get an admission from William that, had the matter become public knowledge, their business would have suffered; that they had prevented the *Daily News* from publishing information on the labour conditions in São Tomé and that if the *Daily News* had carried on the same kind of agitation against slave-grown cocoa as they did against indentured labour in the Transvaal, Cadbury's business would have suffered. William, in a very disingenuous answer, said that he had no interest in the *Daily News* as a shareholder and maintained that if the public knew the whole truth, including the efforts being made by Cadbury's to improve conditions in São Tomé, their business would not have been affected. William had to admit that Cadbury's tried to stop Nevinson writing an article condemning the British cocoa manufacturers for buying cocoa from São Tomé (the Rowntrees never bought cocoa from the islands) and said, amid laughter, that it was done 'because condemning the British Cocoa makers meant condemning the British Government'. He insisted, 'We went on buying the cocoa because we were absolutely advised by the highest authorities we could consult that it was the best thing we could do in the interests of the reform of labour conditions in West Africa.'

Carson asked, 'Had you no conscientious objection to going on buying cocoa produced under these conditions?'

'I should have had very serious objections if we had not been doing our utmost to secure reform,' Cadbury replied. 'My conscience and common sense I try to work together and I thought that for me to sit down and say, "I will have nothing more to do with the matter by ceasing to buy," was not the best and right thing to do. I thought it best to go to the people who were in a position to give me advice – and to take it.'

After Joseph Burtt had given his evidence, George Cadbury entered the witness box. He was seventy and seemed, compared to William, less assured. He said that when he and his nephew had seen Sir Edward Grey at the Foreign Office he had asked whether a gunboat could not intercept a vessel carrying native labour to São Tomé, but was told this was impossible owing to Britain's friendly relations with the Portuguese government. His own counsel had some difficulty getting him to refute the suggestion that 'in this matter you were not acting honestly, not to benefit the natives but to protect yourselves'. George Cadbury replied that he had said all along that they would lose very little by giving up buying cocoa from São Tomé. Isaacs tried again and George Cadbury replied, amid laughter, 'It is not suggested by anyone whose opinion we care for.' At the third attempt Isaacs got from the witness the answer he wanted, that there was no truth in the suggestion whatsoever.

Carson, cross examining George Cadbury, came back again to the question of conscience. 'You have always looked on slavery as an accursed thing?'

'Yes.'

'You are incapable of making a profit out of anything produced by slave labour?'

'One has to use common sense and sentiment. Sentiment told me I should give up buying at once, but common sense told me it would do no good.'

Carson asked, 'As an ordinary proposition, would not you say that anybody who made a profit out of the produce of slave labour was doing a wrong thing?'

George Cadbury answered rather lamely, 'I would say the whole profit made during that time has gone to benevolent purposes. Nothing would have given me greater joy than to feel we could have given up using the cocoa without damaging the blacks.'

After Sir Edward Carson had announced, to the surprise of the court, that he was calling no witnesses and would simply address the jury himself, a course of action which Rufus Isaacs later described as 'the sheltering of the *Standard* behind Counsel's gown', the public galleries were even more crowded. Carson started his speech for the defence from a high moral point of view. 'The *Standard*, like every other high-class newspaper, was bound . . . if they had written an article, not on a private matter, but on a great public matter of importance to civilisation itself, to save neither trouble nor expense in vindicating the position they had taken up . . . as they believed they were performing one of their highest functions in calling attention to the matter . . .' He was interrupted by Rufus Isaacs, who pointed out that as the defendants had called no evidence they were not entitled to say what the defendants believed. Carson took the intervention in his stride and said, 'The *Standard* stood by their article.' He went on to say, 'Messrs Cadbury had always, by the action they had taken, put themselves forward as the champions of the proper conditions of labour. Whether at home or amongst the coloured races abroad, by their action they had put themselves on a very high pinnacle of public morality . . . They made no little boast of what they had done towards improving conditions of the people in their works . . . In the years in which they were dealing, certain of the plaintiffs had the control of the *Daily News*, which set itself up as the great champion of the conditions of labour in South Africa and the Congo.'

If Messrs Cadbury's real anxiety was to promote the welfare of the labourers on the plantations, would not their first act have been to cease their contribution to the men who were holding down the slaves in São Tomé and Principe? Painting a vivid word-picture of men, women and children driven like beasts through the 'hungry country', the children, like the calves of a cow or the lambs of a sheep, becoming not the property of their parents, but the property of the owners of their parents, Carson led dramatically to the point he wanted to hammer home. 'When you say that slavery is not an issue in this case, I say slavery is a vital issue.' And to cries of 'Shame!' he went on, 'I say it because for eight long years that condition was supported by money that came from the Cadburys – those perfect gentlemen. One million three hundred pounds paid from this country by the Cadburys to the slave dealers in Portugal.'

Their explanation, said Carson with heavy irony, was that they did it much against their will, in the interests of the people of São Tomé and Principe. It would have been reasonable to have given the planters six months' notice to improve conditions, instead of which, in one year they purchased more than 60 per cent of their raw material from the islands. Carson said that for the Cadburys to say, 'What was the good of giving up the "accursed thing"? If they did, someone else would take it,' seemed to him an extraordinary moral position for them to take up.

Carson went on to ask what had been the effect of their negotiations – they were in exactly the same position in 1907 as they had been in 1903. 'In 1908 nothing effective was done except that Messrs Cadbury made efforts to keep the matter from becoming public and finally communicated to the public that Messrs Cadbury had found matters so bad in São Tomé, Principe and Angola that they must give up their humanitarian project to benefit the labourers, must abandon their "lever" and give up using slave-grown cocoa.'

In what the *Birmingham Daily Post* called 'an elegant peroration', Carson called on the jury to look at the matter as a public one on which the press were entitled to comment. Rufus Isaacs immediately objected and said this had not been raised by the defendants in the particulars and the issue was not that it was a matter of interest proper for public comment, but that the plaintiffs charges were justified.

Accepting that his last remarks were not fair comment, Carson, after two hours and thirty-five minutes on his feet, sat down.

When Rufus Isaacs rose to answer, he acknowledged that no one could excel Sir Edward Carson in the art of scoffing and sneering at witnesses whose evidence was against him. William Cadbury, he suggested, had shown, by his 'quiet, simple, modest, unassuming, straightforward demeanour that he was a man upon whose word they could rely'. The defence were asking the jury to say that Messrs Cadbury had been acting in collusion to present a series of deceitful, wilfully lying statements before the world in order that they might fill their pockets out of the dealings in São Tomé cocoa. They were not being asked whether, with the knowledge Messrs Cadburys had before them, they had adopted the wisest course to secure reforms of São Tomé labour conditions, but did they adopt those measures which bona fide they believed most likely to attain their purpose?

Rufus Isaacs then took his revenge on Carson and referred in scathing terms to the fact that the defence had not called a single witness. They dared not, he taunted them, 'put one witness into the box to give evidence upon the charges – how the article came to be written, why it was written, or whether the writer believed it to be true at the time it was written'. The defendants had not even put Mr Nevinson in the witness box because they knew he would destroy the whole fabric of their case. Nevinson himself commented on the fact that he had not been called and thought it was because the plaintiffs had accepted his book, A Modern Slavery, as true beyond dispute, although he regretted not being given the opportunity to refute the allegation that his story of the barbaric hunting-down of escaped slaves was not true.[12] However, since Nevinson had written to the Cadburys acknowledging the part they had played in bringing to light the conditions of the slave traffic after Joseph Burtt's visit to São Tomé, Carson's cleverly constructed defence, making the matter of slavery the issue, could have been put at risk had Nevinson made this declaration in court.

Isaacs ended by saying that in January 1908 William Cadbury had satisfied himself that the promises of reform were illusory and decided to buy no more cocoa from the islands. The defendants said of Mr Cadbury's visit that he went with the 'alleged purpose' of ascertaining whether the planters had reformed the slave system, but that really he went out only to enable the firm to put more money in its pocket. 'Could anything be more cruel, more wounding, more offensive and more insulting to Mr Cadbury?' demanded Isaacs. There was applause for Rufus Isaacs from the gallery, quickly suppressed by the judge, who then began his summing-up.

The judge, as The Times said, stated the issues in a manner not unfavourable to the Cadburys. He narrowed the question down to the point for the jury: 'Was this a dishonest plot to delay the matter being brought before the British public in order to enable the plaintiffs to go on buying slave-grown cocoa which they knew they ought to give up?' That was the matter for the defendants to prove and that alone was the issue they had to try. After less than an hour the jury returned with a verdict for the plaintiffs with damages of one farthing.

The Cadburys were awarded costs by the judge, which must have been considerable, for both sides were represented by formidable legal teams – five KCs were involved and altogether nine counsel received instructions. But the amount of the damages awarded, a derisory farthing, made the trial an interesting one – still more interesting for reasons that go beyond the actual matter in dispute.

Carson and Isaacs had faced each other in court two years previously, in a case which had many similarities with the Cadbury libel action. Then William Lever brought an action against Lord Northcliffe (1865–1922) the newspaper proprietor, for attacking proposals by Lever Brothers aimed at creating a mammoth 'soap trust'. The *Daily Mail*, the *Evening News* and the *Daily Mirror* had denounced Lever's business practices. (Cynics were not slow to point out that the advertising receipts of the Harmsworth press would also be affected by the proposed merger.) Lever was particularly offended to see Port Sunlight, his model workers' village outside Liverpool, caricatured as 'Port Moonshine' in the *Daily Mirror*. Incensed, as a Liberal and a free trader, at being accused of engaging in a form of self-protection at the expense of the poor, but still more hurt, as a businessman, by the sudden drop in his companies' sales, Lever persuaded Carson, then Unionist MP for Dublin University, to take on the case, while Rufus Isaacs, Liberal MP for Reading, defended the *Daily Mail*. Lever came out a clear winner. Isaacs called no witnesses, and Northcliffe had fled to France to avoid being called. Northcliffe had to pay damages and costs to the tune of £150,000. However, Lever did not escape unscathed, and his hopes of building a soap combine were defeated.[13]

In the Cadbury libel action, the question of why the jury chose to award the insulting one-farthing damages has been the subject of considerable comment. It has been seen as a political gesture by Chamberlain supporters unable or unwilling to give an unbiased verdict, but after Carson's shocking description of the lives of the slaves, they may well have felt morally justified. *The Times*, taking the view that the good name of a widely known firm is a public possession, said, 'We have no sympathy with those who would gladly see an honourable reputation ruined or besmirched,' and went on to say that 'it would always be a nice question for moralists what should be done in the circumstances revealed by this trial'. The leading article also said, 'We do not care to dwell much on the contrast between the policy pursued at Bournville and the hideous state of things in São Tomé.'

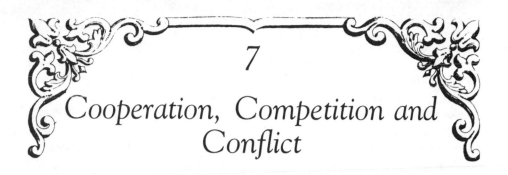

7

Cooperation, Competition and Conflict

By the turn of the century Cadbury Brothers and Rowntree and Company had grown from small provincial cottage industries to highly mechanised businesses nationally known, but J. S. Fry & Sons was on the downward slope. As competition between the Cadburys and the Rowntrees intensified, it throws an interesting new light on the relationship between the founders and their families.

While Cadbury's and Rowntree's were still small there was friendly cooperation between the two companies, and both George and Joseph from time to time appealed to Joseph Storrs Fry for help and advice. When Joseph Rowntree decided to manufacture chocolate creams, he wrote to Joseph Fry saying that he did not wish to seem to undercut and damage Fry's, for it was after all they who had pioneered the idea. 'I do not wish to do anything recklessly to injure what ought to be a lucrative branch of our business . . . Of course thou will only answer my questions just so far as thou inclines . . .' He was also anxious to discover what Fry and Cadbury did about price cutting and went on to say that Rowntrees were strict with discounts 'from a wish not to cut down the profits of the trade'.[1]

When business interests were only marginally affected and matters of principle in question, the firms could be generous towards each other. In 1900 a Rowntree relative in Scarborough had organised what was meant to be a peaceable meeting to discuss the questions raised by the Boer War in South Africa, then in its second year. Unfortunately tempers became frayed and there were riots and damage to property. The Rowntrees of York felt obliged to put a disclaimer in the press to try to limit the damaging consequences which the affair had caused their trade. In a gesture of solidarity Cadbury's sent Rowntree's a copy of a letter they had sent to their travellers, saying they would be distressed if it were found they had profited from the prejudice against Rowntree's of York.

But there were underlying tensions between the businesses as they grew and competed for markets. Both Fry's and Cadbury's had made full use of advertisements since the early 1870s, to their mutual benefit. Joseph Rowntree's extreme reluctance to enter this field certainly held back his company's development. He held strong views about the morality of advertising; disliking the element of conflict. He also believed that it was speculative and compelled the business to take short-term views rather than adopt a continuous policy. He was worried by the fact that the claims made in advertisements did not always correspond to the truth and had been very disturbed by the way in which Cadbury's, through their aggressive advertising of Cocoa Essence, had attempted to destroy the business of the other cocoa manufacturers. Joseph had been able to maintain his views about advertising in the 1870s because Rowntree's were in any case unable to afford to advertise. He had issued a letter giving his views on the subject: 'As we do not advertise we are enabled to give greater value for money than those firms whose sales depend on advertisements. We prefer to trust to quality . . . Steadily increasing sales strengthens our opinion that this is a sound method of doing business.'[2]

Nevertheless, during the period from 1897 to the outbreak of war in 1914, Rowntree's actually spent more on their advertising budget, relative to their sales volume, than either Fry's or Cadbury's. Cadbury's had been forging ahead and Rowntree's, despite Joseph's insistence that if goods were of sufficiently good quality they would sell, was not prospering to anything like the same degree. Though idealistic, Joseph was also shrewd and practical. Once he accepted that advertising was the key to increased sales and profits, he sanctioned it.

The Rowntrees had been disappointed that their own bold but ephemeral attempts to publicise Elect Cocoa had met with so little success; they knew their product was good and that it could be very profitable if only it could be successfully marketed. Joseph needed money to finance his new factory at Haxby Road which was coming on stream; Arnold, his nephew, was very anxious to try new marketing methods; and Joseph was anxious to prove that Rowntrees could make and market a cocoa every bit as good and popular as Cadbury's Cocoa Essence.

When Joseph finally agreed that Rowntree's must seek professional help, S. H. Benson was the firm selected. Unlike some of the advertising agencies of the time, Benson's had always had a reputation for integrity and they were able to meet the standards demanded by Rowntree's. Samuel Benson had attempted to set up an organisation to enforce advertising standards and levels of service, but was unable to get agreement on who was eligible. Joseph must also have found Benson a congenial colleague to work with because he took a personal interest in the welfare of his staff and drilled the messenger boys working in the agency after hours to ensure their wellbeing – a habit noted by Dorothy Sayers, who later worked at Benson's and used the agency as background for her thriller *Murder Must Advertise*.

Benson's whole approach to advertising would have done much to reconcile Joseph Rowntree to the use of this relatively new profession. Benson was a thinker and his writings show that he believed in studying the consumer, the trade and the competition as well as ensuring the product was right before any thought was given to its promotion.[3] He did not believe in making exaggerated claims, which, he argued, was a short-sighted policy, because the aim of the advertisement was to buy the good will of the customer. Benson's wrote later about the way in which they tackled the problem of advertising the Rowntree cocoa and how they found an immediate solution:

25 A Cadbury's advertisement.

26 A Fry's advertisement.

27 The famous Beggarstaff's poster for Rowntree's, 1896.

In the face of colossal advertising by other cocoas, probably then at the aggregate rate of over a quarter of a million sterling per annum, the grocers were, naturally, shy at a new cocoa and the travellers could not get in edgeways. It was, however, imperative to get the article stocked. Willy nilly the trade must buy. We had to devise a scheme which would stock the trade and at the same time make the public talk about the cocoa. The scheme adopted was called the *Daily Telegraph* Scheme, and it provided a penny stamp and a sample of cocoa in exchange for a coupon from the paper. Simple as it was, it was extraordinarily effective, a thousand accounts were open in a fortnight and every grocer's shop on the list was besieged.[4]

The year they were appointed, Benson's pulled off a spectacular coup. They contacted two leading London bus companies and got their agreement to having the buses decorated with Rowntree advertisements and their conductors also suitably dressed, and on 3 December 1897 the *Daily Mail* asked its readers, 'Have you had your ride on a Rowntree Bus? Every lady passenger gets a free trial tin of Rowntree's "Elect Cocoa".' The public responded with such enthusiasm to this novel attraction that the police threatened to stop the whole exhibition as being contrary to the regulations of the City. They grudgingly allowed it to go on, the superintendent of police remarking, 'But mind, never again.' The following day the *Daily Mail* gave the stunt half a column, headlining it; 'The Cocoa War: a brilliant engagement in London yesterday'. Several other newspapers also commented on the dramatic way in which Rowntree's had drawn attention to themselves and their cocoa.[5] What the staid and peace-loving Joseph can have thought at seeing his business described in military terms as the instigators of a cocoa war is not recorded. However, he could at least comfort himself with the knowledge that they were, in fact, giving the public the opportunity of judging the quality of the Rowntree product for themselves and not making claims which, by inference, called in question the quality of the cocoa manufactured by competitors.

Rowntree's, under the guidance of Benson's, were one of a handful of firms that made use of the brilliant posters designed by Beggarstaff's. Although commercially unsuccessful, the Beggarstaff posters with their enigmatic figures gazing into space, lacking any apparent connection with the product being advertised, were amazingly eye-catching as posters. The Rowntree poster, which in its original form measured 15 feet in height and had to be carried into the Benson offices by both the two designers, became world famous. Beggarstaff's, because of the innovative techniques used by the agency, have been held to represent 'perhaps the shortest and most significant episode in poster history'. The Rowntree poster was dramatic and simple, and Benson's wanted it used again the following year. Rowntree's disagreed. They were not the only firm to have doubts about the wisdom of using so unusual a poster. Beggarstaff's succeeded in selling only a few of their designs before abandoning the poster business.

Rowntree's returned to the more comfortable type of poster such as the one showing Rowntree's Elect Cocoa being carried on a tray by the maid, the strings of her apron being playfully pulled by two children. The caption reads 'Mother's Cocoa in danger'. The scene is one with which the public could identify, if not put off by the whimsical nature of the design, and one which made sense in terms of their philosophy of building up a relationship with their customers. There was nothing aggressive or competitive about the brand identification at the top; 'Rowntree's High Class Chocolates and Cocoa'.

Benson's must sometimes have found their relationship with Rowntree's a somewhat difficult one. It may well be that Dorothy Sayers had the Rowntrees in mind when she wrote, in *Murder Must Advertise*, 'A visit was expected from two directors of Brotherhoods Ltd, that extremely old-fashioned and religiously-minded firm who manufacture boiled sweets and non-alcoholic liqueurs.' By linking the non-alcoholic chocolate liqueurs with the innocuous fruit gums, Dorothy Sayers put her finger on the almost obsessive concern shown by chocolate manufacturers with the problem of drink. All three chocolate manufacturers had been disturbed by the successful sale of liqueur sweets introduced in 1903 by Stollwercks, a German manufacturer with whom they had close links. The confectioners James Pascall were the first to raise the matter, and after some discussion on the morality of selling such sweets, it was agreed to support Pascall's who took up the matter with the Band of Hope in an effort to stop the sale of this new, and to them, pernicious novelty.

When Rowntree's received the royal warrant in 1899, there was a natural desire to make the most of this honour. But the proposal to send out a selective display in special tins, known as the Queen's Gift Tins, ran into an unexpected difficulty. The idea was dropped, not only because it was thought that it would be upsetting to those shopkeepers not chosen, but also because it would be 'pandering to some degree to the present war fever'. The Boer War made even patriotism suspect. Fortunately there was nothing to stand in the way of exploiting the coronation of King Edward VII. Rowntree's offered half a million tins of cocoa or chocolate, at the cost of a penny or tuppence a tin, to the organisers of the King's coronation dinner for the poor of London. The same offer was also made to the 60,000 stewards who were serving the meal because, as was noted, 'they would be of greater importance to us socially than the 500,000 poor'. Rowntree's hoped to make the gift appear as though given by the King because 'it would be more gratifying to the recipients'. It would also have been a neat way of making the point that Rowntree's enjoyed royal favour. Other coronation committees were offered gifts, and Sheffield was one of those who accepted. The gifts were, no doubt, appreciated but so too was the value of the advertisement, which was said, in the case of Sheffield, to be of far greater value than the apparent loss of £70. Rowntree's duly received the royal warrant from the new king in November 1902.[6]

From having a budget with practically nothing allocated for advertising, Rowntree's had increased their spending until it was relatively greater than their competitors' and a very large proportion of that budget was being spent on the promotion of just one product, Elect Cocoa. It is tempting to see this as Rowntree's way of responding to the damaging campaign waged by Cadbury's when they were promoting their Cocoa Essence. Some of the other Rowntree lines, which had relatively little advertising, had consistently higher sales than did Elect, but Elect was made to carry the weight of the advertising budget and expected to show a profit.

There were some well-known examples of the chocolate manufacturers cooperating over matters of public importance to themselves; less well known was the extent to which they cooperated over business matters, particularly over the setting of prices and on policy over profit margins. It was the Quaker view that vigorous trading in business could be a true vocation and of benefit to the whole community, so in setting prices Joseph made sure that adequate margins were allowed, not only for the manufacturer, but for the wholesaler and the retailer as well. And Quakers were among the first to mark their goods with a fixed selling price, feeling this to be fairer to the customer.

All three manufacturers agreed to adopt a set of principles, and there were regular meetings between Fry's, Cadbury's and Rowntree's, sometimes also Caley and Clark, chocolate manufacturers of Norwich, to agree price rises. According to the Rowntree minutes, Cadbury's did not always play the game. They reduced the price of one of their chocolate assortments without informing Rowntree's[7] and, what was worse, it was noted that 'Fry's have followed suit'. Characteristically, Rowntree's decided not to cut their prices as 'this would be contrary to recently agreed profit margins'. There was also a pact not to poach staff from one another, and agreement was reached over the vexed question of gifts to customers at Christmas in kind or in money.

Very occasionally there was agreement about the level of advertising, and Rowntree's, who monitored Cadbury's every move, were always quick to adjust the amount of their advertising to every variation made by Cadbury's. There was one occasion when Rowntree's felt so strongly about the way in which Cadbury's were advertising their cocoa that they approached Conrad Fry, one of the Fry directors, on the subject. Conrad Fry arranged for Joseph Storrs Fry, who was chairman of J. S. Fry & Sons, to see George Cadbury privately and represent to him the views of both Fry's and Rowntree's.[8] This was probably the last occasion on which Fry's had the moral authority to play the role of arbiter; they were soon to lose their dominant position as market leaders to Cadbury's.

Notwithstanding the competitive tension, extensive cooperation between the chocolate manufacturers was to their mutual benefit. Fearful, however, of running into the kind of hostility from the press that had arisen over Lever's attempts to create a combine of soap firms, Cadbury's and Rowntree's corresponded over the danger of appearing to be too closely involved in pricing policy. Following a speculation on whether 'there is or is going to be a "Cocoa Trust" more or less comparable to the "Soap Trust" now attracting so much attention in the press',[9] it was agreed that travellers should be instructed to be circumspect in what they said. All phrases like 'owing to an agreement with our competitors' were to be avoided and the existence of price agreements was to be kept from the public.

The years 1905 and 1906 were important ones for Cadbury's, for it was during those years that they launched two new products, Cadbury's Dairy Milk and Bournville Cocoa, which were to provide the basis for their rapid prewar expansion.

Until then Swiss manufacturers had had a virtual monopoly of the milk-chocolate market in Britain, with only Rothwell's competing in a small way. Milk chocolate had first been produced by Peters in Switzerland in 1876, but the problem of combining milk and chocolate had baffled most manufacturers. In America, Milton Hershey was spending days sloshing round in hip boots in his new creamery, built from some of the million dollars he received from the sale of his caramel business, trying to solve the problem, while Cadbury's were also experimenting with different formulas. In the same year that Hershey perfected his secret recipe for the Hershey bar, Cadbury's found a chocolate that suited the British taste. Rowntree's noted with anxiety that the sales of their Queen chocolate were almost extinguished by the success of Cadbury's milk chocolate. Their only response was to continue to advertise on a modest scale.[10] In 1911 Cadbury's set up the first of their subsidiary factories at Knighton, on the borders of Shropshire and Staffordshire, an area surrounded by dairy farms, to process the milk needed at Bournville. By 1913 CDM, as it was known both inside and outside the firm, had become Cadbury's biggest selling line.[11] Rowntree's never succeeded in producing a milk chocolate to compete in quality with Cadbury's Dairy Milk.

The success of the advertising campaign to promote Elect Cocoa had undoubtedly affected the sale of Cadbury's Cocoa Essence, and the public now preferred the flavoured and alkalised cocoas, which were also being imported from Holland. Bournville Cocoa was Cadbury's answer, and they spent heavily on publicising their new cocoa. Competition between the two firms was intensifying, Rowntree's had no new product and could only reply by increasing their own advertising. The gift-coupon scheme which Rowntree's were using to promote their cocoa certainly affected Cadbury sales; Cadbury's twice approached Rowntree's to ask them to give it up and twice Rowntree's courteously refused.[12] But the very popularity of the scheme made it expensive for Rowntree's, for they could never tell how many gifts they would be called on to provide, and after a third approach they agreed to standardise the weight of purchases and to set a limit on the value of the gifts.

Although Rowntree's successful advertising made life difficult for Cadbury's, Elect itself was under pressure, not only from Bournville Cocoa but from other proprietary brands, and the size of the advertising budget needed to sustain sales was causing concern. The Rowntree board discussed the possibility of approaching Cadbury's to negotiate a standstill in the level of advertising, but Joseph, interestingly, vetoed the suggestion. Joseph's obstinate determination not to give way when faced with strong competition from Cadbury's appears to have come from a strong sense of pride in his firm's achievements and a definite wish not to allow Cadbury's to dominate the market. However, when Cadbury's made a similar proposal shortly afterwards, Rowntree's were glad to agree to cut advertising by a third. Fry's weaker trading position was acknowledged by the other two manufacturers, and they were permitted to cut their advertising by only a quarter.[13] But the recent Cadbury–Rowntree involvement in the newspaper betting controversy, which had led their papers to become collectively known by their political opponents as the 'cocoa press', made them cautious of being seen to be cooperating.

In 1910 the agreement over the pricing of cocoa came to an end and Cadbury's immediately undercut the price of Elect Cocoa by a penny. Rowntree's decided to stick to their price, advertise heavily and give greater bulk discounts. The market at this time was flooded with cheap cocoas and the Rowntree travellers were finding it hard to compete. Joseph had made his views known to the travellers in 1907.

> Speaking for myself, I remember that often in old times when bringing out a new article of the finest quality, it was urged by members of the staff that if the goods were so made they would yield no profit, and my reply used to be to the effect that the price must be fixed to suit the quality and not the quality to fit any low price. Acting on this principle we have not hesitated to sell some important lines at a price higher than that charged by our keenest competitors. Our experience has fortified us in the view that there is plenty of room in this country for a firm who will manufacture the very best goods, charging them at a price higher than that of other English makers.[14]

Fry's had lost their premium market completely by concentrating on the cheaper end of the market, and even Cadbury's Welfare Cocoa, their cheapest product, was said to be losing ground. Rowntree's managed to defend Elect Cocoa without lowering the price, but at the cost of heavy advertising.

The years of the First World War were difficult for all three chocolate manufacturers and drew them into closer collaboration. Regular conferences were held at Cheltenham to discuss matters of common interest. The question of the level of prices was of perennial interest and when, in 1917, Cadbury's declined to raise the price of their chocolate Rowntree's minuted their response in the following disingenuous way: 'It is thought we may have to raise prices whether Cadbury does or not, but we do not want to put ourselves in the position of being less obliging to our customers than our competitors.'

At the next conference, Arnold Rowntree found Cadbury's 'much more candid than recently'. Rowntree's considered their gift-coupon scheme as part of their advertising, not as a price reduction;[15] Cadbury's argued that if Rowntree's continued with their scheme it gave them the right to reduce the price of their chocolate. It was agreed that it might be wise to have an advertising agreement, but Rowntree's were averse to making any agreement that would interfere with the way in which they marketed their cocoa. However, the most startling piece of information that Arnold Rowntree brought back with him was the news that Fry's were seeking a merger with Cadbury's as a way out of their difficulties, which had become acute during the war years.

Owing to their weak trading position, Fry's had opened negotiations with Cadbury's the previous year. Cadbury's would have liked a three-year trial merger, but they had competition. A hustling outsider, the Swiss chocolate firm of Nestlé, was casting covetous eyes at the ailing Fry business. Could Rowntree's afford to remain independent? Arnold Rowntree discussed the implications of fusing the three firms with Barrow Cadbury, Richard Cadbury's eldest son and a vice-chairman of Cadbury Brothers, but he was worried about the possible popular objection to combines. After talking to Barrow Cadbury, Arnold thought there was no need to rush the matter. But Fry's made it quite clear that they would not allow time for lengthy discussions. By early 1918 it was known that Fry's had considered selling out to Nestlé, something that Cadbury's certainly would not wish to see happen. Cadbury's were afraid, as it was, of increasing opposition from American combines, and Arnold Rowntree was told that they favoured the idea of a holding company, because Fry's had not delegated authority and such a company would enable them to achieve economies of production.

The Rowntree directors discussed the matter at length at a special board meeting on 5 February.[16] Arnold Rowntree was in favour of widening the existing arrangements, but the practical Joseph saw at once that Fry's had made this impossible. Seebohm Rowntree believed that Rowntree's had no option but to join Cadbury's and Fry's, and there was much anxious talk about provision to safeguard the workers under possible new arrangements. John Stevenson Rowntree felt the proposed consortium would become nothing but a moneymaking concern. Joseph remained unhappy about the whole idea. He still hoped, as he had outlined to his sons in 1890, to create a business in which the workers could be partners in a profit-sharing scheme. Amalgamation would be a threat to his long-held belief that the best form of philanthropy was a well-run business making profits for the good of all.

When William Cadbury told the Rowntrees that a dummy company had been registered under the name of the British United Chocolate and Cocoa Company, Joseph remained uneasy, fearing such an amalgamation would lessen the individual life of each of the three firms (and Rowntrees were the smallest) if ultimate control and authority rested with a joint board on which a number of directors of the separate boards had no voice. It was decided to invite two directors representing Cadbury and Fry to York, and Barrow Cadbury and Walter Barrow met the Rowntree directors on 26 March.[17]

Joseph had now made up his mind and took his own board by surprise. He said his view was definitely against Rowntree and Company amalgamating with Cadbury and Fry, and that he would be very uncomfortable with any pooling arrangement. It might be possible to join with Cadbury and Fry in a few years, but Rowntrees needed time to carry out a 'variety of things which we have in mind'. This definitive statement seems to have come as something of a shock to the other Rowntree directors, who had expected to be able to make some kind of proposal to Cadburys. Arnold Rowntree wrote explaining the situation:

> After Tuesday's discussion, however, you will not be surprised to learn that at present our Board is not unaminous on the advisability of taking steps to amalgamate and without complete unanimity we should not be prepared to act. This being the case, we think it only fair to state this to you quite frankly now, because we know how anxious both you and Messrs Fry are to come to an early decision . . .[18]

It has been said that Joseph's refusal to consider amalgamating with Cadbury and Fry was a matter of personal pride, and there may be some truth in that argument.

But Joseph had a vision of the role and purpose of his business and it was primarily to defend that vision that he took the decision to block amalgamation. In a memorandum addressed to the board the following year, Joseph spelled out his business creed:

1. The present industrial organisation of the country is unsound for the following reasons.
(a) It is based upon competition, a euphemism for war.
(b) It has divided the country into classes, the holders of capital on one side and the workers on the other, who have separate interests and are largely antagonistic to each other.
(c) It is a system which has so worked out that 'large masses of the people are unable to secure the bare necessities of mental and physical efficiency'. "The Human Needs of Labour".

2. That such a firm as ours, which seeks to minimise the evils of the existing system, necessarily occupies a transition position, and its capacity for helping in social advance will greatly depend upon the frank recognition of this transition period.

3. That the goal, whatever may be the exact form which it takes, should be one which should gain for oneself and seek to secure for others a fuller life on all sides, the fullest life of which an individual is capable.

The election of the first central works council had given Joseph great satisfaction and he saw the election of the works council as the first phase in the democratisation of industry. He wrote, 'We look to those Councils for the future spirit of cooperation between those who are responsible for the direction and management of the business and those upon whose labour also depends the successful working of the factory.'[19] Fifty years later, at a dinner to celebrate its half century, the Rowntree Central Works Council was extolled as being an example to trade unions and employers for the way in which it had used the machinery of joint consultation and voluntary collective bargaining. Its first and greatest achievement had been to discuss, amend and approve a code of works rules which were to govern the conduct and working conditions of the employees. These rules could only be amended by agreement of the council and the company, a remarkable step forward in joint control.[20]

In 1921 another of Joseph's aims was fulfilled when the Central Works Council adopted a profit-sharing scheme. Joseph wrote of his pleasure in the thought that all over eighteen years of age 'will become interested in the financial results of each year's trading' and that this would 'form one more bond in the close union between all those who contribute to the success of the undertaking'.[21] Unfortunately the substance of the scheme was more apparent than real for several years, for the cost of independence from the Cadbury/Fry consortium was high and there were few profits to distribute.

Joseph may well have feared that merging with Cadbury would have made these

28 The famous Cadbury's
Cocoa Essence tin.

29 An advertisement for
Cadbury's Cocoa Essence,
1870.

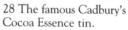

30 An early Rowntree's
advertisement for White
Rose Drinking Chocolate,
1891.

31 A Typical Cocoa Nibs
advertisement, early 1920s.

32 A Rowntree's Elect Cocoa poster,
1911–13.

developments impossible. Although there was an elaborate consultative system between management and workers at Bournville, and working conditions were second to none, there was no intention to democratise the company or to introduce profit sharing. The reins of power were firmly in the hands of the Cadbury family.

Seebohm Rowntree, who in 1923 took over the chairmanship of Rowntree and Company from his father, was very close to him in thought. He believed that under any satisfctory industrial system there were two conditions that had to be observed. Firstly, in the process of wealth production, industry must pay the greatest possible regard to the general welfare of the community and pursue no policy detrimental to it. And, secondly, that the wealth produced must be distributed in such a manner as will best serve the highest ends of the community.

Seebohm was conscientious to a degree, but what Rowntree's desperately needed was someone with flair and resolution to take the firm forward. Seebohm was basically an academic, a skilled negotiator, a man who had the welfare of the work-force very much at heart, but he was not an innovator and he lacked the fighting spirit of his father, which had twice saved the independence of the business. Rowntree's had no answer to Cadbury's popular milk chocolate and they were forced to admit that Bournville Cocoa, although made from beans of not as good quality, had a more chocolaty flavour than Rowntree's Elect Cocoa and sold twice as much.

With no outstanding product to market and with sales of Elect slumping, the Rowntrees were forced to consider other ways of keeping their name before the public. They were determined to remain ahead of other firms in quality, but the question was, how could this be conveyed to the public? The answer was Plain Mr York of York, Yorks, a dapper, plump little gentleman with large grey topper, elegant waistcoat and eyebrows raised in perpetual good-natured surprise. He was created to promote the idea that Rowntree's sold quality goods at a reasonable price. He was used to promote their plain chocolate, Motoring Chocolate and generally to make the name of Rowntree known. Like everyone's favourite uncle, Plain Mr York was very popular. He could be used in all sorts of contexts – electric models of Plain Mr York were made, games were created featuring the little man who didn't threaten anyone and exuded bonhomie.

Less attractive were the Cocoa Nibs, 'two of the jolliest kids imaginable.' L. A. G. Strong, in his unpublished book on Rowntree and Company, commented that little needed to be added to this nauseous description, but the Cocoa Nibs, for all their spurious gaiety, were very popular with children, who followed the weekly adventures of the Cocoa Nibs with keen anticipation. They could be said to have been the forerunners of that other famous pair, the Bisto Kids. Cadbury's had led the way into the children's market with a special children's cocoa and Rowntree's could not afford to allow them any advantage.

Throughout the 1920s competition remained fierce. Rowntree's were dropping further and further behind Cadbury's, who could afford to advertise three times more at any time without making inroads into their overall profit. So any advantage Rowntree's might gain from advertising could be neutralised by Cadbury's, or, as

33 Rowntree's grocery lines.

ROWNTREE'S
GROCERY LINES

ROWNTREE'S ELECT COCOA

SIZE	PACKED IN	SELLING PRICE
2 oz. tins	1 dozen	3d. each
¼ lb. tins	1 dozen*	5½d. each
½ lb. tins	1 dozen	10d. each
1 lb. tins	¼ dozen	1/7 each

* You can save 1d. off the dozen price by ordering ¼'s in 6 dozen cases.

TABLE JELLIES

4½d. each   packed in 1 dozens
in decorated outers

Assorted Flavours	Orange
Blackcurrant	Pineapple ....
Cherry	Port Wine ....
Greengage	Raspberry ....
Lemon	Strawberry ....
Lime Fruit	Vanilla ....

CHOCOLATE BISCUITS

Trumps—Assorted, 6d. per ½ lb.—5½ lb. tins
10 o'clock Biscuits—2d. each—¼ gross outers
2d. Chocolate Crisp—2d. each—¼ gross outers

SPECIAL—ROWNTREE'S COCOA IS THE DIGESTIVE COCOA. BY A
SPECIAL MANUFACTURING PROCESS ROWNTREE'S COCOA
ACTUALLY HELPS THE DIGESTION OF OTHER FOODS.

FIRST SEE INSTRUCTIONS OVERLEAF:-

PLAIN Mr. YORK'S
TIME CARD

Visitor's Name

Week ending

1929

DAY	IN	OUT
MON		
TUE		
WED		
THU		
FRI		

The Time
you clocked in
at the
Model Factory of
Plain Mr. York.

ANYTIME
passes happily
with
Rowntree's

34 Plain Mr York's Time Card.

35 A window display advertising Rowntree's and Fry's goods, 1915.

the board conceded, worse than neutralised. Mr York of York was very effective, but Cadbury's retaliated and Rowntree's were unable to reply. An added problem was the rival Quaker York chocolate manufacturers, Terry's, who had now got hold of the best trade and were making the best chocolate.[22] The onset of the Slump made the market for cheap goods a lucrative one, but it was one for which Rowntree's found themselves unable to produce at a profit.

Although George Cadbury had retained the chairmanship until his death in 1922, his sons and nephews had been working alongside him for many years, and there had been a gradual transition of power, so there was no abrupt change when Edward Cadbury took over. George Cadbury's successors inherited a thriving business and they continued to exploit their opportunities and to expand. The installation of automatic moulding machines in 1927 for milk-chocolate production brought increased productivity. That, combined with vigorous advertising, led to rising sales and price reductions and ensured for Cadbury's their dominant position in the moulded-chocolate market.[23] Two years later a new cocoa block was completed, the most up-to-date factory of its kind in the world with the potential for enormous output. A network of distribution depots were set up all over the country, advertising was decentralised and an outside factory was bought to relieve the congestion at Bournville. In 1931 Cadbury Brothers celebrated the centenary of the business.

The way in which Cadbury's advertised themselves – as makers of fine chocolates, benefactors to the public and initiators of price reductions – had had the effect, cumulatively, of making Rowntree's seem inferior. Joseph had retired from the chairmanship of Rowntree and Company in 1923, when the firm was growing and showing a modest profit. He remained to the end of his life chairman of the trusts he had set up, and closely involved with their work. Their continued successful development owes much to his sane, clear and well-balanced judgement. He died in 1925, and A. G. Gardiner wrote truly of him that there was in him 'an unusual fusion of the idealist and the realist and his dreams were always within the firm grasp of an instructed and practical genius'.[24] However, the business legacy he left his successors was not an easy one. Having fought to keep Rowntree's independent in 1918, his sons, nephews and other board members had an uphill struggle all through the 1920s to keep Rowntree's profitable, a struggle made all the more difficult by the seemingly unstoppable success of Cadbury's.

With the onset of the Depression at the end of the 1920s, Seebohm Rowntree could no longer disguise from himself or the board that the business was not healthy.[25] Fruit gums and cocoa were still the leading products, but only heavy advertising was holding up the trade in both cocoa and chocolate. Competition with Cadbury's had degenerated into an advertising war which Rowntree's could not win. They could claim to be leaders only in the Christmas fancy trade, and that was small comfort.

Once again the Rowntree board discussed the possibility of opening talks with Cadbury's with a view to some rationalisation of price reductions. They already knew that they had little hope of success because the Nestlé Company, by lowering its prices, was forcing Cadbury's into something like a price-cutting war with them. It was gloomily minuted that 'Cadbury's interests were concentrated on their own Cadbury business to an extraordinary degree'[26] so that the possibility of making contact with them on the subject of either advertising or prices was thought to be difficult.

The only alternative was to discuss the question of a merger. It was agreed that Seebohm was to write to the Cadburys to sound out the possibilities of a meeting, on the pretext of wanting to discuss his ideas on the rationalisation of the trade. He made the point that the board 'no longer felt bound by Joseph's views'.

> You will recall that you approached us in 1918. At that time the whole Board, except Joseph Rowntree, were favourably inclined to accept your proposals. He made it a personal matter (not at all I need hardly say out of any feelings against you, but because of certain ideas and principles with which he had grown up) and out of affection for him we accepted his view, though it was against our own business judgement.[27]

On 15 April 1930 Seebohm went to Bournville and met with Edward, William, Paul and Laurence Cadbury. Five weeks later the Rowntree board heard that the Cadburys were not interested in a merger. The Cadburys could have been under no misapprehension of the reasons that had prompted Seebohm to make the visit, so when they said that they hoped the present working relationships would continue, it must be suspected that they perhaps hoped to be able to absorb Rowntree's on more favourable terms at a later date.

George Harris, a relative outsider, provided the inspiration and driving force that was to revitalise the Rowntree business in the 1930s. He had married Friedl Rowntree, daughter of Frank Rowntree, Seebohm's cousin, and come into the firm in 1923, the year Seebohm took over the chairmanship. Until 1930 he had held appointments which kept him away from York, and his return coincided with the failed negotiations with Cadbury's.[28] There was a sense of pessimism and despair throughout the business. By 1931 the factory was working a three-day week and its very survival was in doubt. Even the buoyant Arnold Rowntree, whose optimism and dash had sometimes led to his getting at cross-purposes with his more reserved and cautious cousin, Seebohm, had no answer to the problem.

Rowntree's had long known that the one thing they most needed was a new product, something which would not compete with Cadbury's already well-established lines. Under the dynamic influence of George Harris a whole new range of products was developed, beginning with Black Magic in 1933 and followed by Kit Kat, Aero chocolate, Dairy Box and Smarties, enabling Rowntree's not only to recover financially, but to compete directly with Cadbury's.

George Harris had an almost obsessive desire to end Cadbury's dominant position and he set himself to learn how others had come to take the largest share of the market. He was a friend of Forrest Mars, whose brilliant marketing skills had made the Mars bar a household name. Simon Marks of Marks & Spencer and John Sainsbury were also friends from whom he learned much. From them he came to understand that it was not only creativity that counted, and he sought to apply to the Rowntree business the principles that had brought them success. Besides introducing a more professional approach to selling, replacing the large number of rather undistinguished products by a smaller range, Harris also emphasised the importance of consumer research. Statistically based research was used to test ideas with the aim of increasing the popularity of the Rowntree products among consumers. Harris used sophisticated advertisements to back up his consumer research.

Benson's were no longer the agency to promote the new-look Rowntree's. They had told Rowntree's, rather depressingly, that they did not think their prestige justified their advertising in the way that Cadbury's did, so when Philip Benson, Samuel Benson's son, died in 1931, Rowntree's took their custom to J. Walter Thompson. At first a fairly cautious policy of peaceful penetration was decided upon, using a conversational type of advertising, frontal attack being eschewed for fear of retaliation by Cadbury's. But by 1935 more money than ever was being spent on advertising Elect Cocoa, fruit gums, Black Magic and Aero chocolate, with the result that profits rose significantly that year. The sophisticated and romantic advertisements for Black Magic surprised and pleased the public and were no threat to Cadbury's, but the sharp copy used to promote Aero chocolate, in direct competition with Cadbury's, was a different matter. Just as Elect Cocoa had been chosen to challenge Cadbury's Cocoa Essence, so Aero chocolate was picked to challenge Cadbury's Dairy Milk, and a confident Rowntree's took out patents to protect the new chocolate. The aim was to counter the pulling power of Cadbury's famous slogan 'A Glass and a Half . . .', showing the actual amount of milk used in each bar of Dairy Milk chocolate. Cadbury's first move was to say that Rowntree's had no grounds for taking out patents on their new process, but the Rowntree directors warned Cadbury's that they would take legal proceedings if Cadbury's brought out an aerated chocolate.

Rowntree's did not mince their words when making claims for Aero. 'It digests twice as quickly as old-fashioned milk chocolate' . . . 'There are no lumps in Aero' . . . 'Aero has no cloying after-taste.' 'Scientific' copy, which would never be allowed today, was included, purporting to show the texture of ordinary chocolate as compared with the smooth texture of Aero, with its delicate surfaces, which were said to make it more palatable (by inference, than Dairy Milk) and easier to digest.

Some directors queried the desirability of advertising that decried other products, but this was a minority view; the majority were happy to feel they had their competitors worried and the board waited with interest to see what move Cadbury's would make next. They knew that Aero was affecting Cadbury's sales, and wondered if Cadbury's would cut prices or even go so far as to require the newspaper proprietors to exclude Rowntree advertising as a condition for keeping the Cadbury account.[29] It was decided that it might be politic to make some concessions at the forthcoming Cheltenham conference, when the leading chocolate manufacturers met to discuss matters of mutual interest, and the word 'milk' was deliberately left in the advertising copy as a bargaining counter, which could be withdrawn later.

At the Cheltenham conference in July 1936 Cadbury's told Rowntree's that they considered the Aero advertisement constituted a challenge to the good will which existed between the companies and strongly objected to the disparagement implied by the wording. At this time Seebohm Rowntree retired from the chairmanship of the York board, perhaps somewhat out of sympathy with the confrontational aspect of the advertising policy being adopted by Rowntree's. He nevertheless remained company chairman of the Rowntree board until 1941. His place was taken by F. G. Fryer, a long-serving member of the board who had at one time been in charge of the engineering, chemical and research departments before moving on to marketing and distribution. After one meeting with Paul Cadbury, Fryer reported to the board that Cadbury's appeared very disturbed by the progress Rowntree's were making, which they saw as dangerous to them. Paul Cadbury made it clear to Fryer that if the two firms could not come to terms which, in their view, would slow down Rowntree's progress, then Cadbury's would take strong and very expensive measures to meet the situation.[30] Far from being deterred, Rowntree's decided that while they held the advantage they must profit from every available month in which to advertise, even if this meant advertising during the summer months, which were usually not considered cost-effective. On no account would Rowntree's contemplate being driven back into a position where they might once more become impotent in the hands of Cadbury's, as they had a few years previously.[31]

By 1937, both firms were weighing up the financial consequence of taking legal action. Cadbury's to challenge the legality of the Aero patents and Rowntree's to defend them. When in July Rowntree's discovered that Cadbury's had actually taken legal action on whether the Rowntree patents were valid or not, Fryer, who had been negotiating with Paul Cadbury over the payment of a royalty on the manufacture of cellular chocolate, felt that he, too, should take legal advice on whether he should even continue to meet Paul Cadbury in the circumstances.[32] At the end of the month, Rowntree's received a petition for the revocation of their product patent from Cadbury's. They replied that if this was proceeded with they would take legal action which would cancel all the offers they had so far made to Cadbury's in an attempt to reach a mutually acceptable agreement.[33] This was probably the closest the two firms came to open conflict.

The possible outcome of any legal action was so finely balanced and the damaging consequences so correspondingly great for both firms that reason prevailed.[34] A contributory factor that induced Rowntree's to settle was the knowledge that Cadbury's had invented another process for aerating chocolate, not covered by the Rowntree patents, and Rowntree's did not want to find themselves debarred from using the process if it was better and cheaper than the ones they were currently using.

Negotiations between the two sides continued throughout August until a settlement was finally reached. No cellular chocolate was to be sold by Cadbury's, Fry's (by this time a wholly owned subsidiary of Cadbury's) or Nestlé until after June 1938; and various agreements were made with regard to pricing and the payment of royalties. Rowntree's had not got all they wanted, but they had stood up to

Cadbury's and from now on they would be a force to be reckoned with. Ironically, despite all the controversy surrounding the advertising of Aero chocolate, it was not the most successful of the Rowntree products. That honour went to Rowntree's Chocolate Crisp, better known as Kit Kat, which outsold Aero then and has continued to outsell every other Rowntree product up to the present day.

With the outbreak of war in 1939, past controversies were forgotten and, in a spirit of friendliness and cooperation, pledges of mutual assistance were exchanged. George Harris, who had been a member of the York board since 1931, became its chairman in 1938. When Seebohm Rowntree retired in 1941, Harris succeeded him as company chairman. But it was only after the Second World War that the true measure of George Harris's success could be assessed, when the products he had launched with so much enterprise and drive began to make their real impact on Rowntree's in terms of increased sales.

Peter Rowntree was the last member of the family to be on the board, and when he retired in 1951 the family no longer had any direct involvement with the business. In this they differed from the Cadburys. George's sons, Edward and Laurence, were successively chairmen of the company, and Laurence's son, Sir Adrian Cadbury, is the present chairman. Paul Cadbury, who became chairman of the company in 1959, said that in his opinion, since 1962, when Cadbury's had become a public company, they could no longer be considered a family concern. Now that they were a publicly quoted company, outside considerations predominated over what had heretofore been matters of family policy. The names of both firms are now no longer solely connected with those of their founders; Cadbury Brothers have become Cadbury Schweppes plc, a company capitalised at some £1000 million and Rowntree and Company, who merged with John Mackintosh and Sons in 1969, are known as Rowntree Mackintosh plc, and were capitalised at some £900 million in January 1987.

8

Death of the News Chronicle

George Cadbury died in 1922, full of years and honour, though not of the worldly kind, which he steadfastly refused all his life. Although for many years he had left the management of the *Daily News* to his two sons, Edward and Henry, the death of so towering a personality marked the end of an era.

If the Liberal press in the 1920s had had the benefit of the same degree of talented editorship as they previously enjoyed, the Parliamentary Liberal Party might not have found itself in such distress after the First World War. A. G. Gardiner of the *Daily News* and H. W. Massingham of the *Nation* had lost their jobs, and soon so did Robert Donald of the *Daily Chronicle* and J. A. Spender of the *Westminster Gazette*. H. W. Nevinson, in typical form, said that he thought that all the best editors of his generation had been deposed because of their very excellence. A more sober view is taken by Stephen Koss, the historian and writer, who thought that party allegiances and professional attitudes counted against them. The decline in the spirit and talent of the Liberal press mirrored the divisions and disarray within the Liberal Party itself.

Although by 1920 few insolvent newspapers, struggling to enlarge their audiences, could take an independent line, the *Daily News* and the *Daily Chronicle* suffered less than most from such inhibitions. Lloyd George may have thought that in Gardiner he was rid of one opponent, but Henry Cadbury had no intention of letting the *Daily News* be seen as an uncritical supporter of the Liberals. Since Gardiner's dismissal in 1919 there had been few changes on the paper. Unlike Arnold Bennett, who could afford to write that he was leaving 'partly because now that Gardiner has gone my original distaste for the Cadburys has free rein', most journalists were unable to give up their jobs for personal reasons even had they wished to do so.

Lloyd George, as leader of one faction of the Parliamentary Liberal Party, was anxious to have a paper that would give him unequivocal support, and as early as 1917 he had conceived the idea of obtaining custody of the *Daily Chronicle*. The *Daily Chronicle* had started life as a modest suburban newspaper. It was bought in 1876 for £30,000 by Edward Lloyd, a paper manufacturer, and a massive injection of capital had successfully transformed it into a vigorous London daily paper. Lloyd already owned *Lloyd's News*, which he had started in 1842 as *Lloyd's Penny Illustrated Newspaper*. By 1896 it had become the first newspaper to reach a circulation of one million. Lloyd, a tough, hard-headed businessman, was a regular Victorian paterfamilias. Twice married, he had nineteen children. His son Frank was designated chairman and left to carry on the business.[1]

The new chairman was very different in character, of gentle disposition. He encouraged the paper to pursue a broad Liberal policy and developed the artistic and literary side of the *Daily Chronicle* under a good team of journalists. However, Robert Donald, his editor, found it increasingly difficult to disguise his hostility to Lloyd George. Frank Lloyd had no wish to be drawn into this political infighting, so for a good price he was willing to sell his inheritance, United Newspapers.

In 1918, Henry Dalziel (later Baron Dalziel of Kirkaldy), a fervent supporter of Lloyd George, made an offer. Donald, unaware of the danger, continued to attack Lloyd George and Frank Lloyd's price had gone up to £1 million, which seemed an impossibly large sum to find. But between them Lloyd George and Dalziel raised the necessary finance; a new holding company with Dalziel as chairman and with absolute political control was set up. Within a month of a particularly sharp attack by Donald on Lloyd George, all details for the purchase of the *Chronicle* were complete. The first Donald knew of the matter was when he asked his proprietor to issue a contradiction to settle the rumours that had been circulating about the sale of the *Daily Chronicle*, only to be told by Lloyd that they were true. Lloyd George's victory over Donald was complete, and the former editor had only that afternoon to clear his desk.

William Pringle, a Liberal MP of independent mind, during question time in the Commons took the opportunity to ask whether 'the attention of the Chancellor of the Exchequer had been called to the recent purchase of London newspapers for the purpose of changing their political policy, whether the Government would set up a Committee to enquire into monopolistic control of the Press, and, whether a supply of paper would be granted for new newspapers to promote the policy of the newspaper's purchasers'.[2] Dalziel, reluctantly forced to reply to 'the base allegation', tried to imply that Frank Lloyd was in 'failing health' and that only after others had tried and failed to relieve him of his vast responsibilities had Dalziel come to his aid. (Nothing could have been further from the truth.) 'The suggestion . . . that because the *Daily Chronicle* appeared to criticise the Prime Minister and therefore I rushed in . . . is entirely incorrect,' Dalziel said in the House. It was said that Frank Lloyd only realised a month later to whom he had actually sold the paper.

The *Daily Chronicle* continued as a self-professed Liberal and democratic organ. The former news editor, E. A. Perris, became editor. J. A. Spender, editor of the *Westminster Gazette*, fully alive to the importance of the coup Lloyd George had brought off, categorised Perris as 'merely a news gatherer without politics or writing capacity . . . the sort of man loved by newspaper bosses'.[3] Lloyd George, whose only motive for buying the *Daily Chronicle* had been to silence the opposition to him before the general election, now found that the paper was proving financially rewarding. By 1925 it was making £50,000 a year, but it took up more time and energy than Lloyd George was prepared to give to it. Writing to his wife he complained that his son, Gwilym, was indolent, that the new chairman of the Chronicle board, C. A. McCurdy, National Liberal member for Northampton, who had succeeded Dalziel, was lazy and flabby, and the editor, Perris, spent too much of his time at the Kit Kat Club instead of behind his desk. Nevertheless, recognising the financial advantages, he wrote that despite all the calls on his time he meant to keep at it.[4]

Within two months of writing that letter Lloyd George had changed his mind. It did not prove difficult to find purchasers who were prepared to find the asking price, which was said to be in the region of £3 million.[5] Lord Reading, the recently retired governor-general of India, agreed to become chairman of United Newspapers Ltd, and Lloyd George, satisfied that the paper was in friendly hands, took the profit and relinquished his interest in it.

By 1928, however, the *Daily Chronicle* was once again in need of financial underpinning and Lord Reading withdrew from the chairmanship. A merger between the *Daily News* and the *Westminster Gazette* had been agreed in January 1928. A further merger between the *Daily Chronicle* and the *Daily News* would have made economic sense and would have ensured that the *Daily Chronicle* remained in Liberal hands. The possibility was discussed with Sir Walter Layton (later Lord Layton), then managing director of the *Daily News*, but the discussions came to nothing. The *Daily Chonicle* was sold to William Harrison, a practising solicitor, who was building up a newsprint and publishing empire, which collapsed with the stock exchange in 1929. A merger between the *Daily Chronicle* and the *Daily News* now seemed more than ever the obvious solution, but Henry Cadbury and the Cadbury family had difficulties of their own to resolve.

At the time of the merger with the *Westminster Gazette*, Lord Cowdray, chairman of the holding company, Westminster Press Ltd, had given the *Daily News* a cash injection of £100,000, enabling it to restart its northern edition. He became vice-chairman of the reconstructed Daily News Ltd. Cowdray believed there were a million people in the country who were Liberal in interest and would therefore want to read a Liberal paper. The question was what kind of political news service the *Daily News* should provide. Should the paper seek, Henry Cadbury asked,

> to satisfy those who are interested in the political organisations of the Liberal Party, or is our Liberal appeal to be so based as to swing a considerable part of the doubtful votes . . . ? In other words, how far should the *Daily News* and the *Westminster Gazette* be a journal of opinion, or how far should we administer the Liberal point of view in such well-coated sugar pills that we may affect the vote of a considerable number of waverers at the time of a General Election?[6]

Cowdray made it clear that he did not believe the paper could attempt to satisfy political organisations, but could only hope to improve their quality.

It seems evident that in its attempts to remain competitive, the *Daily News* could only continue its drift away from the spirit of philanthropic radicalism that had been its hallmark. The Cadbury family were divided over whether or not they should continue with their involvement in popular newspapers. Both Henry, who was suffering from weak eyesight, and Edward Cadbury wanted to retire; Laurence did not find it easy to come to a decision. Layton, who was negotiating with the representatives of the ailing *Daily Chronicle*, threatened to withdraw altogether unless some agreement was reached.

Finally Laurence, the elder son of George's second wife, Elizabeth, agreed to carry on the Cadbury tradition of newspaper ownership, perhaps more out of loyalty to his father than anything else. In 1930 Sir Walter Layton became chairman of the amalgamated *News Chronicle*, which acquired the *Daily Chronicle* for a knock-down price. United Newspapers owned 50 per cent of the capital of the *News Chronicle*, but Laurence Cadbury became chairman of the holding company, Daily News Ltd, which in turn was firmly in the hands of the Daily News Trust. The new multi-tiered structure which controlled the *News Chronicle* reached agreement on a policy for the paper, but it was not a body to inspire much confidence. Two of the five trustees were representatives of United Newspapers and only interested in the paper as an investment. Over the next few years the board was further infiltrated by conservative businessmen linked to the United Newspapers interest. Cowdray and Cadbury, unlike their fathers, were primarily businessmen, and Walter Layton was the only dedicated Liberal.

Laurence Cadbury, reserved by nature, had no desire to be in the public eye. He was a well-read man with a remarkable memory and, if the story of the demolition of the old power station at Bournville is true, one who liked to get his own way. He was planning to modernise the factory at Bournville and was seriously put out when the board turned down his scheme to pull down the old power station and build an up-to-date new one. One night soon afterwards the building went up in flames, and when the Bournville fire brigade arrived, Laurence was already on the scene, wearing his First World War tin hat. His version was that he had seen the flames from the Manor House and driven over immediately, but there were other versions of the story in circulation.[7]

His wife, Joyce, managed the household and brought up the children, and also found time to become heavily involved in youth work, for which she was awarded an OBE. Interested in education, she served on the Birmingham City Education Committee and was given an honorary LL.D. by Birmingham University for her work.[8]

Laurence Cadbury had been appointed a managing director of Cadbury Brothers in 1919, with a wide range of responsibilities, at a time when the senior members of the board were suffering from the strain of the war years. He turned out to be an able director of business enterprises and his knowledge of economics was to prove valuable to Cadbury's. On entering the firm he saw that the expanding postwar demand would need new methods of production. He replaced the existing premises with multistorey blocks capable of housing the necessary mass-production machinery. By the end of the 1930s Cadbury's, as a result of improved productivity and vigorous promotion, dominated the moulded-chocolate market. Laurence also played a leading role in the coordination of the Cadbury and Fry businesses after the merger of their financial interests into the British Cocoa and Chocolate Company. Perhaps his success in the chocolate business emboldened him to enter the field of newspaper management, perhaps it was respect for family tradition that was the deciding factor, but, in retrospect, Laurence Cadbury would have done better to have paid greater attention to the doubts he clearly felt for he was not at home in the world of newspapers. Nor was he a committed Liberal; his instincts were Tory and he moved further to the right as he grew older. His eleventh-hour decision to step in and take on the responsibility for the *Daily News* was to be his personal misfortune.

Walter Layton had been Laurence Cadbury's tutor at Cambridge and a colleague of Keynes before 1914. He was a man with a wide range of interests and he remained editor of the *Economist*, which he had been for ten years, when he took up the editorship of the *News Chronicle*. His was a strangely aloof personality but his mind was keenly incisive and he held strong views about the paper's policy, which he set out in a leading article in the first issue on 2 June 1930):

> The combined paper will stand, first and foremost, for peace. It will seek by every means in its power to support and forward the ideals of the League of Nations. It will oppose both reaction and revolution with equal firmness. It will oppose waste, and fight steadily for real economy in public expenditure. Believing that tariffs are an attack upon the people's livelihood, it will resist both. It will champion, on the other hand, the social reforms which both papers have always insisted are demanded, both by common justice and common sense; and the liberties of speech, of thought and of religion for which both have always stood. And it will defend these causes for the future – at a time when many of them are gravely menaced – with the vigour and consistency which unity can alone assure.

The sheer necessity of making the reconstructed paper popular and successful undermined its independence and idealism. Although Laurence Cadbury wrote to Layton that 'the paper has as always been and still continues to be, independent and under no obligation to any political party', the words had a hollow ring.[9]

The annual report of the Westminster Press Ltd of 1931–32 showed the paper to be holding its own financially, but in personal costs the unification of the two papers was very much less satisfactory. The *Newspaper Press Directory* in 1931 saw the sudden and sensational collapse of the *Daily Chronicle* and its amalgamation with the *Daily News* as the most disastrous event in the journalistic year. The loss to the parent company in that year was reduced to £27,215, which was easily offset by profits from its subsidiaries, but the numbers of the unemployed – and politically unemployable – were considerably increased. A third of the *Daily News* staff were dismissed to make way for the same number from the *Daily Chronicle*, the same formula that had been used when the *Morning Leader* was merged with the *Daily News* in 1912.

Layton was both chairman and, effectively, editor-in-chief of the *News Chronicle*, and even without the intervention of the Cadburys he would have had problems enough. But Layton was not the owner, and all four Cadbury brothers felt they had a right to express their own very strong views on policy and management. Layton's relationship with Laurence Cadbury was particularly difficult, and Layton was often irritated by Laurence's frequent letters of criticism. Laurence for his part found his position vis-à-vis Layton difficult. The fact that he had once been Layton's pupil coloured their relationship and he could not forget that he, who actually owned the paper, had no real power. He wrote in a letter he described as 'frankly egotistical', 'I want to take a major part in the paper and not to be just a nagging outsider.'[10]

The *News Chronicle* staff were divided between supporting Asquith and Lloyd George. Tom Clarke, the editor, and A. J. Cummings, who had left the *Yorkshire Post* to take on the position of principal leader-writer on the *Daily News*, were both supporters of Lloyd George. Cummings in particular greatly displeased Cowdray, who thought him 'entirely intolerant of anything except the most labour view'.[11] J. A. Spender, whom Cadbury had persuaded to write old-style Asquithian political leaders, wrote that Tom Clarke 'hardly disguises that he thinks me a nuisance and a burden'.[12] Yet the *News Chronicle* was virtually the only paper the Liberals could count on to reflect their policies and ideals. In doing so it mirrored the increasing divergence of opinion among Liberals, and the story of the *News Chronicle* can be seen as the story of the decline of Liberalism. The agreement between the three interested parties – United Newspapers, the *Daily News* trustees and the holding company – had sought to ensure that 'consistent support should be given to the promotion of unity in the Liberal Party', a demand that the paper could not possibly meet.

Following Layton's hint that it would be better if he went, Clarke resigned, to be replaced by Aylmer Vallance in 1933. At almost the same time Cowdray suddenly died. The new Lord Cowdray, young and inexperienced, was represented by his uncle, Clive Pearson, who, trying to find common ground with the Cadburys, suggested a new formula as a basis for editorial policy. But when Pearson received Layton and Cadbury's reply he regarded it more as a declaration of socialism than a fair declaration of liberalism. Laurence Cadbury tried to mediate, but when the *Evening Standard* on 26 July the following year stated that the *News Chronicle* had gone socialist, there had to be a full meeting of trustees to sort matters out. The *Standard* based its claim on the impression that the *News Chronicle* had sympathised with H. L. Nathan (later Lord Nathan), the Liberal MP for Bethnal Green, on his defection to Labour.

The meeting revealed how the aspirations of the trustees of the *News Chronicle* differed fundamentally one from another and how far Laurence Cadbury was having to compromise and bend the principles of the Daily News Trust in his attempts to accommodate the incompatible interests of the dissident parties. Sir Herbert Grotian, a Conservative who managed the United Newspaper interests, said he did not care whether the opinions expressed in the *News Chronicle* were consistent with the 1930 agreement or not, but his shareholders did care very much about the financial success of the paper, which he thought had been jeopardised by making it a feeble imitation of the *Daily Herald*. From the advertising point of view the readers of the old *Daily News* were much more valuable than any socialist readers who might be attracted to the *News Chronicle*. Pearson, in his desperate attempt to retain the *News Chronicle* as the standard-bearer for liberalism, was demanding tighter editorial control, demands which, if Layton accepted them, would have had an even more adverse affect on the circulation figures of the paper.

Vallance, feeling himself under attack from all sides, protested in a series of memos to Cummings and Laurence Cadbury that he had only accepted the editorship on the understanding that he would be free 'to run the paper as an independent radical organ – opposed, naturally to revolutionary socialism but not tied to any of the groups which once formed the Liberal Party and – *a fortiori* – hostile to Toryism'.[13] It was not his fault, he wrote, that the Liberal consensus had since eroded, with the result that moderate-minded gradualist Labour leaders most nearly approximated the spirit of philanthropic radicalism that George Cadbury had enshrined in the memorandum of 1911. Vallance reserved his most biting attack for the 'elderly Reform Club Whigs' who, if they had their way, would swing the paper right. Layton himself sometimes found it useful, when dealing with the Cadbury family, to quote George Cadbury's testament calling for 'taxing the rich for the benefit of the poor and the nationalisation of monopolies better administered by the community itself for the benefit of all'.[14]

It may be wondered if Laurence Cadbury found himself entirely comfortable with his brilliant editor in spite of these declarations of high principle. Vallance had a penchant for the low life, and the orgies and debaucheries that took place in the office of the *News Chronicle* scandalised and titillated Fleet Street. It must be presumed that the Cadburys did not know at the time, but for those who did the situation was ironical. Collin Brooks, one-time editor of *Truth*, enjoyed in the privacy of his diary 'the story of the Aylmer Vallance episode at the *News Chronicle* when the austere Quaker newspaper office became a veritable brothel'. The editor and his companions were said to have fornicated 'all over the place . . . Even Arthur Cummings's sacred desk was violated.'[15]

Despite all these troubles, the *News Chronicle* was profitable, and Laurence Cadbury was able to arrange for the Daily News Ltd to buy out the Westminster and United Newspapers interests in 1937. Layton, though appearing kind and gentle, could be tough. Against Laurence Cadbury's advice he sacked Aylmer Vallance and appointed Gerald Barry in 1936. Described as bland and pompous by a fellow journalist, Barry during his ten-year stint in the editor's chair was very much under the direct guidance of Walter Layton. Layton would have liked a greater stake in the enterprise and the status of governing director. He wrote, 'The *NC* in its present form is from the financial point of view my creation; politically I have kept its head above water at a time when the appeal of the Liberal party was almost nil; I have reconstructed its editorial staff.' He went on to point out that it was no longer losing money but he was adamant that there could not be 'two kings at Brentford'. He was happy to collaborate with Laurence Cadbury, but made it quite clear that the *News Chronicle* must represent his point of view.[16]

It is clear from Layton's unpublished memoirs that he would have liked to be in a position to buy the *News Chronicle* from Laurence Cadbury, but Laurence was never willing to sell. Although no longer interested in the paper for the same social and political reasons as his father, he had perhaps invested too much personal effort in it to give it up, particularly to Layton, towards whom he felt a certain jealousy.

The stresses and strains of the years immediately before the Second World War, when Neville Chamberlain's policy of appeasement divided not only the country but families as well, did not leave the Cadburys unscathed. Outraged by the *News Chronicle*'s attack on Chamberlain, Paul Cadbury wrote to Laurence, his cousin, that he was giving up the paper in favour of the *Birmingham Post* and added that he thought many thousands of readers would do the same.

During the war, when Layton was seconded to the Ministry of Supply, Laurence Cadbury took over control of the *News Chronicle* and found it somewhat difficult to keep his staff, with their various and deeply held opinions, in line. Despite the shortage of newsprint, all the newspapers increased their circulation during the war, the *News Chronicle* making a modest recovery in 1942. Some thought this was because there was less political news to report, and certainly those papers which went in for entertainment, like the *Express* and the *Daily Mirror*, surged ahead.

The lack of a political dimension suited Laurence Cadbury, whose own commitment to liberalism had noticeably weakened, as had his former close association with the Society of Friends. Indeed, the Cadburys took the view that the *News Chronicle* would be compromised if Layton accepted the presidency of the Liberal Party. Laurence Cadbury was more disturbed by the spread of socialism than attracted to conservatism. So far removed was he from his father's original objectives that he feared the *News Chronicle*'s propensity to support progressive causes was a drain on its circulation, always his first concern. Egbert Cadbury, Laurence's cousin, who had succeeded Henry Cadbury as a trustee, was a Liberal activist, who had stood as a Liberal for Stroud in the 1945 election. He was 'exceedingly annoyed at the lack of criticism of the Government' and could only hope that the *News Chronicle* would get a little punch into its leading articles. Winston Churchill referred to the *Manchester Guardian*, as 'the only Liberal paper, for who would apply that great name to a paper which, like the *News Chronicle*, is moved only by nervous hysteria?'[17]

After the 1950 election, when the *News Chronicle* had sat on the fence, Laurence Cadbury, in the light of the Labour Party's tiny majority, felt brave enough to say that paper should back the government, as their minuscule majority would compel them to drop their nationalisation programme. He instructed the staff to give all party news but to refrain from propaganda. That year saw great changes at the *News Chronicle*. Walter Layton retired as chairman in favour of Laurence Cadbury, but remained vice-chairman of the Daily News Trust. Bertram Crosfield, who, it is said, never received the credit that was due to him as managing director from his Cadbury in-laws, also retired and was succeeded by Frank Waters from *The Times*.

The *News Chronicle*'s uncertain political stance was reflected in its typography, which veered from giving the paper an appearance more *Express*-like than the *Daily Express* itself to reviving its erstwhile *Daily News* image. It also expanded and contracted at a surprising rate, shrinking from forty-two pages in January to thirty-six in June, which reflected the papers difficulties in maintaining its advertising revenue.

During the decade which ended with the demise of the *News Chronicle*, two possible opportunities were missed which might have saved the paper, had Laurence Cadbury been willing to sell. Lord Beaverbrook, aware of the rumours circulating about the future of the *News Chronicle* and *Star* offered Layton the financial backing to buy both papers if he were willing.[18] Although many problems lurked beneath the seemingly straightforward proposition, Layton cited only two reasons for refusing Beaverbrook's offer, the main one being that Laurence Cadbury had no wish to sell. The fact that, as he said, he was sixty-eight, not fifty-eight, could perhaps have been overcome, given that he had a son whose interests he was anxious to promote in the newspaper world. Had this opportunity been taken, it is possible that the *News Chronicle* might have survived.

Two years later with his paper's circulation still falling, Robin Cruikshank, who had been appointed editor after the war, wrote Laurence Cadbury a letter in which he spelled out his anxiety about the state of alarm and depression that prevailed at Bouverie Street. A brilliant man and gifted writer, Cruikshank lacked the ability to build and inspire an editorial team. Laurence Cadbury's uncertain temper was known to his employees as 'the Birmingham Reaction' and Cruikshank's letter, instead of giving Cadbury pause for thought or causing him to enquire into the reasons for the malaise, provoked him to fire Cruikshank and replace him by Michael Curtis, the deputy editor. Curtis, although a paid-up member of the Labour Party, had helped Walter Layton to draft the Liberal Party manifesto. He had no great commitment to the paper, and three years later he resigned to become personal aide to the Aga Khan, a strange choice for a Labour man.

Frank Waters, trying to identify a role and a purpose for the *News Chronicle*, took a hard-headed look at its problems. There seemed to him no radical wing in either the Conservative or Labour party that the paper could endorse; in fact, he wondered if it were possible to have a radical spirit in a welfare state. Laurence Cadbury he considered to suffer from 'weakness and timidity and a lack of news instinct'[19] and Layton, who had played such a major role earlier on, was now somewhat detached and in any case enmeshed in the unworldly political aims of the enfeebled Liberal Party. It was therefore with some interest that he weighed up an offer to join Cecil King's Mirror Group, but he died before anything could come of this. His death, given the lack of leadership from any other quarter, in effect sealed the fate of the *News Chronicle*.

In spite of the stimulus received through the acquisition of the Manchester *Daily Dispatch* in 1955, the paper continued on its downward curve. Layton had entered into negotiations with Odhams Press to explore the possibility of creating a composite paper of the left, but the TUC would not accept any scheme that would release Odhams from its political tie to the Labour Party and the scheme came to nothing. Layton, disheartened by this failure, took no further action. It was said that the end of the *News Chronicle* and *Star* would have come in 1958 if the Cadburys had not needed the newspapers to help them obtain the Tyne Tees Television franchise,[20]and the fact that this profitable sideline was retained by the Daily News Trust only added to the bitterness and outrage at the manner in which the two papers were sold to the *Daily Mail.*

Margaret Stewart, a journalist on the *News Chronicle*, gave a graphic description of what it felt like to be on the receiving end of the decision to close in a piece in the *New Statesman* entitled 'The night the blow fell'.[21] On 17 October 1960 she was at her desk completing a story about tally clerks when the telephone rang at 5.20 p.m. All work on the paper stopped, her story remained in her typewriter, a message to ring the Ministry of Labour went unanswered. The staff learned, at a meeting of the NUJ chapel at seven o'clock that evening, that in the biggest mass close-down in journalistic history, 3,500 people had lost their jobs. Most were too dazed to speak, but that night anger rather than self-pity was the dominant reaction. Anger that the *News Chronicle* should be sold like a piece of cake, anger that two newspapers with their valuable sites, combined circulations, printing plant, wharf, and other interests should have fetched so little as £1.5 million; anger above all at the meanness of the compensation – the cocoa handshake, as it was called.

Francis Williams, under the title 'Murder of the News Chronicle' wrote bitterly in the *New Statesman* that 'none has been buried so cynically as the *News Chronicle* and the *Star*, and accused Laurence Cadbury of allowing neither 'morals nor politics' to come into it. 'The soul of these newspapers was not his concern', he simply dispatched their bodies to the mortuary after 'extracting from the Daily News Trust Ltd. the profitable share in the commercial TV contract for Tyne Tees, which it secured as a publisher of newspapers and now intends to keep, although the newspapers no longer exist'. It was also the first time a national newspaper had been sold overnight to an owner of diametrically opposed views. Admitting that the *News Chronicle* was losing money, Williams blamed management for not taking action earlier. It was economic lunacy, he wrote, to print in London and Manchester; resources should have been concentrated, and management should have gone out more vigorously for quality and appropriate advertising.[22]

The Times in its leading article the following day wrote that though the *News Chronicle* had been a 'very alligator among newspapers', having swallowed the *Morning Leader*, the *Westminster Gazette*, the *Daily Chronicle* and the *Daily Dispatch*, it had always remained in essence the *Daily News*. And no one could expect the *Daily Mail* to be appreciably altered by the incorporation of the *News Chronicle*. One of the few papers to commiserate with the Cadburys, *The Times* recalled the family's sixty-year-old unbroken link with the newspaper and wrote, 'In this bitter hour for them tribute should be paid to their long record of public-spiritedness and their devotion to what they conceived to be the paper's interests.'[23]

Geoffrey Crowther, the editor of the *Economist*, was soon to succeed Layton as chairman. Crowther and Layton, as the only two members of the Daily News Trust who were not connected with the beleaguered Cadburys, wrote in defence of the action taken in a letter to *The Times*, starting a correspondence which went on for several days. They maintained that the decision to sell was made in the interests of the staff. 'Would critics really have preferred that the *News Chronicle* and *Star* should have been carried on until the last gasp, until all the assets had gone, until they no longer had saleable value, and until there was no hope of compensation for displaced staff?' They maintained that in the interests of the staff they could not accept any of the offers made. No prospective purchaser had enough money

> not only to provide working capital and to meet trading deficits but also, if and when he eventually failed, to provide the very large sum for the staff that is now available. The secrecy and speed with which the decision had to be made was defended on the grounds that Associated Newspapers would only have parted with such a substantial sum of money if they could be assured of having the maximum possible start over competitors and to that end negotiations had to be kept private.[24]

The staff of the two papers rejected all the arguments put forward. They said that they knew of two substantial offers that had been made and virtually ignored by Laurence Cadbury. The *Observer* in a provocative article, unkindly called 'Poison in the Cocoa', added its voice to the chorus of disapproval.[25] It found it astonishing 'that the prudent Cadburys, long famous for their Midland thrift and their advanced notions on labour relations, seemed to have made only vague arrangements for pensioning staff. Instead of a self-supporting pension fund, holding securities to cover its obligations, there seems to be only a tangle of good intentions that will take months to sort out.' Only in 1958 had a start been made to provide pensions for the staff. The financial reasons put forward by Layton and Crowther sounded lame and inadequate, given the Bournville tradition.

The *Observer* made the further point that if the sale of the paper was solely to provide adequate compensation for the staff, the owners could simply have liquidated. The necessary funds could have been raised

> without any necessity for the *Chronicle* readers to wake up one morning with a paper of the opposite political colour in their letter boxes. The fixed assets of the Daily News Ltd. alone are written down at £1,100,000. This must be an underestimate for two buildings just off Fleet Street, a wharf and a site on the South Bank, a sports ground in the suburbs where land values were booming, a building in Manchester and great deal of trucks, plant and incidentals.

The *Observer* then gave a long list of all the possible alternatives, including a considerable offer from Sir Frank Packer's Australian Consolidated Press. Why, it asked, as a businessman, did Mr Cadbury ignore all offers except one? Why, as a philanthropist, did he allow himself to treat his staff in a way which has made them feel betrayed? Why, as a Liberal, did he sell out to the truest and bluest Tory of all who came forward with offers?

Caught between the public's perception of all that the Cadbury name had come to mean of Quaker philanthropy, and his own private inclinations, Laurence

Cadbury was the recipient of all the dashed hopes and frustrated ambition of the dispossessed Liberals. His treachery seemed all the greater in that the Liberals had just won the Torrington by-election and had gained a few extra seats in the 1959 election. Geoffrey Hoare, the paper's former Paris correspondent, was furious that Laurence Cadbury, 'that silly little rabbit, should throw away the only popular Liberal newspaper, and at the birth of some sort of Liberal revival too'.[26] It was almost as though, by selling the *News Chronicle*, Laurence Cadbury had provided the Liberals with a convenient scapegoat to berate for their financial and political impotence.

James Cameron, whose appointment to the paper had been one of its few recent successes, was the most bitingly critical. In a letter to the *West London Press* on 21 October 1960, Cameron wrote:

The death of the *News Chronicle* is the biggest journalistic tragedy for many years – I think it is the most meaningful collapse the newspaper business has seen this generation. For the vestiges of independence in Fleet Street the writing on the wall is up to 72 point. If the *News Chronicle* could not survive, with its extraordinary advantages of tradition, and loyalty, and talent, who can outside the great chain-stores of the trade? . . .

Here is the most insoluble problem of what we rather fulsomely call the 'Free Press': how is it possible to equate the commercial success that is indispensable to a liberated paper with the business interests that will always encroach upon that liberation?

Well, as far as the *News Chronicle* is concerned, it couldn't be done. The newspaper with the most admirable free-thinking radical tradition withered on the bough precisely at the moment when the nation was ripe to appreciate these liberal qualities.

Its greatest opportunities opened out before it, and it surrendered because there was nothing at the top but timidity, conventionality and emptiness. In its closing days, the *News Chronicle* was a potential warhorse ridden by grocers. And thus it died, and great numbers of the most gifted, loyal, frustrated, trained, perceptive, and heartbroken men and women are now without a job while the grocers survive.

Many journalists, including the last editors of the *News Chronicle* and the *Star*, Norman Cursley and Ralph MacCarthy, never worked in Fleet Street again. There is a further irony in the circulation figures of the *Daily Mail*: at the time of the merger it was selling just over 2 million, a decade later just under 2 million copies.

Reviewing the situation in 1970, Tom Baistow, a former *Chronicle* journalist, saw many and complex reasons for the *Chronicle*'s fatal illness. He picked out as the terminal disease the paper's advertising anaemia; the root cause of its decline was 'a sudden and severe change of personality by ham-handed, pre-frontal leucotomy in the early 1950s when Laurence Cadbury, a Conservative industrialist, took over the chairmanship from Lord Layton, an enlightened if rather woolly Liberal'. He regarded the whole operation as a classic demonstration of what happens when the managerial mind mistakes a newspaper for just another market.[27]

The Times, in its obituary of Laurence Cadbury in November 1982, although less than fair in its coverage of his other achievements, accepted that it was Laurence Cadbury's misfortune to be in control of two famous British newspapers at a time when the qualities he could supply were not those needed to ensure their survival.[28] It was also his misfortune that his handling of the demise of the *Chronicle* should inevitably be compared to the high idealism of his father, whose sense of moral duty had caused him to shoulder the burden of newspaper proprietorship in the early years of the century.

9

The Trust Makers

George Cadbury is remembered for his success as a manufacturer of chocolate and cocoa and for the village he created at Bournville; he was not a trust maker in the sense that Joseph Rowntree was. But when Joseph created his trusts, he intended them to have limited lives. So the trusts which today bear his name, and are among the most important in Britain, do so, in a sense, almost accidentally.

George Cadbury was the first chocolate manufacturer to create a trust. He held that money ought to be spent 'while it is fresh', and once the Bournville Village Trust was established, he regarded the spending of wealth as a duty and a responsibility. His newspaper proprietorship was a costly venture, and while he gained some satisfaction from it, he saw it more as a responsibility that he could not give up. He spent money for the promotion of causes that he believed to be for the public good, some more overtly political than others. The extent to which he helped to finance the Labour Party and some of its candidates is something which now probably cannot be known.

George Cadbury's biographer stated that he had no pleasure in saving and believed that great inheritances were a curse rather than a blessing to children. But despite countless acts of generosity, George Cadbury died a millionaire, one of the richest of the new breed of successful manufacturers. No more than Andrew Carnegie, whose famous dictum was that 'the man who dies rich dies disgraced', could George Cadbury divest himself of the mantle of wealth.

It is likely that Richard Cadbury, had he not died relatively early, might also have become a trust maker. He had already built the Friends' hall and institute in Moseley Road, Birmingham, 'for the carrying out of schools either for children or adults . . . for the holding of meetings for religious, educational, philanthropic or other charitable or benevolent purposes . . .'[1] Unfortunately he died within twelve months of executing the trust deed in 1898, which became void under the Mortmain Act. Barrow Cadbury, his son, took on where his father had left off and executed another trust deed in 1899, couched in similar terms. The institute has flourished, as extracts from the minutes show; among the necessarily mundane reports of everyday events there are occasional reminders by the trustees of what was expected from those in charge. In 1899 a note was printed giving instructions on how to prepare a substitute for brandy in case of sudden illness or pain. 'Tincture of ginger (strong), aromatic spirit of ammonia (sal volatile), chloric aether, of each equal parts, in faintness, spasm of stomach, diarrhoea, or sudden pain, one teaspoonful (one drachm) mixed with one tablespoon of hot or cold water may be taken . . .'[2] In April 1902 it was deemed 'quite unsuitable that the Young Women's Class should be taught by a young man, as at present. The Superintendent is requested to terminate this arrangement at once.'[3]

There was a flurry of trust making by George's and Richard's children in the 1920s. Barrow and Geraldine Cadbury founded a trust bearing their name in 1920. According to Ronald Tress, director of the Leverhulme Trust, it can be said to be one of the first trusts in Britain to which the term 'foundation' can be applied, Carnegie's United Kingdom Trust being the first.[4] In the American sense of the word, foundation is the generic term used for a permanent institution founded through a large gift of property (most often in the form of a stockholding in private enterprise), the income from which is to be used for charitable purposes. Barrow and Geraldine Cadbury set up their trust so that they could regularise their support for those causes in which they had an interest or support wholly new schemes which they had initiated. Four years later Barrow Cadbury set up another fund bearing his name, which was intended to supplement the incomes of those who had devoted their lives to religious and social causes, and also to enable him to make grants to organisations not recognised as charities. William Cadbury, another of Richard's sons, set up a trust of his own, called the William Adlington Cadbury Charitable Trust, but not before the habit of trust making had reached the third generation. The year before, in 1922, the G. W. Cadbury Trust had been set up by George Woodall Cadbury, one of George Cadbury's grandsons.[5]

The Cadbury family have continued to be prolific trust makers. Paul S. Cadbury, Barrow Cadbury's son, set up his own trust in 1931, to further his special interest in town and country planning, as well as in the handicapped and matters pertaining to the welfare of the family. A whole group of further Cadbury trusts were set up after the Second World War, no fewer than four in the 1960s.

The most unusual of the Cadbury trust makers was certainly Beatrice Boeke, the youngest daughter of Richard Cadbury, Barrow and William's sister. The story of the Boeke Trust has a particular poignancy because it demonstrates so dramatically the near impossibility of any of George or Richard Cadbury's children escaping the powerful legacy bequeathed to them. Beatrice caused her family much anxiety through her desire to return to earlier Quaker principles, live a simple life, share her wealth and create a new society where all would be united by Christian love. But her loving and wealthy relations came to the rescue when she and her family became virtually destitute as a result of the extreme lengths to which she and her husband went in an attempt to put into practice these views.

In 1898, after the death of her father, Richard, Beatrice did all that a dutiful daughter should do. She lived with her mother and accompanied her on her journeys until her death, caused by a fall down a companionway in rough weather, on a return voyage from the United States. Beatrice then joined her sister, Helen, who was married to Charles Alexander, and went with them on missionary journeys to China and the United States. During this period her interest in the missionary side of Quaker work developed.

Beatrice met her future husband Klaus Boeke, or Kees, as he was always known, when he applied for the headmastership of a Quaker school at Brummana in Lebanon.[6] Kees, born in Alkmaar in the Netherlands in a devoutly Christian home, was deeply impressed by the Quakers' reliance on inward guidance and practical simplicity. He married Beatrice in 1912. The outbreak of war in 1914 forced them to leave the school in Brummana and return to England. They lived in a comfortable house belonging to Beatrice's sister Helen, who with her husband spent the war years in America. Feeling oppressed by the relative luxury of her sister's house, Beatrice and her family moved to a small house in Anderton Park Road, Moseley, Birmingham, where Beatrice, with little help, brought up her four young children. As dedicated workers for peace, the Boekes joined the Fellowship of Reconciliation, a body set up to promote understanding and friendship between Britain and Germany, at a time when conscientious objectors were subject to imprisonment. Kees was a talented speaker, much in demand. In early 1918 he was arrested at an open-air meeting and deported. Beatrice and the children followed him to Holland.

The Boekes made the house they acquired in Bilthoven a centre for peace and international studies. Three more children were born and, although life was hard and Kees was imprisoned for preaching peace, the real difficulties only started when the Boekes put their own belief, 'that private ownership of capital was at the root of nearly all social and economic trouble in the world', into practice. In September 1920 Beatrice Boeke wrote to her brothers, William and Barrow, of her intention to inform 'all who are co-operating in the Works known as Cadbury Brothers Limited, Bournville' to say that she wished to hand over the ownership of 'the Ordinary Shares (of the British Cocoa and Chocolate Co.) I now possess, to you collectively'. Beatrice Boeke wanted, in so far as possible, that 'the money be spent alleviating "the acute suffering caused by the capitalist order of society", in studying better methods of production and distribution, in work for the reconciliation between those estranged through national or class war and in preparing the minds of people for a new order of society'.[7]

There is a certain similarity between Beatrice Boeke's desire that the workers should not only dispose of part of the income of the business but also take a share in the running of it, and Joseph Rowntree's long-term objectives. The big difference was, of course, that Joseph felt that the only way to effect such a change was gradually to introduce measures that would promote worker participation and profit-sharing and had the wisdom to see when the time was right to take each small step in that direction; Beatrice, doubtless influenced by her strong-willed husband, went at the problem like a bull in a china shop. But in fact Joseph Rowntree and Beatrice Boeke both used the same words on different occasions to express their fears that the chocolate business might become nothing more than a 'money-making machine'; Joseph at the time of the proposed merger in 1918 and

Beatrice in 1920, when she was attempting to give away her inherited shares.

Tom Hackett, the Cadbury works foreman, one among many trying to advise Beatrice, told her that, although he had the deepest admiration for her and was himself a socialist, fewer than one in ten of the Bournville factory workers shared her ideals of pacifism and internationalism. He warned 'The new power you propose to give to the workers would have to be carefully thought out.'

The Cadbury family were concerned about the Boeke children and felt they should not be bound by their parents' extreme views. After learning of the horrors of the Russian famine, the Boekes gave all their disposable wealth to the Quaker Food Relief Famine Service; they at one time attempted to live without money at all, which resulted in the seizure of their furniture and led to the family being forced to camp out on the dunes in tents. The experiment came to an end in 1925, when Barrow Cadbury and his wife came to Holland and bought another house for the Boeke family in Bilthoven.

Beatrice's desire to give her shares in the family business to the workers created the most extraordinarily complex legal problems, which were finally solved by the setting up of the Boeke Trust. It was almost impossible for Beatrice to divest herself of her ordinary shares in favour of the Bournville work force because they carried voting rights. In the opinion of an international lawyer, 'Mrs Boeke's intended disposition of her property in the manner contemplated might create trouble after her death unless in the meantime the capitalist world has come to an end or Mrs Boeke had become a member of a Russian or other idealistic state.'

Matters came to a head when the Boekes announced that they had 'withdrawn from the state' and in conjunction with some others were setting up a local community council, to whom they were going to assign the Bournville shares not taken up on behalf of the Bournville workers. Back at Bournville this put matters in a very different light. As one member of the works council put it, 'I would rather see the money in the hands of the Bournville workers than in those of Dutch visionaries.' The Boekes had won and Barrow Cadbury wrote to say that if the Boekes felt they could not keep the money, then there was no one with a better claim than the Bournville workers. The two works council representatives sent over to negotiate with the Boekes brought back a splendidly original agreement whereby the works council became the 'spiritual owners' of the shares. The Boekes had a conscientious objection to the making of a legal trust, so the document was not even a legal document – but it worked.

Obviously such an unusual transaction was open to misunderstandings. The Works Council initially saw the trust as benefiting the work force itself. When Tom Hackett, who was one of three trustees (Dorothy Cadbury and Walter Barrow being the other two), came to explain the objects of the trust to the council he had to deal with questions concerning the trust's attitude to strikes and wage claims, such as 'Are you prepared to advocate the making-up of wages which are low? If you are not prepared to do this, are you prepared to finance a strike fund?' Understandable from the workers' point of view, but not at all what the trustees had in mind.

Once such difficulties had been dealt with and everyone concerned realised that the trust, substantial though it was, had insufficient resources to bring about the changes in society which the Boekes might have wished, it began to operate in a relatively conventional way. As with all trusts, it took time for the trustees to establish some kind of policy and the proportions first decided on – a quarter for charitable purposes and the remainder divided initially merely under the general heading, 'Bournville' and 'Miscellaneous' – were revised in the light of experience. Internationalism in the form of support for peace movements, travel and the promotion of fellowship between nations, care of the Boeke family themselves (in so far as they would allow it), social service, education, relief of distress and suffering, movements for working-class unity – all were given their due proportion of support.

The Boekes' interests now began to focus on the next generation and need to give children the kind of education which would enable them to build the new and more equal society Beatrice and Kees dreamed of. Their new experimental school in the house in Bilthoven proved a success. Kees gained so much respect and renown for his work in the educational world that the Dutch royal family sent their children to the school.

Joseph was already nearly seventy when the success of the Rowntree business made him a wealthy man. George Cadbury had had the satisfaction of dispensing patronage while he was still relatively young. Joseph, on the other hand, realised that he would be unlikely to be able to oversee or guide to completion the projects in which he was interested, particularly because he never wished to give to remedy what he called the 'superficial manifestations of weakness or evil, while little thought or effort is directed to search out their underlying causes'.[0] Writing of the emotional response to obvious distress, he said that 'it is much easier to obtain funds for the famine-stricken people of India than to originate and carry through a searching enquiry into the causes of recurrence of these famines', words that remain as true today as when Joseph wrote them. He noted that the soup kitchen in York never had any difficulty in obtaining adequate financial aid, but that an enquiry into the extent and causes of poverty would enlist little support. Underlying Joseph's philosophy was the hope that once the cause of evil was known, steps could and would be taken to remedy it.

Joseph devoted an enormous amount of time to investigating the problem of drunkenness among the poor. He and an associate Arthur Sherwell, published a best-selling book in 1898 with the title *The Temperance Problem and Social Reform*. The book may have attracted a wide readership, but the suggestion put forward, that the sale of drink should be through private companies and that private profit should be eliminated, as had been done in Gothenburg in Sweden, was not received with enthusiasm. Joseph was not discouraged and a series of books on the subject were published in the following years, written in collaboration with Arthur Sherwell.

Joseph and his son Seebohm were actively concerned with the problem of housing for the low-paid, seeing it as one of the most important underlying causes of poverty. In 1901, he purchased an estate three miles outside York. New Earswick was created in an attempt to raise the standards of design in houses let at low rents and to provide a better environment for wage earners to live in. As New Earswick took shape, Joseph realised that he would need to make provision for the future, if new ideas in site planning, house design and community organisation were to continue to be developed.

To finance both the needs of New Earswick and research into matters in the social, religious and industrial fields in which he and his family were interested he created three trusts. He had consulted George Cadbury and, convinced of the advantages in the way the Bournville Village Trust was set up, he wrote,

> The almost indefinite expansion which attaches to George Cadbury's scheme constitutes, I think, its great strength. If in twenty-five years the accumulated Bournville rents amount to a sum which would enable a similar model village to be established elsewhere, one feels there is hardly any limit to the possibilities of the scheme; for at the end of another ten or twelve years the rents of the two villages would form a third sum capable of starting another experiment and so on indefinitely.[9]

His optimistic expectations of the villages' financial success never materialised in the way he envisaged, still less was there any collaboration with the Cadburys in this field. Fifty years later, the income of the trust had greatly increased, but the need to repeat the housing experiment of New Earswick had disappeared; local authorities and their architects were initiating experimental work. The trustees were left with the dilemma of deciding what projects the trust should be supporting and what initiatives they should be taking, a dilemma made all the more awkward in that the two other Rowntree trusts, originally created to complement the work of the Village Trust, were still in being – this despite Joseph's clearly expressed view that they should cease work after a period of not more than thirty-five years, because he believed that each generation should provide for its own needs.

Joseph created two further trusts, the Joseph Rowntree Charitable Trust and the Joseph Rowntree Social Services Trust. The first was designed as a social and religious trust, able to undertake enquiries into social work, to promote adult education and to interest itself in the life and work of the Society of Friends. The Social Services Trust was also a social trust, but Joseph did not want the objects he had in mind hindered by legal restrictions. It was a noncharitable, taxpaying trust, set up in the form of a close company limited by guarantee, with no other obligation than to send its annual report and accounts to the Register of Companies. The trust is still almost unique as a substantial grant-giving foundation free from the restraints of a legal charity.

The first trustees under Joseph's chairmanship were mostly members of his family, who served on all three trusts. This small family group of like-minded men were also largely responsible for the company which provided their income, and for the first twenty-five years all the trust meetings were held at the cocoa works. The administration of the trusts was carried out by part-time secretaries.[10] In 1904 Joseph

36 A Cadbury's advertisement in the *Christian*, the Analyst bearing a marked resemblance to Richard Cadbury, 1891.

37 'A Casket of Chocolate being handed to Neptune to make known to the Countries of the World.' Frontispiece from *Cocoa: All About it*, Richard Cadbury.

38 Girls enjoying the opportunity to relax at the Rowntree's swimming pool, 1933.

wrote a memorandum for the guidance of his trustees, a remarkably far-seeing document, yet it carried within it the seeds of many of the difficulties which beset later trustees as they struggled to relate its meaning to the changed conditions in which they found themselves. In spite of all the care with which it was drafted, it was done with the original trustees in mind. Joseph expected the same men to administer the two trusts until they came to an end, men 'who are closely in sympathy with my general thoughts and aims, and will, I believe, give to the administration of these trusts the same thought and direction which I should have given to them myself'. Joseph began and ended the memorandum by saying that it was not intended to have any legal or binding force, that he fully realised that 'new occasions teach new duties' and that 'time makes ancient good uncouth'. He believed that he had given the directors and trustees very wide powers and few directions of a mandatory nature, as indeed he had.

The problem was that the memorandum was not written to apply to permanent substantial foundations, which is what the Joseph Rowntree Charitable Trust and the Joseph Rowntree Social Services Trust, were to become. Those in charge of the trusts at the time when radical alterations were made to the way in which they were originally conceived can be seen, in a sense, as the trust makers of the next generation. Alan Pifer, president of the Carnegie Corporation from 1967 to 1982, has no doubt that although a foundation may have a certain reputation inherited from the past, 'this can fairly quickly be altered through the fresh outlook and changed actions of new trustees and staff'.[11] This observation is borne out by the later development of the three trusts, who, in the years immediately after the Second World War, 'increasingly went their separate ways.'[12]

Joseph's 1904 memorandum was written in conjunction with one for his children upon the 'opportunities of wealth and the dangers connected with it'. Taken together, the two memoranda provide a remarkable picture of a Quaker businessman, whose life had been guided by the principles he was anxious to pass on, and whose concern for his family was the mirror image of his wider concern for humanity as a whole. He had given half his fortune toward the setting up of the three trusts, but he realised that if the cocoa works remained moderately profitable his children were likely to inherit large incomes. He was concerned with the danger that faced those who inherited wealth and quoted his own father, who had written warning of that 'ease-loving and self-considering spirit which makes us dwarfs in all that is great and beautiful'.[13] He warned against expensive habits, which he thought did not increase the real richness and fullness of life but only added to its burdens. He saw it as a piece of 'culpable stupidity' on the part of those with sufficient means if they lived in a style which meant they were continually worried by financial consider-ations and had neither time nor energy to make 'their mental powers or their wealth available for local or national needs'.

The opening paragraphs of the 1904 memorandum reflect his view that money is best spent by persons in their lifetime, but since this was not possible in his case he wanted to make known the principles he had followed in setting up the trusts so that his successors might be familiar with his thoughts. He thought it undesirable that money be given to hospitals, almshouses or similar institutions that emphasise relief over research. Joseph divided the objects of the Charitable Trust and the Social Services Trust under three heads – religious, political and social – and it is clear that he meant the trusts to work together.

When Joseph established his trusts it was only just over a decade since the much-debated declaration in the House of Lords in 1891 that income-tax relief was due to all charities devoted to the relief of poverty, the advancement of education, the advancement of religion or other purposes beneficial to the community – a classification which might be thought to be sufficiently wide to enable Joseph to further his ideas. But Joseph's ideas went beyond what might be considered solely charitable, and the Social Services Trust was set up to deal with matters which, in Joseph's words, might be 'at least of equal importance to the well-being of the community' but could necessitate pressing for an alteration to the law of the land and would thus fall outside the definition by the House of Lords. Joseph believed that rightly directed grants could change the face of England, and it is a mark of his wide vision that he took the precaution of ensuring that no mere legal impediment should stand in the way of desirable change.

He expected that the Social Services Trust might be in a position to hand part of its resources over to the Charitable Trust before the expiry of thirty-five years, because the Social Services Trust had been given the greater endowment in view of the heavy demands which the establishment and support of newspapers might involve. Joseph gave some indications of how the trusts should come to an end if they had not exhausted their principal as well as their interest. He thought the trustees might create new trusts and hand over the property to new trustees or transfer the remaining property to the Joseph Rowntree Village Trust. As for the Village Trust, Joseph's one permanent creation, he plainly expected that if New Earswick was successful the trustees would repeat the experiment. In re-emphasising his wish that nothing should be done to prevent the growth of civic interest and the sense of civic responsibility in any community existing on the property of the trust, he wrote of village communities in the plural.

Joseph's ideas for the future of his trusts were eminently understandable in the light of his idea that money should be spent in a man's own lifetime. Besides his own wide interests he was deeply committed to the interests of his sons, John Wilhelm and Seebohm, and saw the trusts as enabling them to continue and finish the work they had started. With such considerations in mind it was a logical step to create time-limited trusts, designed to extend beyond his own expected life span, to enable work started by his sons to be completed.

John Wilhelm Rowntree, worried by the dominant Quaker strain of evangelical fundamentalist theology which he believed to be stifling the life of the Society of Friends, had set up a series of summer schools and study circles. This led to the idea of a residential centre for the systematic study of religious questions and related social and international problems. George Cadbury had also had doubts about the adequacy of Quaker worship as traditionally practised and had been concerned at the stagnation of the movement and the spiritual torpor that seemed to have overcome Quakerism. The idea of a centre where such matters could be studied on a more permanent basis made an instant appeal. George Cadbury, writing about the Woodbrooke settlement, said that while he was out riding 'it was strongly impressed upon my mind that the house and gardens of Woodbrooke should be handed over to the Society of Friends as a college for men and women'.[14] The foundation of the Woodbrooke settlement rapidly followed, notwithstanding some opposition from Friends, who, it seemed to George Cadbury, 'would rather see the Society disappear than make any change'.[15] Despite his strictures on making gifts to establishments, Joseph Rowntree made an exception of Woodbrooke, writing that 'the need for religious teaching to members of the Society of all ages, is also something which is not clearly seen . . . but upon which a powerful ministry depends. I therefore entirely approve of support to the Woodbrooke Settlement or to kindred efforts.'[16] John Wilhelm lived only a year after Joseph wrote his memorandum.

The meeting of the Joseph Rowntree Charitable Trust, in April 1905, authorised their first grant:

> Edward Grubb MA [to] be employed by the Trust as from 1st January 1905 at a salary of £150 per annum on giving under the direction of the Trustees religious teaching to Members of the Society of Friends . . . the Trustees realising the value of the services he might render . . . upon lines that would have commended themselves to John Wilhelm agree to pay him the additional salary yearly of £250 from the time he . . . agrees to devote the whole of his time to the above named work.[17]

Grants were made to Woodbrooke for bursaries, books and toward general expenses. By 1905 the minutes record that arrangements had been made for the writing of the 'History of Quakerism', 'a work to which John Willhelm attached such great importance, and which he had so much at heart . . .'[18] In 1907 at Arnold Rowntree's suggestion the annual series of Swarthmore Lectures was launched as a systematic commitment to the publishing of Quaker thought and experience. For seventy-seven years the trust supported the lectures, until in 1984 they became self-financing through an endowment fund.

There was no discussion within the official structure of the Society of Friends about the developments initiated by John Wilhelm. Roger Wilson, in an essay in the 1982–84 report of the Joseph Rowntree Social Service Trust, believes that without John Wilhelm's vigorous spiritual and intellectual leadership, which was supported by the trust, the very future of the Society itself might have been at risk. Instead, at the end of the 1914 war, the Society of Friends emerged confident of a bright future as part of the Christian church.

Seebohm Rowntree's seminal work on poverty had appeared six years before Joseph founded his trusts. Both the Social Service Trust and the Charitable Trust made important contributions to his continued research. Nor was Joseph's own special interest in the drink problem overlooked. He founded and chaired the Temperance Legislation League and his Social Service Trust gave substantial funds to it and to work associated with it. The Trust also continued to be involved with newspapers and periodicals and, during the first thirty-five years, to 1939, nearly half the income of the trust was spent on publishing.

When the time came in 1939 for the Joseph Rowntree Social Service Trust and the Charitable Trust to come to an end, in accordance with Joseph's expressed wishes, the trustees found little difficulty in agreeing that the trusts should continue. A new generation of trustees had been appointed and there were many new needs for them to try to meet. The trusts had been developing in different ways, the new trustees bringing differing experience and new interests to the work. Not least, the capital value of the trusts had increased considerably and this undoubtedly influenced the thinking of the trustees. The two trusts, which were once considered to be essentially the same, and which Joseph hoped might in time be integrated, have continued, with no change of name, on very different lines. Joseph, in all probability, never took into account the insidious satisfaction that trusteeship brings with it, giving to those who serve in that capacity the power to act as philanthropists at one remove.

The history of the Joseph Rowntree Village Trust is, if anything, more unexpected. At the fiftieth anniversary of the trust's foundation, in 1954, Seebohm Rowntree, the last of the foundation managers, had just died, and the trustees were very much aware that this marked the end of an era. They had in front of them an account of the past, *One Man's Vision*, an advance copy of the book, written by Lewis Waddilove, of the story of New Earswick. They had also to consider at this meeting a memorandum written by Thomas Green, the headmaster of Bootham School, a trustee since 1949. He was the first to raise the question of what new initiatives the trust should now be taking. He made the point that since local authorities had taken over the responsibilities for housing and their architects were initiating much experimental work, there was little reason for the trust to repeat elsewhere the housing experiment of New Earswick. Like the other trusts, the Village Trust had benefited from the increasing prosperity of Rowntree and Company, and Thomas Green felt that the trustees should exercise initiative and not merely wait for other people to come along with ideas.[19]

It was finally agreed, in 1957, that the trustees should undertake work of research or social enquiry. This was in the sphere of the Charitable Trust, but they had kept very close to the wishes of the founder in that they had supported only projects which were the personal concern of individual trustees; many of their trustees had been appointed because of their knowledge in the field of social services. The Village trustees wanted to adopt a radically different approach, being willing to support projects initiated by outside bodies and to allow their staff to monitor the work they were supporting. Since Joseph Rowntree's death there was no machinery to perpetuate the founder's original ideas of how the trusts should operate. If the Village trustees went ahead with their ideas they would effectively drive a coach and horses through Joseph Rowntree's conception of an interrelated trio of trusts. Although some informal arrangements for cooperation were set up, they were stillborn. The trustees appointed to the different trusts were unknown to each other and their ideas of how best to carry out their obligations under the different trust deeds were bound to vary.

The trustees of the Joseph Rowntree Village Trust were faced with the problem of a trust which had greater resources than it could use. Where necessary, they wanted to carry out field operations to test in practice the results of their research. The trustees felt that they could make the greatest contribution by the discovery of facts and by drawing certain conclusions from those facts. But they were not sure whether they could do this under the terms of the trust deed, so after long drawn-out negotiations with the Charity Commission they had it changed by act of Parliament in 1959. The name was changed to the Joseph Rowntree Memorial Trust. The trustees were told by their advisers that they could now benefit 'the public or any section of the public in the United Kingdom or elsewhere', they could engage in social or allied research, and they could publish their findings, but if they tried to promote policies suggested by their findings they might well lose their charitable status. Joseph Rowntree knew the inherently conservative nature of charity and had created the noncharitable Social Services Trust specifically to deal with matters which Joseph or his trustees might wish to promote but which fell outside the legal definition of charity. There was nothing to impede the Social Services Trust from promoting any number of policies which their sister trust might identify as being in the public interest, but the possibility of cooperation seems not even to have been discussed.

The Inland Revenue decreed that, in the light of recent court decisions, provision of housing for the benefit of the community was no longer charitable. It was only by limiting its housing work to those who needed it by reason of 'poverty, youth, age, infirmity or disablement' that the clause was accepted for tax-exemption purposes.[20] Having gained wider powers in some areas, the trustees lost their former freedom to administer and develop their own housing estate, but felt that their new powers more than outweighed those they had lost.

A further blow fell in 1965, when the government introduced a rent bill designed to give security of tenure to tenants of rented houses. This meant that the trust remained a housing association but could no longer claim to be a housing trust as defined by statute, and all housing developed under its powers as a housing trust would be subject to the new rent-regulations procedure. The only way around this new obstacle, the trustees were told, would be to divide the trust and create a new housing trust to which they could transfer the property together with a sum of money as working income.[21] The Joseph Rowntree Memorial Housing Trust came into being on 1 January 1968. The trustees had first changed the objects of the original Village Trust and then created a new trust which effectively destroyed Joseph Rowntree's original conception of three interlocking trusts. But they were not the first to do so. The trustees of the Social Services Trust, much to the dismay of their sister trusts, had themselves set up a new charitable trust in 1955 to cover aspects of its work which were legally charitable. In so doing they had further underlined their independence and distanced themselves from the Charitable Trust, who could, in theory, have undertaken such work. So, gradually, the successors to the Rowntree family trustees altered Joseph's grand design, and enlarged both the number and scope of the trusts he had set up. The question remains whether this really was the most effective way in which the trusts could have developed or whether the separation and proliferation occurred because of the problem, as Alan Pifer puts it, 'of sand in the works – petty jealousies, minor obstructionism, turf protection and the "not invented here" phenomenon'.[22]

Perhaps the most unexpected and unusual development was the creation of the Family Fund. The government, as a result of the public outrage at the Thalidomide disaster, when children whose mothers had used the drug in pregnancy were born with terrible handicaps, realised that there were other families whose children were equally handicapped, but for whom no compensation from the Distillers Company (the makers of the drug) or any other source would be available. The Government in the person of Sir Keith Joseph, asked the trustees of the Joseph Rowntree Memorial Trust if they would administer a £3 million fund to 'ease the burden of living on those households containing very severely congenitally disabled children'.[23] Lord Seebohm, then chairman of the trust, agreed to do so on the understanding that the trust could not act as an agent of government, and the government accepted this condition. The trustees made it clear that the money would become part of the trust's funds and that the decisions about individual grants would be made by the trustees alone, and when certain broad guidelines had been agreed, the Family fund came into being and started to operate in April 1973.[24] The trust was initially invited to administer the Family Fund for a period of three years but in 1981 the trustees agreed to continue to manage the Fund without a definite term, provided discussions were held about future developments.

Administrative costs have amounted to less than the growth that has accrued to the fund through good husbandry so that there has been more money to distribute to the families of the congenitally disabled and less demand has been made on government resources.[25] This may be seen as merely letting the government off the hook by doing its work for it. There is a danger that as the Trust becomes increasingly competent in the discharge of its responsibilities, there will be fewer incentives for the government to develop new policies to bring such work within the framework of public administration. A more constructive and hopeful view is that this unique experiment between the government and a trust has opened up new possibilities for creative cooperation. After all, public money can only be spent according to legislative mandate, while money under the control of a trust can be quickly used to meet a sudden need.

Trusts and foundations are characterised by unusual freedom, by their dual private and public nature, private because they are incorporated as private entities and public in the sense that they are tax-exempt and exist for public benefit, and because they control a most precious resource, uncommitted money. The example provided by the Family Fund has shown that a certain amount of government money in the hands of trusts or foundations can sometimes prove to be of more benefit to the public than either direct government funding or funding in the shape of annual grants to voluntary organisations. The government has made a promising start as a trust maker in its own right. It will be interesting to see if this experiment will be repeated.

10

Changing Legacy

Annual reports, cocoa-works magazines, facts and figures, family histories, all help to build up a picture of the chocolate business, but one visit by an intelligent and thoughtful man, brilliantly reported, brings the scene alive. J. B. Priestley (1894–1984), the novelist, visited Bournville while writing *English Journey* in 1933. He had just completed a visit to the Daimler works in Coventry and was anxious to visit another highly organised giant factory. Being in Birmingham and very fond of chocolate, he found Bournville the obvious choice. His descriptions of the works, the village and the Cadburys are vivid and idiosyncratic.

Priestley, like many others before him, started by believing that the village had been built for the work force and thought it was simply part of Cadbury Brothers. Admitting that Bournville was no longer the 'eye-opener' that it must have been when it was new, Priestley says the houses were infinitely superior to most of the huge new workmen's and artisans' quarters that had recently been built, but the village would have been more attractive had the houses and villas not all been detached or semidetached. Describing the long road 'on which tiny villas have been sprinkled, as if out of a pepper-pot' as 'at once fussy and monotonous', he longed instead for rows, courts and quadrangles. He also criticised Bournville for the lack of frivolous meeting places, if not for the excess of public halls of religion. But Priestley was generous in his praise, saying that Bournville village was a 'small outpost of civilisation, still ringed around with barbarism'.

At the time when Priestley made his visit to Bournville, Cadbury's were enjoying one of their most successful periods. They had installed modern machinery and, taking advantage of the low price of raw materials, the business was expanding by leaps and bounds. Paul Cadbury, only son of Barrow and Geraldine Cadbury, was in charge of sales. Cadbury's became the leaders in the chocolate industry. They would soon be taking over the Fry business completely; they had refused to consider a merger with Rowntree's a few years previously, leaving the York business to struggle on as best it could in the face of their overwhelming domination of the market. Chocolate was immensely popular, as Priestley noted. 'This is the age, among other things, of chocolate.'

Priestley said the Cadbury factory was more like a small town than a factory, describing how he had spent hours being rushed from one part of the colossal works to another. He marvelled at the warehouse he was shown where more than 100,000 bags of cocoa beans could be stored. The bags were hoisted to the top of the building and as their contents passed from floor to floor they were 'shelled, winnowed, baked, crushed, refined, pressed and finally pack themselves neatly into tins'. He did not even attempt to describe the more elaborate process of chocolate manufacture, except to say that there were miles of it and thousands of men and girls looking after hundreds of machines that 'pounded and churned and cooled and weighed and packed the chocolate'.

Priestley was most impressed by the room where the cardboard boxes and labels were made. He was astonished at seeing hundreds of white-capped girls on either side of a kind of gangway running down the centre of the room, feeding the insatiable machines with shiny purple and crimson paper. He noted with surprise that the girls preferred the monotonous work with the machines to cutting up coloured marzipan to decorate the chocolate eggs.

One might think that no one working in the factory, breathing the sickly smell of chocolate and seeing huge rivers of it cascading ever onward would ever want to eat the stuff, but chocolate is addictive and Priestley was told that the firm consider their staff among their best customers.

The intense seriousness with which every process was considered, specialists and learned men with degrees in solemn conferences to consider the fate of a bit of coconut dipped in chocolate, struck him as part of the fantastic quality of the times. He found it disturbing that what he saw as trifling bits of frivolity should assume such terrific importance. Of course, enormous financial rewards result from such meticulous attention to detail, which does indeed make it a serious matter to some.

Priestley was interested in human nature and intrigued by the way in which the Cadburys had interpreted their role as employers. And, as he frankly admitted, he used his visit as a peg on which to hang his own thoughts on democracy and industrial relations. Priestley saw the Cadburys as having long been 'in the top class of the school of benevolent and paternal employers'. He believed that the Cadburys genuinely would rather spend a good part of their money on their factory and amenities for their employees than on horses, yachts or gambling.

Priestley wrote that there was no form of self-improvement that was not available at Bournville, no pastime that was denied save 'the ancient one of getting drunk'; magnificent facilities for recreation were provided, from a concert hall to sports grounds and a club room fitted up for old employees to play billiards or any other game; there were works councils for the purposes of consultation and, of course, Cadbury's were one of the earliest companies to provide medical care and pensions for their employees, before the creation of the National Health Service and the introduction of state pensions. Long before Japanese industrialists had developed the concept, Priestley noted that no Cadbury employee need look beyond the factory for his welfare. 'Once you had joined the staff of this firm you need never wander out of its shadow,' he wrote, but found it difficult to decide whether this really was for the best. He argued that owing to a system of paternal employment, good management and the public passion for chocolate, factory workers at Bournville had a better chance of leading a decent and happy life than workers almost anywhere else, even in America during its prosperous years. But in the longer term he felt doubts about making the factory the centre of people's lives and thought the paternalistic system of employment militated against genuine democracy.

Priestley noted that in Australia, where the Cadburys had opened a factory, the workers had refused recreation grounds and concert halls in favour of higher wages, which they could spend as they wished. By selling his labour and nothing else, the Australian employee kept his spirit of independence, Priestley felt, and was in a sounder political situation. He did not have to treat his employer as a superior being, whose 'benevolence fell on him like the rays of the life-giving sun'. Notwithstanding the security and pleasure provided by pensions and bonuses, entertainments and outings, such things could, Priestley feared, end up becoming injurious to the growth of men as intellectual and spiritual beings. He saw the danger that a trading concern run entirely for private profit should so entirely dominate the lives of the people working there that they risked losing their spirit of independence and that the workers should come to see their often monotonous work at the factory as an end in itself rather than a means to an end.

Priestley went on to speculate about the effect if such paternal factories were taken over by the state, and came to the conclusion that, apart from the fact that the factory would no longer be run for profit, the same weaknesses would remain for the individual worker. There is a certain unreality about such arguments because the Bournville factory was essentially an industrial experiment. It must also be remembered that a large proportion of the work force were girls who left work when they married, and as for the men, Priestley admitted that, in spite of the dangers in the system, they were better off, probably more contented than ordinary factory workers and therefore better citizens.

But what of Bournville village today? In ninety years it has grown from 313 houses on 330 acres of land to 7500 on 1000 acres with a population of over 23,000.[1] Until the end of the Second World War the village continued to develop and experiment in size and style of houses, remaining self-financing. Many members of the Cadbury family have served and continue to serve today as trustees, but it was under the chairmanship of Paul Cadbury who was appointed in 1922 and personally involved for sixty years, that the biggest changes took place. He played an important role in the replanning of Birmingham in the 1950s, and the Village Trust collaborated with the city of Birmingham on the Shenley Neighbourhood Development Scheme which was only finally completed in the 1970s.

Government policy in the shape of leasehold reform, building regulations and the listing of buildings has made experiments like those George Cadbury started difficult to continue and impossible to initiate. The passage of time and changed life styles have created new problems – some of the houses are not so attractive to live in as more convenient modern ones and many of the gardens, such a feature of the early days, are now too large for their owners to manage.

When an inspector of historic buildings went to Port Sunlight and Saltaire he had no difficulty in deciding to list both villages as buildings of architectural and historic interest. When he came to Bournville he was at a loss to know what to recommend. The chief inspector himself paid a visit and was equally perplexed, for Bournville had grown to such an extent that it was more like a small town than a village. It was finally decided to list only the centre of the village as a conservation area, so that part of George Cadbury's brave experiment is now preserved as it was created.[2]

Nothing stands still, and Priestley's description of Bournville has been succeeded by more serious studies, in particular one that attempted to evaluate the results of George Cadbury's attempt to introduce a social mix into housing policy which has now been followed for nearly a century. The rather surprising conclusion is that George Cadbury, were he alive today, would have been disappointed.[3] Bournville has become a homogeneous community, homogeneous because the sense of belonging to a community which is historic and unique has created patterns of social behaviour which, in effect, override class distinction. It is, perhaps, an indicator of how society itself has changed over the last half-century. With a more egalitarian philosophy of housing and with home ownership now widespread, the need that George Cadbury saw for a specific policy to encourage a housing social mix has been obviated.

But that is not to say that the trust has outlived its pioneering role. A solar village has recently been built at Rowheath on the southeast edge of Bournville village[4] and, if the experiment is positive and if low-cost energy-efficient homes can be seen to be cost-effective, this will be one further step in the history of the trust's endeavour to improve the quality of life of lower-income groups. No local authority could undertake such an experiment, only a body like Bournville which has the practical experience of design, building, letting, maintenance and other costs to set against measured benefits. The influence Bournville still commands internationally can be measured by the large number of visits, the amount of correspondence and the many requests to attend planning seminars that the trustees receive.

The Rowntree Village trustees had to grapple with problems similar to those of the Bournville trustees, but perhaps made more acute since a major part of the original trust funds had been taken over by the Joseph Rowntree Memorial Trust to fund its experiments in social research and social policy. If New Earswick was not to become merely a museum but remain a living community, as the founder had wished, something had to be done. Many of the houses were old-fashioned and dilapidated, so refurbishment was the first priority. Other objectives were identified: to raise the quality of living for the elderly, to achieve a better balance among the population, and, unusually, to provide more facilities for the single person. Lewis Waddilove, who was the first director of the Joseph Rowntree Memorial Trust, in his book *Private Philanthropy, Public Welfare*, has given a detailed account of some of the problems that have had to be overcome in New Earswick.

Perhaps one of the most notable contributions to housing policy made by the Joseph Rowntree Village Trust was when it supported an investigation into the effects on mothers trying to bring up young children in high-rise blocks. The results led to other studies of the problems of living in high-rise buildings, and now the disadvantages of tower blocks are well known.

Although the majority of the trustees of the different Joseph Rowntree trusts now had no direct connection with the Rowntree family, the trusts were still linked to the Rowntree cocoa works in that their income came, almost entirely, from their shareholding in the business. The arrangement was simple and convenient. Twice a year two large dividend cheques arrived from the company. Even the Memorial Trust, which had a special investment committee as a result of the act of Parliament which had brought it into being, had invested 90 per cent of its fund in Rowntrees. There was no reason for the historic link between company and trusts to be broken.

In 1968, however, General Foods of America tried to take over Rowntree and Company and made a cash offer to shareholders substantially above the current price of the shares. Here indeed was a dilemma. The trustees had no desire to see Rowntree's taken over by a foreign company, but on the other hand their duty was to do their best for their trusts. Even if the trustees vetoed the offer, other shareholders might well resent the trustees preventing them from making an immediate financial gain. All the trustees came to the conclusion that Rowntree's would do better financially in the long term if they remained independent; their judgement was proved right when a year later the value of the Rowntree shares was substantially higher than the cash offer made by General Foods. The following year Rowntree merged with John Mackintosh and their name changed to Rowntree Mackintosh Ltd; the company also made an agreement with Hershey Foods Corporation to market and manufacture selected group products in the USA, and these moves had a dramatic effect on the share price.

There had been discussions of what might happen if there was serious disagreement between the trusts and the company over policy. These problems could be resolved as long as most of the company directors were also trustees, but by the 1970s that was no longer the case. A series of incidents called into question the appropriateness of the link between the company and the trusts.

In 1971, Lord Gifford, chairman of the Committee for Freedom in Mozambique, Angola and Guinea, attended a meeting of the Joseph Rowntree Social Services Trust to put the case for giving help to those who were attempting to overthrow colonialism in Mozambique. The trustees were told that the governments of Holland, Sweden and Denmark had each given £50,000 to the welfare wing of the Frelimo. The trustees agreed to give £30,000 and were surprised at the dismayed reaction of their sister trusts.[5] They stoutly maintained that they believed that a certain amount of controversy was healthy. But there was strong pressure from the other Rowntree trusts, who were deeply concerned at the action of the Social Services Trust, to persuade it to change its name, a move which was equally firmly rejected.

Rowntree Mackintosh were even more dismayed at the action of the Social

Services Trust and the company chairman, David Barron, attended the next meeting to underline the damage that had been done to the company. They were particularly embarrassed by the effect the grant to the Frelimo had on the workers in Wilson Rowntree, a subsidiary that had been established in East London, South Africa, in 1925. They said that the grant had undermined the morale of the work force, who were said to feel that by working for Wilson Rowntree they were being unpatriotic, and as a consequence the company had held back a wage increase for their Bantu workers. There was a lot of publicity in Portugal; markets in that country had been made impossible for the time being and would all have to be reworked. The Trustees were adamant that their support for the liberation movements in Africa did not imply any approval of the use of force by the so-called freedom fighters or guerrillas; the grants were for medical, educational and relief work.[6]

Two years later Rowntree Mackintosh had more trouble with their South African subsidiary. Wilson Rowntree refused to recognise the black South African Workers' Union, and Rowntree's troubles had been highlighted by a TV documentary on the subject. On top of that, Rowntree Mackintosh had done some unwise buying in the cocoa-futures market. The company lost millions of pounds as a result and its future as an independent company was questioned. These crises brought the three trusts together to protect their interests and an inter-trust committee on finance was set up. The Social Services Trust had diversified its holdings after the Frelimo fracas, and now decided to sell its remaining shares, and the other trusts, the Charitable Trust excepted, decided on a policy of diversification to distance themselves from the company.

The Charitable Trust retained up to 90 per cent of its shareholding in Rowntree Mackintosh, to its great advantage. This policy, however, brought difficulties of another kind. Some of those who accepted grants from the Charitable Trust were concerned that some of the money came from the Rowntree Mackintosh subsidiary in South Africa. The trustees of the Charitable Trust were all members of the Society of Friends, and they decided to seek first-hand information about the problems that had arisen at Wilson Rowntree in East London. After the trust secretary and one of the trustees had visited the area they discussed their ideas with the company, and obviously it is their hope that through continuing dialogue the problem will be resolved.[7]

Perhaps because of its major interest in Rowntree Mackintosh, the Charitable Trust used some of the remaining part of its portfolio to involve itself in the problematic field of ethical investment. It took two initiatives; it set up the Stewardship Unit Trust and gave a grant to the Ethical Investment Research and Information Service. The objective of the Stewardship Unit Trust is to enable individuals and charities who do not wish their money to be invested in companies which are involved with South Africa, the manufacture of armaments, or to a substantial degree, in brewing, gambling and tobacco, to invest their money for the positive wellbeing of society. With the exception of South Africa and tobacco, neither of which were, in Joseph Rowntree's time, matters for concern, the areas mentioned all reflect the continuing interest of trustees in subjects with which Joseph himself had been involved.

In the two years from 1976 to 1978, the Joseph Rowntree Social Services Trust alone gave grants to more than 150 different bodies; the Barrow and Geraldine S. Cadbury Trust, together with the Paul S. Cadbury Trust, in their report for the year 1984–85, take eleven pages to list the grants made to the Society of Friends and other churches, to organisations or bodies concerned with peace and international relations, race relations, education, penal affairs, social service, housing, land and community planning, employment, health and handicap, and minority arts. The amounts vary – little more than £100 for penal affairs in 1985, while £170,000 was spent on race relations. Similar variations in expenditure are shown by the Charitable Trust, who in their report for 1979–81 gave £150 to one-parent families in York for group work and £68,000 to Sussex University's Armament/Disarmament Unit.

Nonetheless the two groups of trusts differ in some marked respects. The Rowntree trusts were originally set up by one man, Joseph Rowntree, who had specific ideas about the way in which the trusts and the company would interact. There is no doubt that the way in which the trusts are set up today is very far from what the founder originally intended. The trusts all retain the prefix 'Joseph Rowntree', although there is now minimal family representation. As Alan Pifer has said, trusts are not 'liberal' or 'conservative', 'stuffy' or 'imaginative' of themselves.[8] A trust may inherit a certain reputation from the past, but that reputation can be quickly altered by new trustees and new staff. The Joseph Rowntree Charitable Trust is probably the least changed of the three because of its continuing close links with the Society of Friends.

The Joseph Rowntree Memorial Trust is the most radically different, in that it is a new creation, brought into being by the trustees themselves. Incidentally it is interesting to note that when the Charities Act became law in 1960 there was a clause in the act which effectively prevented any body of trustees from using money from trust resources to prepare any bill for submission to Parliament without the express authority of the courts or of the charity commissioners. Had the act been in force before 1959, would the Joseph Rowntree Village trustees have been allowed to create their new trust? Was the clause a direct consequence of the action of those trustees? These questions remain matters for speculation.

In a surprisingly frank final summing-up of the first twenty-five years of the work of the Joseph Rowntree Memorial Trust, Lewis Waddilove, its chief executive officer during those years, makes clear, with hindsight, his own doubts about the rightness of the trustees' action in going to Parliament to create an entirely new trust. He recognised that the Charitable Trust had all the powers necessary to carry out the work of the Memorial Trust; that in creating a second general purpose trust, as the chief charity commissioner and the chairman of the Charitable Trust had pointed out, the founder's intentions as to the relationships between the three complementary trusts has been completely negated. Living together under one roof, the trusts now come together mainly when they feel their joint interests are threatened, although a recent joint initiative to combat unemployment has been announced.

The author of *English Philanthropy*, David Owen, wrote approvingly in 1964 of the Joseph Rowntree Memorial Trust that 'of all the assorted institutions and organisations that go to make up the British charitable world, none has shown . . . a more imaginative understanding of the use of private philanthropy in semi-collectivist Britain'. Lewis Waddilove, looking at the activities of the trust in the light of developments in the 1980s, questions whether it would not have made a more abiding contribution to social policy if it had stuck to its original objectives and concentrated on the ever present problem of meeting the changing need for homes. Like many other trusts, the Memorial Trust not only responded to the demands of an expanding welfare society, it was in the forefront of those who stimulated new expectations, looking for innovative proposals for social research or social action.

The trustees of the Rowntree Trusts, bound together by name but no longer by structure or family involvement, hold up Joseph Rowntree's 1904 memorandum as a basis for their work, interpreting its widely quoted passage, that future trustees must be free to respond to the needs of changing times, as justification for their actions. The passing years are likely to accentuate their independent roles, but nothing can detract from the fact that it was because of the vision and energy of one man, Joseph Rowntree, that the trusts have been able to play such a creative role and to contribute, on a national scale, so positively to the wellbeing of society.

The Cadbury legacy has taken a slightly different form. George Cadbury created the Bournville Village Trust but he was also head of a tightly knit and affectionate family circle. The fact that so many of his children, and his brother's children, subsequently created trusts of their own must owe a lot to the values he and his brother believed in. The trusts reflect the diverse interests of different members of the family; the legacy is a continuing one, for members of the second and third generation of the family are involved as trustees. Another book would be needed to chart the scope of their work. It is pleasing to think that not only has chocolate itself given pleasure to millions, but the proceeds of its commercial success have been so constructively used that countless others have benefited from the success of George Cadbury and Joseph Rowntree.

Bibliography

—— Books and Papers ——

Alexander, Helen, *Richard Cadbury* (1906)

Binfield, Clyde, *Business Paternalism and the Congregational Ideal* (paper given at London meeting of the Historians' Study Group, 24 February 1982)

Bourke, Algernon, *The History of White's* (no date)

Bradshaw, A. N., *The Quakers: their story and message* (1921)

Bradshaw, J., *The Family Fund: an Initiative in Social Policy* (1980)

Briggs, Asa, *Victorian Cities* (1963)

    Social Thought and Social Action, A study of the work of Seebohm Rowntree 1871–1954 (1961)

Cadbury, Adrian, 'Quaker Values in Business' (paper given in 1985)

Cadbury, E., *Experiments in Industrial Organisation* (1912)

Cadbury, E., and Shann, G., *Sweating, Social Service Handbook No. V* (1908)

Cadbury, L. J., *Post War Problems of the Cocoa and Chocolate Industry* (1946)

Cadbury, R. (Historicus), *Cocoa: All about it* (1892)

Cadbury, W. A., *Labour in Portuguese West Africa* (1916)

Castner, C. S., *One of a Kind, Milton Snavely Hershey, 1857–1945* (USA 1983)

Chadwick, Owen, *The Victorian Church, 1966*

Child, J., 'Quaker Employers and Industrial Relations' (*Sociological Review*, N. S. Vol.12, 1964)

Corley, T. A. B., 'How Quakers coped with Business Success, Quaker Industrialists, 1860–1914' (paper given at London meeting of the Historians' Study Group, 24 February 1982)

    Quaker Enterprise in Biscuits: Huntley and Palmers of Reading 1822–1972 (1972)

Crosfield, John, *The Cadbury Family* (privately printed, 1986)

Crutchley, G. W., *John Mackintosh* (1921)

Davis, R., *Woodbrooke, 1903–53* (1953)

Dictionary of Business Biography, 5 vols, ed. David Jeremy (1984–86)

Doncaster, Phoebe, *Joseph Stephenson Rowntree: His Life and Work* (1908)

Forrest, Denys, *Tea for the British* (1973)

Fox, Joseph John, *The Society of Friends: an enquiry into the causes of its weakness as a Church* (1859)

Fry, William, *The Frys of Corston, Wilts.* (privately printed, 1929)

Gardiner, A. G., *Life of George Cadbury* (1923)

Glass D. V., *Social Mobility in Britain* (1954)

Glendinning, V., *A Suppressed Cry: The Life and Death of a Quaker Daughter* (1969)

Goodall, Francis, see *History, Markets and Bagmen*, ed. R. P. T. Davenport (1986), chapter on 'Marketing consumer products before 1914: Rowntree and Elect Cocoa'

Goodenough, Simon, *The Greatest Good Fortune* (1985)

Grubb, E., *Christianity and Business* (1912)
  What is Quakerism? (1917)

Hancock, Thomas, 'The Peculium: an Endeavour to throw light on some of the causes of the decline in the Society of Friends, especially in regard to its original claim of Being the Peculiar People of God' (1859)

Harris, William, *Life so Far* (1954)

Harrison, Brian, *Drink and the Victorians: The Temperance Question in England 1815–72* (1971)

Head, Brandon, *The Food of the Gods* (1903)

Heasman, Kathleen, *Evangelicals in Action: An appraisal of their social work* (1962)

Henslow, P., *Ninety Years on: An Account of the Bournville Village Trust* (1984)

Hubback, David, *No Ordinary Press Baron* (1984)

Inglis, K. S., *The Churches and the Working Classes of Victorian England* (1963)

Isichei, Elizabeth, *Victorian Quakers* (1970)

Jones, G. G., 'Multinational Chocolate and Cadbury Overseas 1918-1939' (*Business History*, 27, 1985)

Journal of George Fox, ed. John L. Nichalls (1975)

Joyce, Patrick, *Work, Society and Politics: The culture of the factory in late Victorian England* (1980)

Jubb, *Cocoa and Corsets* (1984)

Kitson Clark, George, *The Making of Victorian England* (1962)

Knapp, A. W., *Cocoa and Chocolate* (1920)

Koss, Stephen, *Fleet Street Radical: A. G. Gardiner and the Daily News* (1973)
  The Rise and Fall of the Political Press in Great Britain, vol. 2 (1984)

Loyd, C., *The British Seaman, 1200–1860: A Social Survey*

Loyd, C., and Coulter, J. L. S., *Medicine and the Navy* (1961)

Marsden, J. B., *A History of the Later Puritans* (1852)

Mathias, Peter, *First Industrial Nation* (1969)

Mayhew, Henry, *London Labour and the London Poor* (ed. 1951)

Montagne, Prosper, *Larousse Gastronomique* (NY, 1961)

Morris J., *The Climax of Empire* (1968)

Mumford, Lewis, *Culture of Cities* (1938)

Nevinson, Henry, *A Modern Slavery* (1906)

More Changes, More Chances (1925)

Last Changes, Last Chances (NY, 1929)

Othick, J., 'The Cocoa and Chocolate Industry in the Nineteenth Century' in *The Making of the Modern British Diet*, eds. D. J. Oddy and D. S. Miller (1976)

Pakenham, T., *The Boer War* (1980)

Peters, T., & Waterman, R., *In Search of Excellence* (USA, 1982)

Phillips, Hugh, *Mid-Georgian London* (1964)

Pifer, Alan, *Speaking Out: Reflections on 30 Years of Foundation Work* (Council of Foundations Inc., 1984)

'The enduring value of Philanthropy in a changing world' (paper given at Carnegie Sesquintennial Conference, Dunfermline, 1985)

Pollnitz Lewes, Baron de, *Letters* (written in 1733, published 1745)

Porter, B., *Critics of Empire: British Radical attitudes to colonialism in Africa* (1969)

Prescott, W. H., *History of the Conquest of Mexico* (1843)

Raistrick, A., *Quakers in Science and Industry* (1968)

Rickards, M., *The Rise and Fall of the Poster* (1971)

Rogers, B., *A Century of Progress: A History of Cadbury Bros.* (1935)

Rowntree, A., *Woodbrooke, Its History and Aims* (1923)

Rowntree, B. S., *Poverty, A Study of Town Life* (1901)

The Human Needs of Labour: Land and Labour (1910)

The Human Factor in Business (1921)

Industrial Unrest (1922)

Profit Sharing (1922)

Rowntree, J. S., 'Quakerism past and present: Being an Enquiry into the Causes of its Decline in Great Britain and Ireland' (1859)

Sarkissian, W., and Heine, W., *Social Mix: The Bournville Experience* (1978)

Scott, Richenda, *Elizabeth Cadbury, 1858–1951* (1955)

Shippen, K., and Wallace, P., *Milton S. Hershey* (USA, 1959)

Strong, L. A. G., 'The Story of Rowntrees' (unpublished manuscript, courtesy of Rowntree Mackintosh)

Taylor, H. A., *Robert Donald* (1934)

Tress, Ronald, 'British Foundations and Humanities' (lecture delivered in 1981)

Trevelyan, G. M., *The Life of John Bright* (1913)

Vernon, A., *A Quaker Businessman: The Life of Joseph Rowntree 1836–1925* (1958)

Vipont, E., *Arnold Rowntree: A Life* (1955)

Waddilove, Lewis, *One Man's Vision* (1954)

'Foundations and Trusts: Innovators or survivals'

(Eileen Younghusband Lecture 1979)

Private Philanthropy and Public Welfare: The Joseph Rowntree Memorial Trust (1983)

Whitney, Janet, *Geraldine S. Cadbury 1865–1914; A Biography* (1940)

Whymper, R., *Cocoa and Chocolate: their chemistry and manufacture* (1912)

Williams, Francis, 'The Murder of the News Chronicle' (*New Statesman*, 22 October 1966)

Williams, I. A., *The Firm of Cadbury 1831–1931* (1931)

Wilson, C., *The History of Unilever*, 2 vols (1954)
Woolf, V., *Roger Fry: A Biography* (1940)

—— REPORTS ——

'Report on the Conditions of coloured Labour on the cocoa plantations of São
   Tomé and Principe and the methods of procuring it in Angola' by Joseph Burtt
   and Claude W. Horton (privately printed, 1907)
Barrow and Geraldine S. Cadbury Trust
The Paul S. Cadbury Trust
The Barrow Cadbury Fund Limited
1975–1977; 1977–1980; 1980–1982; 1982–1983; 1983–1984; 1984–1985
Joseph Rowntree Memorial Trust, Triennial Report 1979–1981
The Joseph Rowntree Social Services Trust Limited 1979–81
The Joseph Rowntree Charitable Trust 1979–81; 1982–1984
The Future of Voluntary Organisations; Report of the Wolfenden Committee, 1978

—— PARLIAMENTARY PAPERS ——

Parliamentary Paper H.C. 1874 Select Committee on the Adulteration of Food
   Act 1872
Parliamentary Papers 1877 xi Select Committee on Intemperance
Parliamentary Debates (Commons) 5th series cxviii 78–98

—— UNPUBLISHED THESES ——

Martineau, Erica, 'Quakerism and Public Service, chiefly between 1832–1867,
   being a study of the emergency of the Society of Friends and its members into
   social and political activities' (University of Oxford, B.Litt. thesis, 1938)
Bailey, Maurice H., 'The contribution of Quakers to some aspects of Local Government in Birmingham 1828–1902' (University of Birmingham, MA, 1952)

—— NEWSPAPERS AND PERIODICALS ——

Annual Monitor, 1813–1920
British Friend, 1843-1913
Bournville Works Magazine, 1902–04
Cocoa Works Magazine 1902–20
Fry's Works Magazine, 1909–11
*The Monthly Record. A Journal of Home and Foreign Missions, First-Day Schools,
   Temperance and other Christian Work*, Society of Friends, 1869–91

One and All. The Organ of the Midland Adult School Association, 1891
Birmingham Daily Post
Daily News
News Chronicle
Observer
Star
The Times
National Review
New Statesman
Pall Mall Gazette
The Spectator
Nation
Somerdale Magazine

—— MSS ——

Cadbury Papers, University of Birmingham
York Board Minutes, Rowntree Archive

—— PAMPHLETS AND BOOKLETS ——

'Memories and Minutes, Friends Hall and Institute, Moseley Road, Birmingham, 1898–1983'
'The Bournville Village Trust 1900–1955'
'The Making of a Solar Village and Demonstration House in Bournville', 1985
'So Numerous a Family: 200 years of Quaker Education at Ackworth', Ackworth School, 1979
'Rowntree Central Works committee 1919–1969: 50th Anniversary Dinner'
'The Story of the Boeke Trust', ed. T. Insall, 1978
'History of J. S. Fry and Sons' (unpublished typescript, courtesy of Cadbury Schweppes)
'King's Index to Birmingham Charities'
'Christians in the Business World' (three papers given at the London meeting of the Historians' Study Group, 1982)

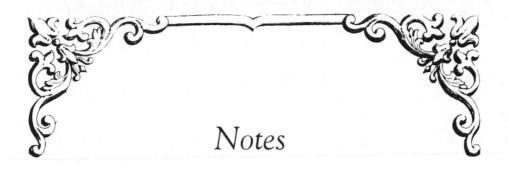

Notes

―――― CHAPTER 1, THE VOGUE FOR CHOCOLATE ――――

1 Knapp, *Cocoa and Chocolate*, p. 8
2 Algernon Bourke, *The History of White's*
3 Williams, '18th Century Chocolate Maker', *Somerdale Magazine*, December 1968
4 *The Gazeteer and New Daily Advertiser*, 20 March 1779
5 'Two Hundred Years of Advertising', *Quiver*, July, 1928
6 Sloane bought the Manor of Chelsea in 1712 and when one of his daughters, Elizabeth, married Colonel Charles Cadogan she carried much of Sloane's Chelsea property into that family   such names as Sloane Square and Hans Crescent, in Chelsea, London, perpetuate Sir Hans Sloane's memory.
7 Rogers, *A Century of Progress: A History of Cadbury Bros.*, p. 20
8 C. Loyd, *The British Seaman, 1200–1860, A Social Survey*
9 C. Loyd and J. L. S. Coulter, *Medicine and the Navy*
10 I am indebted to Admiral Sir Desmond Cassidi for the story and for the information concerning the issue of chocolate and cocoa to the Royal Navy.
11 Katherine Shippen and Paul Wallace, *Milton S. Hershey*, p. 19

―――― CHAPTER 2, QUAKER HERITAGE ――――

1 W. Fry, *The Frys of Corston, Wilts.*
2 *Somerdale* Magazine, August 1969
3 Sir Edward Fry's younger son was Roger Fry (1866–1934), the distinguished artist and art critic. Dame Margery Fry (1874–1958), one of Edward's seven daughters, was known for her work for social reform and education. She became principal of Somerville.
4 Courtesy of Cadbury Schweppes plc
5 *Dictionary of Business Biography*, vol. 4, p. 437
6 '200 Years of Quaker Education at Ackworth'
7 *Dictionary of Business Biography*, vol. 4., p. 966

8 Vernon, *A Quaker Businessman*, p. 81
9 Jubb, *Cocoa and Corsets*, 1984
10 Gardiner, *Life of George Cadbury*, p. 9
11 Gardiner, op. cit., p. 17
12 Gardiner, op. cit., p. 32
13 Letter from George Cadbury to Maria Cadbury, 22 May 1857, quoted by John Crosfield in his privately printed *The Cadbury Family*, 1986, p. 435
14 Gardiner, op. cit., p. 25
15 Ibid., p. 29
16 Francis Goodall, in *History, Markets and Bagmen*, ed. R. P. T. Davenport, p. 50

—— CHAPTER 3, THE SOCIETY OF FRIENDS ——

1 J. S. Rowntree, 'Quakerism Past and Present'
2 Marsden, *A History of the Later Puritans*, p. 240
3 *Journal of George Fox*, ed. John Nickalls
4 J. S. Rowntree, op. cit., p. 68
5 The Religious Census, 1851, p. 65
6 Vernon, op. cit., p. 47
7 Ibid., p. 26
8 Corley, 'How Quakers coped with Business Success: Quaker Industrialists 1860–1914'
9 Child, Quaker Employers and Industrial Relations, *Sociological Review*, N.S. vol. 12, 1964

—— CHAPTER 4, INDUSTRIAL PATERNALISM ——

1 Joyce, *Work, Society and Politics*, p. 193
2 Gardiner, op. cit., p. 30
3 'History of J. S. Fry and Sons' (courtesy Cadbury Schweppes plc)
4 Williams, *The Firm of Cadbury 1831–1931*, p. 67
5 Crosfield, *The Cadbury Family*, p. 443
6 Williams, op. cit., p. 67
7 Wilson, *The History of Unilever*, vol. I, p. 146
8 *Dictionary of Business Biography*, vol. 3., p. 360
9 Williams, op. cit., p. 220
10 Gardiner, op. cit., p. 155
11 Williams, op. cit., p. 236
12 Gardiner, op. cit., p. 188
13 Crosfield, op. cit., p. 463
14 Gardiner, op. cit., p. 128

15 Isichei, *Victorian Quakers*, p. 265
16 Vernon, op. cit., p. 51
17 Isichei, op. cit., p. 265
18 Ibid., p. 273
19 Ibid., p. 275
20 Vernon, op. cit., p. 98
21 *Dictionary of Business Biography*, vol. 4., p. 966
22 Vernon, op. cit., p. 98
23 Strong, *The Story of Rowntrees*, unpublished MS, p. 24
24 Ibid., p. 25
25 Goodall, op. cit. p. 27 Archive, Memorandum to Travellers, 30 January 1891
26 Vernon, op. cit., p. 26
27 Ibid., p. 63
28 B. S. Rowntree, *Poverty*, p.vi
29 Ibid., p. 385
30 Waddilove, *One Man's Vision*, p. 7
31 Clyde, Binfield, 'Business Paternalism and the Congregational Ideal'
32 Waddilove, op. cit., p. 6

—— CHAPTER 5, THE POWER TO INFLUENCE ——

1   *Dictionary of Business Biography*, vol. 3, p. 50
2   Gardiner, *George Cadbury*, p. 217
3   Ibid., p. 214
4   Koss, *Fleet Street Radical*, p. 39
5   Ibid., p. 39
6   Gardiner, op. cit., p. 219
7   Koss, *The Rise and Fall of the Political Press in Britain*, vol. 2, p. 41
8   Goodenough, *The Greatest Good Fortune*, p. 29
9   Koss, *Fleet Street Radical*, p. 34
10 Harris, *Life so Far*, p. 81
11 Gardiner, op. cit., p. 220
12 Ibid.
13 Crosfield, *The Cadbury Family*, p. 522
14 Ibid., p. 522
15 Ibid., p. 569
16 Ibid., p. 572
17 Ibid., p. 573
18 Gardiner, op. cit., p. 231
19 Minutes of the Joseph Rowntree Social Services Trust, 13 January 1907
20 Ibid., May 1913
21 Koss, *Rise and Fall of the Political Press*, p. 147
22 Minutes of the Joseph Rowntree Social Services Trust, 23 January 1907

23 Nevinson, *More Changes, More Chances*, p. 315
24 Koss, op. cit., p. 7
25 Nevinson, op. cit., pp. 322–3
26 Koss., op. cit., p. 78
27 Harris, op. cit., p. 28
28 Koss, *Fleet Street Radical*, p. 115
29 Koss, op. cit., p. 116
30 Koss, op. cit., p. 293
31 Koss, op. cit., p. 255: letter from Cadbury to Gardiner, 30 December 1918
32 Koss, op. cit., p. 255
33 Ibid., p. 266
34 *Nation*, 26 March 1921
35 Harris, op. cit. pp. 198–99
36 Koss, *The Rise and Fall of the Political Press*, p. 362

—— CHAPTER 6, A TIME OF TRIAL ——

1   *Dictionary of Business Biography*, vol. 1, p. 647
2   Quoted in Koss, *The Rise and Fall of the Political Press*, p. 36
3   Koss, *Fleet Street Radical*, pp 77–8
4   See also Cadbury and Shann, *Sweating, Social Service Handbook No. V*
5   Nevinson, *More Changes, More Chances*, p. 27
6   Ibid., p. 80
7   Ibid., p. 86
8   Ibid. p. 86
9   'Report on the Conditions of Coloured Labour on the Cocoa Plantations of S. Tomé and Principe and the Methods of Procuring it in Angola'
10 *Standard*, 26 September 1908
11 The trial was extensively reported in the *Birmingham Daily Post* from 29 November 1909 to 2 December 1909
12 Nevinson, *More Changes, More Chances*, p. 90
13 *Dictionary of Business Biography*, vol. 3, p. 746

—— CHAPTER 7, COOPERATION, COMPETITION AND CONFLICT ——

1   Goodall, in *History, Markets and Bagmen*, p. 21
2   Ibid., p. 21
3   *Dictionary of Business Biography*, vol. 1, p. 290
4   Goodall, op. cit., p. 29
5   Ibid., p. 29
6   Ibid., p. 33

7   Minutes of Directors' Conferences, vol. 5, 17 November 1903, p. 33 (courtesy Rowntree Mackintosh plc)

8   Minutes of Directors' Conferences, vol. 8, 25 September 1906, pp. 145–6 (courtesy Rowntree Mackintosh plc)

9   Minutes of Directors' Conferences, vol. 4, 13 January 1903; 20 January 1903 (courtesy of Rowntree Mackintosh plc)

10 Minutes of Directors' Conferences, vol. 8, 6 November 1906, p. 203 (courtesy Rowntree Mackintosh plc)

11 Business History, vol. XXVI, 'Multinational Chocolate', p. 60

12 Ibid.

13 Minutes of Directors' Conferences, vol. 8, 27 July 1906, p. 76 (courtesy Rowntree Mackintosh plc)

14 Minutes of Directors' Conferences, vol. 10, 17 October 1907, p. 15; 22 October 1907, p. 24; 18 December 1907, p. 72 (courtesy Rowntree Mackintosh plc)

15 Goodall, op. cit., p. 39

16 Minutes of Directors' Conferences, vol. 24, 19 March 1917, pp. 103–104 (courtesy Rowntree Mackintosh plc)

17 Minutes of Directors' Conferences, vol. 24, Special Board, 5 February 1918, pp. 208–10 (courtesy Rowntree Mackintosh plc)

18 Minutes of Directors' Conferences, vol. 26, 25 March 1918, pp. 13–14, (courtesy Rowntree Mackintosh plc)

19 L. A. G. Strong, 'The Story of Rowntree', unpublished MS

20 Ibid., p. 73

21 'Rowntree Central Works Committee, 1919–1969, 50th Anniversary Dinner' (courtesy Rowntree Mackintosh plc)

22 Minutes of Directors' Conferences, vol. 33, 18 October 1927, p. 269 (courtesy Rowntree Mackintosh plc)

23 Dictionary of Business Biography, vol. 1, p. 555

24 From an unpublished biography of Joseph Rowntree (courtesy of Joseph Rowntree Trusts)

25 Minutes of Directors' Conferences, vol. 33, Memorandum on the position of the business, 23 October 1929, pp. 461(a)–461(i) (courtesy Rowntree Mackintosh plc)

26 Minutes of Directors' Conferences, vol. 34, 4 January 1930, p. 13 (courtesy Rowntree Mackintosh plc)

27 Dictionary of Business Biography, vol. 4, p. 970

28 Ibid.

29 Minutes of York board, vol. 1, 22 June 1936, p. 570 (courtesy Rowntree Mackintosh plc)

30 Ibid., 22 December 1936, p. 570

31 Ibid., 18 January 1937, p. 679

32 Ibid., 19 July 1937, p. 774

33 Ibid., 3 August 1937, p. 783

34   Ibid., 10 August 1937, pp. 788–9

—— CHAPTER 8, DEATH OF THE *News Chronicle* ——

1   *Dictionary of Business Biography*, vol. 3, pp. 827–8
2   Parliamentary Debates (Commons), 5th series, cxviii, cols. 78–98
3   Koss, *The Rise and Fall of the Political Press in Britain*, vol. 2, p. 337
4   Lloyd George to his wife, 22 September 1926, Lloyd George family letters
      Koss, op. cit., pp. 206–207
5   Taylor, Donald, pp. 241–5
6   Memorandum from Henry Cadbury to Cowdray, 5 September 1928, quoted
      in Koss, op. cit., p. 472
7   Crosfield, op. cit., p. 66
8   Ibid., p. 679
9   Koss, op. cit., p. 385
10   Hubbard, *No Ordinary Press Baron*, p. 135
11   Koss, op. cit., p. 497
12   Hubback, op. cit.
13   Koss, op. cit. p. 529
14   Koss, op. cit., p. 491
15   Koss, op. cit., p. 138
16   Hubback, op. cit., p. 139
17   Crozier, *Off the Record*, p. 349
18   Koss, op. cit., p. 649
19   Ibid., p. 651
20   *Observer*, 22 October 1960
21   *New Statesman*, 22 October 1960
22   Williams, 'Murder of the *News Chronicle*', *New Statesman*, 22 October 1960
23   *The Times*, 18 October 1960
24   Ibid.
25   *Observer*, 23 October 1960
26   Koss, op. cit. p. 654
27   *New Statesman*, 16 October 1970
28   *The Times*, November 1982

—— CHAPTER 9, THE TRUST MAKERS ——

1   'Memories and Minutes, Friends Hall and Institute, Moseley Road, Birming-
      ham, 1898–1983'
2   Ibid., p. 5
3   Ibid., p. 18
4   'British Foundations and Humanities', lecture by Ronald Tress, 1981

5 'King's Index to Birmingham Charities', pp. 88–90
6 'The Story of the Boeke Trust', ed. T. Insall (courtesy of Cadbury Schweppes plc)
7 Ibid.
8 Joseph Rowntree, memorandum of 1904
9 Waddilove, *One Man's Vision*, p. 6
10 Joseph Rowntree Social Services Trust Ltd., Report, 1976–78, p. 10
11 Pifer, *Speaking Out, Reflections on 30 Years of Foundation Work*, p. 4
12 Joseph Rowntree Social Services Trust Ltd., Report, 1976–78, p. 116
13 Waddilove, *Private Philanthropy and Public Welfare*, p. xxii
14 Gardiner, *George Cadbury*, p. 199
15 Ibid. (letter from George Cadbury to H. S. Newman), p. 201
16 Vernon, op. cit., p. 154
17 Joseph Rowntree Charitable Trust, Report for the years 1982–84, p. 37
18 Ibid.
19 Information on the Joseph Rowntree Village Trust and the Joseph Rowntree Memorial Trust is based on Waddilove's account in *Private Philanthropy and Public Welfare*.
20 Waddilove, op. cit., p. 41
21 Ibid., p. 43
22 Pifer, op. cit., p. 35
23 Waddilove, op. cit., p. 35
24 See also Jonathan Bradshaw, *The Family Fund*
25 Joseph Rowntree Memorial Fund, Triennial Report, 1979–1981, p. 45

—— Chapter 10, Changing Legacy ——

1 Henslowe, Phillip, *Ninety Years On, An Account of the Bournville Village Trust*
2 I am indebted to Antony Dale, chief inspector of Historic Buildings at the time, for this information.
3 Sarkissian and Heine, *Social Mix: The Bournville Experience*, p. 96
4 'The Making of a Solar Village and a Demonstration House in Bournville', 1985
5 Minutes of the Joseph Rowntree Social Services Trust, June 1971
6 Joseph Rowntree Social Services Trust Report, 1976–78, p. 10
7 Joseph Rowntree Charitable Trust, Report for the years 1982–84, p. 10
8 Pifer, op. cit., pp. 3–4

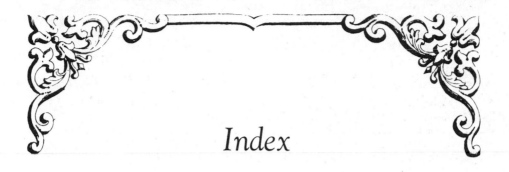

Index